WITHDRAWN

Hemingway and Faulkner:
inventors/masters

by

Linda Welshimer Wagner

The Scarecrow Press, Inc.
Metuchen, N.J. 1975

GRAMLEY LIBRARY
Salem Academy and College
Winston-Salem, N. C. 27108

PS
3515
E 37
Z 9165

Parts of this book have appeared in various
forms in College Literature, Ernest Hemingway: Five Decades of Criticism, The Journal
of Modern Literature, The Journal of Narrative
Technique, MidAmerica I, Modern Fiction Studies, The Sewanee Review, and Studies in Short
Fiction. My thanks to the editors for their per-
mission to reprint the essays.

Library of Congress Cataloging in Publication Data

Wagner, Linda Welshimer.
    Hemingway and Faulkner.

    Includes bibliographical references and index.
    1. Hemingway, Ernest, 1899-1961. 2. Faulkner,
William, 1897-1962. I. Title
PS3515. E37Z9165   813'. 5'209   75-23367
ISBN 0-8108-0862-5

Printed in the United States of America

Copyright © 1975 by Linda Welshimer Wagner

for

DOUG, TOM, and ANDREA

When you start searching for "pure elements" in literature you will find that literature has been created by the following classes of persons:

(1) Inventors. Men who found a new process, or whose extant work gives us the first known example of a process.

(2) The masters. Men who combined a number of such processes, and who used them as well as or better than the inventors.

(3) The diluters. Men who came after the first two kinds of writer, and couldn't do the job quite as well....

--Ezra Pound

We are discussing the Art of Fiction; questions of art are questions (in the widest sense) of execution....

--Henry James

CONTENTS

v

PREFACE

In modern American literature, two authors of proven importance--Ernest Hemingway, great if mannered tough guy; and William Faulkner, modest Southern farmer--appear to be in need of critical reassessment. Both have received the Nobel Prize for Literature, along with other accolades. Both have aroused much critical attention (Faulkner comparatively late in his career; Hemingway from the beginning) and both were consistently suspicious of and depressed by reactions to their writing. As Hemingway wrote in 1924 to Edmund Wilson, from whom he had eagerly sought notice, "I think there's nothing more discouraging than unintelligent apprecia-tion.... Christ how I hate this terrible personal stuff ... it turned me sick."[1]* Later, Hemingway was either silent about his reviews, or vituperative in return. Faulkner's tactic was to ignore criticism.

The most apparent similarity--and the one which this book attempts to describe--is that both Faulkner and Heming-way began their writing careers in search of innovation. ("Make it new" echoes throughout this period of experimenta-tion in all the arts) and grew through their love of method to attain a command of skill that gave them their positions as masters of modern prose. Contrary to the idea that an interest in craft robs the writer of expressive ideas, Faulk-ner and Hemingway show plainly that the writer who has tried many methods of achieving the effects he wants is best equipped to handle whatever story intrigues him. As the writer matures, and his ideas come to philosophical fruition, he is finally able to capture even the most difficult of char-acters, interrelationships, and attitudes.

The careers of Faulkner and Hemingway were out-

---

*Notes to this Preface and succeeding chapters and appendices will be found together in the Notes section at the back of the book.

wardly very different, but the core of each man's life was the same--his dedication to his writing. Each lived the life he did in order to continue his writing career. Hemingway's search for adventure, for power, for prestige was usually directed toward giving himself the materials as well as the confidence in his work to begin again. His relatively few novels --each growing from a climactic experience in his personal life--are testimony to the fearful existence of the sensitive man who knew well how hard it was to write anything, much less the great testaments he had set his course toward.

It is easier to see the artist in the withdrawn and relatively quiet existence of Faulkner, doing his stints in Hollywood for cold cash, but otherwise living without notoriety. His life centered on his wife and family, his home with its horses and mules, and always--superimposed--the writing.

The contrast between the lives of these men is as great as that between their appearances--Hemingway being one of the most striking figures on the literary scene anywhere, at any time; and Faulkner being one of the smallest men in the business--dapper, kind-eyed, droll, but definitely short. Yet they were alike in their devotion to literature, and to the men involved in creating it. Each man, when hardly more than an adolescent, had decided to become a writer, and had begun training for that occupation with wide, eclectic, and often avant-garde reading.

Nearly self-educated, both Hemingway and Faulkner must have found themselves at the mercy of the latest fads in contemporary writing; they read the same little magazines; they followed the same (shocking) writers. As two young, would-be artists, they each were mobile enough to travel where interest took them, and to become part of various literary groups. Not least, they were both from small towns where their literary propensities were, in a sense, encouraged. Bad as their juvenilia seem, most of it was published (Hemingway's in Oak Park High School's Tabula and Trapeze, and Faulkner's in The Mississippian); even while young, they were "important" literary figures, accountable for their artistic judgments. Thus the nearly rural circumstances of their early years seem more important considerations in their development as writers than the geographical fact that Faulkner's small town was in Mississippi, and Hemingway's was in Illinois.

The circumstances of early years are relevant, I believe, because any writer writes as he does at least partially because of his formative experiences. This study is in part a survey of beginnings, of apprenticeships. How did Hemingway and Faulkner come to create their ultimate work? What were they writing before their mastery of the novel? In the work of most great authors there is a progression, a change, as ideas grow and techniques become more polished. Masterful writing usually stems from less masterful, from writing in which there has been the germ of a later idea or a sentence of a later rhythm. Both Faulkner and Hemingway believed that writing well took a lifetime of care and effort, and that such expenditure was merited, because, in Faulkner's words, "Art is not only man's most supreme expression; it is also the salvation of mankind."[2] With more characteristic practicality, Hemingway gives this affirmation to Thomas Hudson who, in Islands in the Stream, muses about a friend's misused talents:

> So now he was going to start new again and how
> would it turn out this time? How could he think
> that wasting his talent and writing to order ...
> could fit him to write well and truly? Everything
> that a painter did or that a writer wrote was a
> part of his training or preparation for what he was
> to do.[3]

This emphasis on the importance of devotion to art joins Hemingway and Faulkner with other dominant figures of modern literature, recalling Ezra Pound's statement that "The mastery of any art is the work of a lifetime,"[4] or Ford Madox Ford's declaration that writing was "a priest's vocation." "To write honestly and well was the most important thing in the world."[5] For, like many major twentieth-century writers, Hemingway and Faulkner were both craftsmen, as the respect that existed between them showed. Each recognized that the other's work was genuine, and admired him for his persistence. Too many of the "promising" writers had dropped out early.

Hemingway and Faulkner are, in fact, the great craftsmen of modern American literature. In their concern for the demands of their craft, we might call them poets, as Faulkner termed himself. Perhaps it seems strange to consider the terse Hemingway and the raconteur Faulkner in that way, but poet seems the most accurate label for designating their obsessive concern with the way they were doing what they were doing. And here the problem of categories rears its head. For Faulkner and Hemingway are considered "novelists" (although each also wrote many short stories, some poetry, an occasional play, and informal essays), and much of the commentary about their writing has been written by fiction experts. Most judgments of their work will rest, undoubtedly, on the strength of their best-known novels, yet one might ask, are their best-known novels their best writing? What criteria are being used to make judgments? Can we measure the force of their accomplishments purely in terms of plot and character? The Old Man and the Sea, reduced to a summary, becomes the kind of story not even a beginning writer would bother with. And Faulkner's Absalom, Absalom! becomes a nightmare of story line, with little apparent justification for its multiple narrators. When their novels are judged by the hard-to-erase criterion of realism, one finds evidence of too much selection, of the detail made to stand for entire scenes, a technique at once Impressionistic and poetic. Even the old tactic of determining the worth of a piece of writing by its moral stance falls far short with these writers' works. Could readers themselves agree on moral absolutes, we would still have as Hemingway heroes Jake Barnes, pimp; Frederic Henry, deserter; and Richard Cantwell, lecher. Summarizing in simplest terms Faulkner's heroes become an even greater travesty--V. K. Ratliff, dupe; Jason Compson, "evil incarnate"; Mink Snopes, twice-murderer.

Ralph Freedman in The Lyrical Novel gives some indication of the complexity of attempting to judge modern fiction, by whatever standards, in pointing out that with such novels as those of Gide, Woolf, and Hesse, traditional narrative methods have changed, techniques have become more poetic in respect to structure, as narrative has been submerged in imagery and what Freedman calls "portraiture, the halting of the flow of time within constellations of images or figures. "6 In such writing, emphasis falls on "formal design" and imagery instead of linear plot; even most characters may appear as "personae for the self." The author's purpose is not simply to tell a story, Freedman conjectures, but to, perhaps more compellingly, create an experience; and since only he who has had an experience can recreate it, the narrator-writer thus becomes the undisguised central consciousness. This shift in the author's role from story teller to participant (and recorder of that participation) has many technical ramifications, but it also--perhaps more importantly --blurs the line between what we characteristically distinguish as fiction and poetry.

Freedman does not suggest that genre distinctions are obsolete, but A. D. Van Nostrand, in Everyman His Own Poet, does conclude that genre studies fail to deal accurately with great American writing. Considering Walden, Leaves of Grass, Emerson's Nature, Poe's Eureka, The Education of Henry Adams, Moby Dick, The Bridge, Williams' Paterson, and the fiction of Thomas Wolfe, Van Nostrand says, "Each of them breaks the conventions of the literary form that ostensibly contains it. Whether in prose or verse or both, each dramatizes a theory of poetry. They are hybrids."7 He goes on to question the very definition of fiction and poetry, pointing out that

> Any comprehensive theory of fiction really concerns what historically has been called poetry ... the generic process of constructing a system of metaphors to explore the relation between one's self and everything else [84].

The theses of both Van Nostrand and Freedman, in varying degree, reflect current critical recognition that literary forms are changing, modulating. It is one of the ironies of literature that as early as 1920 this changing pattern in genre was already acknowledged by many practicing writers. Indeed, Freedman's general observations can be extended from Gide, Hesse, and Woolf to include a great many major and minor writers, in both prose and poetry, of this century; just as Van Nostrand's list of misunderstood works can also be widened. For 1910 to 1930 was an age excited by technique, an age of highly sophisticated writers who knew the ways literature had been created, and chafed under what they felt were cumbersome restraints.

It is hardly accidental that in 1918 Ezra Pound edited the Little Review's special issue honoring Henry James, a writer little known in America then. 8 For James as early as 1884 had described the accurate form of the novel as being one of perfect freedom, of organic proportion. In "The Art of Fiction" he insisted that the novel be allowed to mirror the great variety of life in its own, unprescribed way, and that its technical devices be "as various as the temperament of man." He continues to describe the responsibilities of the artist who works outside established forms:

> The form, it seems to me, is to be appreciated after the fact; then the author's choice has been made ... then we can follow lines and directions

GRAMLEY LIBRARY
Salem Academy and College
Winston-Salem, N. C. 27108

> and compare tones and resemblances ... we can
> estimate quality, we can apply the test of execution.
> The execution belongs to the author alone; it is
> what is more personal to him, and we measure
> him by that. The advantage, the luxury, as well
> as the torment and responsibility of the novelist,
> is that there is no limit to what he may attempt
> as an executant. 9

James in effect here shifts the determination of a novel's
quality from its moral lesson, character, or "meaning" to
its method or technique. This criterion demands a much
more knowing writer, and gives him an exciting impetus for
his work, but it also demands a better-trained reader, and
consequently limits the audience for the best twentieth-century
fiction. As T. S. Eliot pointed out in his 1949 preface to
Djuna Barnes' Nightwood, "it is so good a novel that only
sensibilities trained on poetry can wholly appreciate it. A
prose that is altogether alive demands something of the reader that the ordinary novel-reader is not prepared to give."10

The truth had become--as Ezra Pound, Gertrude Stein,
James Joyce, William Carlos Williams and innumerable others had pronounced with such fervor--that the way a thing
was written was prescribed no longer by external standards
but only by internal necessities of the writing itself. Organic form--shape as a revelation of content--became the
artistic base for nearly all modern writing. This is not to
say that the same harmony between content and style does
not exist in earlier literature, because all great writing is
marked by it; but writers then may have begun at a somewhat different point. Instead of thinking, "Now these are the
rules I must follow" and perhaps later--or in the course of
the writing--letting the work have its head, the modern writer begins with the concept of the work free to go as its own
necessity takes it. Thus, as Warren Tallman suggests, the
reader must recognize that the way the writing moves, the
way the account is structured and presented, has a function
integral to the meaning of the writing; otherwise, critical
error results. Of the great books of this century, Tallman
writes,

> Works that should have been studied in light of
> their linguistic potential were studied instead in
> light of their semantic potential. The consequences
> go on to this day in the vast collection of explica-
> tions and interpretations that have plowed through

the masterworks of our century in attempts to turn
up Truth, Wisdom, Reality and Morality....
    The chief difference, then, between the older
American writing and the new is that between writing considered as a means to an end, sentences
used as corridors leading to further rooms, and
writing considered as an end in itself. The latter
will seem limited only to readers who fail to realize that books contain not persons, places and
things but words. [11]

    William Handy, in his 1971 Modern Fiction, A For-
malist Approach, also discusses the problem of treating fiction in ontological perspective. Quite accurately, he traces
much contemporary writing to Pound's emphasis on presentation through the Imagiste method, justifying his formalist
rationale in this way:

        the narrative images, scenes, and episodes which
        comprise the ontological structure of the fictional
        work may be seen to function reflexively in the
        process of their re-creation by the reader, pro-
        viding finally a single overall presentation which is
        the work.

Handy continues that "the novel or story is better seen as a
single image than a linear progression," and specifies that
the scene in modern fiction is parallel in many ways to the
image in poetry. [12]

    Following the sympathies of these and other formalist
and structuralist critics, I have emphasized in this book the
ways in which Hemingway and Faulkner each learned and followed his craft, the experiments they made in various genre
and techniques, and the eventual writing which resulted. Because part of their self-consciousness about their craft
stemmed from the milieu, Chapter One presents a discussion
of the literary ferment of those years, 1910 to 1925, and
traces Hemingway's relationships with the most established
writers of their time, Pound, Sherwood Anderson, Stein, and
others. Chapter Two is concerned with The Sun Also Rises,
Hemingway's earliest novel, as evidence of his developing
aesthetic. Chapters Three through Six discuss Hemingway's
writing from In Our Time through the last published, and
Chapters Seven through Twelve consider Faulkner's work
from the same perspective.

This study is limited and selective, primarily because it seems unnecessary to over-illustrate a thesis which can be proved by almost random selection from the writings of both men. It was once a much longer book. My apologies for what has been left out; my thanks for the great writing I have had to work with.

Thanks also to Michigan State University for several research expense grants; to the Alderman Library at University of Virginia for access to the Faulkner collection; to my colleagues Joe Waldmeir, Russell B. Nye, Clyde Henson, and Victor Howard for their conversations; and with particular appreciation to Frederick Eckman and Stanley K. Coffman, Jr.

Chapter One

BEGINNINGS

"Currents of energy seemed breaking out everywhere,"
John Dos Passos reminisces. Americans were "groggy with
new things in theatre and painting and music...."[1] Excitement in one area of art led to innovation and equal excitement in others: change was the young writer's aim, the older writer's fresh start. As Malcolm Cowley describes so
vividly in A Second Flowering, the years from 1905 to 1930
were fevered, but hectic in scrupulously satisfying ways.[2]

To understate, it was an exciting time to be alive.
For Faulkner, born in 1897, and Hemingway, born in 1899,
the furor of the 1913 Armory Show passed unnoticed. But
its aftermath--the wild technical experimentation in all areas
of art--bombarded them as well as older artists. In 1913
William Faulkner dropped out of school during his sophomore
year, and became one of the increasingly large group of self-
educated American authors. Reading widely, with particular
interest in contemporary literature, Faulkner developed firm
standards of artistic judgment by the time of his contribu-
tions to The Mississippian when he enrolled at "Ole Miss" as
a special student in 1919. For Hemingway, since college
held no attraction, his reading was also highly eclectic. A
friend recounts Hemingway's reading Browning aloud for
much of the night when the two were cub reporters for the
Star--this, in 1917, when Hemingway was 18.[3] And Dos
Passos recalls their reading the Bible together in 1925,
largely the Old Testament, especially "Deborah and Chron-
icles and Kings."[4]

The self-education of Faulkner and Hemingway is important in that they were each easily impressed by more
traditionally literary colleagues a little later in life. The
wide if somewhat erratic learning of Ezra Pound, Gertrude
Stein, or Ford Madox Ford could not help but appear for-
midable, just as the general mien and narrative ability of
Sherwood Anderson must have been impressive to the quieter
younger men.

15

By the time of the American entry into World War I, April of 1917, Hemingway and Faulkner were both ready to leave home, to join the great crusade, and also to escape what they already felt to be the complacent provincialism of their families. As eldest sons, they each felt the pressures of carrying on in father's footsteps. Hemingway had graduated in 1917, taken a job on the Kansas City Star, and enlisted the following year. Then July 18, 1918, as a lieutenant in the American Red Cross Corps, at Fossalta, Italy, he received 237 shell fragments in his legs. Convalescing through the end of the war and after, Hemingway had ample time to learn more about writing, and to write.

Faulkner, too, had already begun his apprenticeship. His friendship with Phil Stone, whom he had met in 1914, strengthened his ambition to become a writer, and his subsequent years at odd jobs provided time for the reading and beginning writing he was to do before he too entered the war in 1918. Enlistment in the Royal Canadian Air Force gave Faulkner only a few months' flying time (these even now obscured by his own humorous legends), but they did provide a love of flying that was to surface again and again, both in the situations of his novels and in his own private life.

By the time of World War I, America, in its somewhat rambunctious quest for culture, had gone through an assortment of impulses. Although Hemingway and Faulkner may not have been directly aware of such major currents as Impressionism, Futurism, Imagism, and Surrealism, the result of these occasions was to change the entire American artistic experience--to enrich it, to free it, and in some cases to destroy it; but always to emphasize its existence. For the first time in American history, public attention was pointed toward painting and poetry, even if that attention only ridiculed these arts.

New ideas, new currents in art were coming from all directions. The French Symbolist poets, popularized mostly by F. S. Flint, brought new life to a waning formal poetry, just as realism and its resulting naturalism invigorated the popular novel. Soon after the turn of the century, some private and as yet unnamed experimentation was also occurring. Gertrude Stein's Three Lives was published in 1909, although written from 1904 to 1906. Pound had written some free-form poems by 1908 when he first met Ford Madox Hueffer; and the 1905 Fauves, the Autumn Salon, the 1908 Cubist exhibition in Paris, and Picasso and Braque's 1911-12 collages were all influential. Graphic art seemed to have found some of its direction, but in literature these years from 1908 to 1912 were given largely to experimentation, experimentation with no set direction.

By 1913, when Pound was already an elder statesman of American and English letters, the first English translation of Freud's Interpretation of Dreams appeared, giving rationale for a comparatively new emphasis on the subconscious and, more important, on psychological motivation for characters. Also in 1913, Americans first saw the French experimental painters such as Duchamp in the highly publicized New York Armory Show. And in the March issue of Poetry, also 1913, appeared Pound and Flint's statements on Imagism.

Pound's essay, among other things, defined the Image as "that which presents an intellectual and emotional complex in an instant of time." By stressing the inclusive powers of the image, he greatly strengthened the Imagist principle; and his emphasis on speed gave new life to the post-Victorian poem that was nearly buried in expected details. As he continued (and here one must think also of Joyce's epiphany), "It is the presentation of such a 'complex' instantaneously which gives the sense of sudden liberation; that sense of freedom from time limits and space limits; that sense of sudden growth, which we experience in the presence of the greatest works of art."5

Flint's statement stressed the three now-famous "rules":

1. Direct treatment of the 'thing' whether subjective or objective.
2. To use absolutely no word that does not contribute to the presentation.
3. As regarding rhythm: to compose in the sequence of the musical phrase, not in sequence of a metronome.

He went on to explain that Rule 2 was perhaps primary, giving as example the fact that an Imagist poet could often rewrite ordinary verse, "using about ten words to his fifty."6 The vers libre principle (which attracted most of the unfavorable notice) was really just one means of attaining the more elusive structure, organic form, a shape consonant with the mood and subject being expressed. Pound expanded on this notion in his essay by discussing the unity of tone and mood that the best poems maintain: "The term harmony is mis-applied to poetry; it refers to simultaneous sounds of differ-ent pitch. There is, however, in the best verse a sort of residue of sound which remains in the ear of the hearer and acts more or less as an organ-base."

The aim of the Imagists seems to have been, then, a freedom to let the poem achieve its own unity, a wholeness of effect unmarred by artificial and obviously literary con-trivances. In this aim, they were only echoing the great masters of literature. As Flint pointed out, the origins of the Imagists were not exclusive, but rather included elements of oriental, classic and English poetry: "their only endeavor was to write in accordance with the best tradition, as they found it in the best writers of all time--in Sappho, Catullus, Villon."

The value of these tandem essays was twofold: they alerted all modern poets to the fact that something new ex-isted, and respectably so; and they provided a specific list of principles to serve as a guide, however general. Un-fortunately, the statements also served as a reminder that the best art cannot be classified, and hence Pound's turn to "Vorticism" and Williams' to "Objectivism" in escape from the literality of the Imagist principles. Taken as they were in-tended, however, and that was to be generally--as Pound had warned in the 1913 essay--the Imagist principles were of im-measurable value, and particularly in their written form.

Aside from freeing poetry from prescribed rhyme and rhythm patterns which were often unnatural to the phrasing of American English, Imagism was most important in its empha-sis on concentration, on art as craft, and on the use of the natural idiom. Most of Pound's essay relates to ways of cutting dead words, in the hope of making every word in the poem work. A poet is a maker, Pound often said; he must create living things. From Ernest Fenollosa Pound had learned that verbs are the active parts of speech, just as he had come to realize that the Chinese ideogram--relying on pictures of specific objects to create words and, hence, ideas --was the perfect image. As he said later in 1914, "The point of Imagisme is that it does not use images as orna-ments. The image is itself the speech."[7]

"Go in fear of abstractions," Pound warns; "Use eith-er no ornament or good ornament;" "Don't be descriptive;"

instead "Present." Such axioms demanded that the poet constantly choose--whether or not to include this word, or, indeed, any word at all. The poet became a polisher of gems.

The emphasis on craft, necessary as it was as a corrective to some of the Post-Victorian writing habits, grew within the decade to become a near-mania. Pound wrote in 1918, "I believe in technique as the test of a man's sincerity,"[8] and in that strange mixture of terms waves the flag for the coming generation of writers. Richard Aldington goes even further in 1915 when he gives Ernest Dowson his highest praise by saying

> his theories of poetry were solely technical; and
> that proves, if proof be necessary, his authentic
> character as an artist.[9]

And T. S. Eliot made his echo in 1924 by saying that "[The task of the artist is] a task in the same sense as the making of an efficient engine or the turning of a jug or a table leg."[10] One has only to remember William Carlos Williams' famous definition of a poem as "a machine made of words" to see how pervasive this view has become.[11]

It is rather ironic that the chief objection to Imagist poems was that the poems were not "real" poems but instead prose chopped into short lines. For the truth of the situation about Imagism was that most of its principles were applicable to prose as well--and it is this width of reach that makes the movement so significant in modern literature. As Christian Stead wrote recently, Imagism may well be "the most significant revolution in poetry since that initiated by Wordsworth and Coleridge." He goes on to point out that its most important bases were the ideas of "organic form" and the use of "the language and rhythms of common speech."[12] It is interesting that Stead emphasizes principles that relate equally well to prose, for in that direction seems to have gone some of Imagism's greatest influence.

That much of this artistic concentration on the image, the concrete, was traceable as well to the empirical philosophy of William James and, more directly, Henri Bergson--and, later, of Alfred North Whitehead, John Dewey, P. D. Ouspensky, and F. H. Bradley--helps explain the seemingly voracious adoption of "the doctrine of the image" by so many different artists. For people who had already embraced the relative empiricism of James, expressing an emotion through the use of a tangible thing was only a small step forward (similarly, Georgian poetics could only take the modern artist backward). As Bergson wrote in his Introduction to Metaphysics, "the image has at least this advantage, that it keeps us in the concrete.... [M]any diverse images, borrowed from different orders of things, may, by the convergence of their action, direct consciousness to the precise point where there is a certain intuition to be seized."[13] A way of apprehending, a fresh means of cognition--from Gertrude Stein to Pound to Dos Passos, Hemingway, and Faulkner the thread of a tactile, experiential knowledge forms the warp of literary technique.

Pound is one of the first to include prose in his discussion of the poetic principles, doing so in several 1913 essays in both Poetry and The New Age, and in his 1914 essay on Vorticism. In 1915 he praises "prose that gives us pleasure paragraph by paragraph"; in 1917, prose "that one can enjoy sentence by sentence and reread with pleasure." His move to Flaubert's le mot juste is soon to come. By 1922 when Ulysses appeared, Pound saw that novel as the logical fusion of the epic poem tradition and the nineteenth-century novel, and accordingly began in earnest his own Cantos.[14] And as he was to muse nearly forty years later, "the most important critical act of the half-century was in the limpidity of natural speech, driven toward the just word."[15]

Much of Pound's emphasis on the identity between prose and poetry--and, indeed, his own recognition of that identity--came from his relationship with Ford Madox Ford ("It is no secret that I learned more from Ford than from anyone else"[16]). For twenty years, Ford had been stressing all the qualities that Imagism had adopted, but, like many avant-garde artists, Ford had no audience. As Pound recalls, "In 1912 nobody paid any attention to Ford's verse, or to Hardy's."[17] It is Ford who early stresses "hardness," "objective character," using the language of one's own day, and rendering rather than reporting. In 1911 in fact, Ford explained the real rationale for the development of the Image,

> The poet must be content to restrict his attention to the small areas which he can know: 'Nowadays we may contemplate life steadily enough, but it is impossible to see it whole.'[18]

And in 1914, in discussing Impressionism, Ford hit on the

other area of Imagism--that important point that the poem
was to depict not just things, objects, "small areas," but also the poet's emotional reaction to the more tangible facet
("an image presents an intellectual and emotional complex").
According to Ford, "the Impressionist gives you himself, how
he reacts to a fact; not the fact itself; or rather, not so much
the fact itself."[19]

It is as an extension of this subjective involvement that
the writer uses his own conversational idiom. In 1914 Ford
wrote in defense of free verse, commenting--correctly--that
"the unit of vers libre is really the conversational sentence
of the author."[20]

Stanley K. Coffman, Jr., in his classic study Imagism, finds Ford one of the most important figures of the
movement. Coffman thinks the term "Impressionist" was a
clique definition, placing more emphasis on structure than the
other components of the novel, and quotes Ford's own comment to Richard Aldington in 1914 that "he was the only real
Imagist and that all its doctrines were derived from him....
He hoped that Imagism might have profited by its acquaintance
with three of his theories; the word has energies which transcend its sounds or letters; emotions have their own proper
cadence; poetic ideas are best expressed by the rendering of
concrete objects."[21] Arthur Mizener, too, substantiates this
point, that the concern with the craft of writing was to Ford
the real basis of modern literature.[22]

Both in his own writing--poetry as well as fiction--
and in his position as public figure and editor of, first, The
English Review, 1908-1910, and later the transatlantic review, 1923-24, Ford exerted monumental force in the writing
of this century. And although he went without adequate public
recognition, Pound--the other giant of the quixotic times--
praised him highly as early as 1913, by calling his Collected
Poems "the most important book of the season."[23] It is largely Ford as heard through Pound's voice who dominates twentieth-century writing. As Ford himself remarked, "I learned
all I know of Literature from Conrad--and England has learned
all it knows of Literature from me."[24] His discovery of Henry James, his discrimination among the young new writers,
his recurring enthusiasm for Hardy, Pound, Joyce, and Wil-
liams--all these judgments are tributes to his perspicacity.

Admittedly, some critical difficulties arise when the
term Imagism is relegated only to poetry and Impressionism,

to prose. There was never any confusion in terminology for Ford, however, who referred to himself as both "Imagist" and "Impressionist": Paul Wiley notes that Ford "drew no strict line between prose and verse."[25] Ford in 1924 called Turgenev "the greatest of all poets," and then continued to explain,

> We [Conrad and Ford] agreed that a poem was not that which was written in verse but that, either prose or verse, that had constructive beauty.[26]

Stein, too, usually avoided genre distinctions in her discussions of writing, as did William Carlos Williams; to him, good writing was good writing, regardless of its ostensible shape or format. Given this context of writers enjoying the sometimes undetermined fluidity of their writing, perhaps one can better understand the similarities between Imagism and Impressionism: Imagism was attempting to make poetry a valid art form once again, just as Impressionism was trying to promote regard for the novel as an independent and respectable form, the rhythmic unit of Conrad's New Form. In both movements, the use of living language and organic form was essential.

There were important differences, however, and these came to be emphasized largely through Pound's objections to some of the prose which Ford had both admired and had himself produced. Imagism generally created a more intense effect than Impressionism; brevity was the norm, and the writer's role one of selection. And the image, that "intellectual and emotional complex," provided a central focusing device, as well as a means of attaining some objectivity for the writer. With a working image, presentation was easier.

Just at the height of this interest in new art forms, World War I necessarily slowed the momentum.[27] Ford, for one, went to war, as did Richard Aldington, Fitzgerald, Dos Passos, Cummings, Hemingway and Faulkner. England bore its losses among Rupert Brooke, Wilfred Owen, Gaudier Bzresca, Edmund Dulac, T. E. Hulme, Arnold Dolmetsch, and other promising young writers and artists. Pound continued to write, as did H. D., Marianne Moore, and Williams. The message was reaching the second wave of young writers, as Cummings' 1915 commencement talk at Harvard indicates. Titled "The New Art," it discussed such people as Matisse, Brancusi, Satie, Stravinsky, and Stein.[28]

John Dos Passos is another example of an aspiring artist caught in the crossfire of artistic innovation. He wrote poems and fiction, studied architecture, had two one-man shows in New York, and did much stage designing (and play-writing), some for Josephine Baker's Les Ballets Nègres. After graduation from Harvard, Dos Passos was one of the first Americans to join the Norton-Harjes Ambulance Corps; then in 1917 he wrote One Man's Initiation, which was not published until 1920. In style and content, Dos Passos' re-creation of war foreshadowed Hemingway's 1925 In Our Time--disconnected and juxtaposed fragments of scenes, with much emphasis on dialogue recorded "objectively" and a reportorial tone, all stated with the inevitable irony.

For the fact that the techniques of Imagism are here transferred to war fiction, Stanley Cooperman finds explanation in the post-war mood. According to Cooperman, had the world awakened to its usual dull complacency, the tautness and restraint of Imagism would have given way before wordy platitudes.

> The hostility to idealism in the years following the war produced or accentuated a flight from all abstraction, evidenced, for example, in the dictum of Hemingway--and Pound--that the object, the thing, the experience-in-itself, stated boldly and without rhetorical flourish, would recreate truth ....[29]

This is also Floyd Watkins' view, that the verbosity of an inflated patriotism, and particularly that of President Wilson, had convinced writers that "abstract words were a shallow pose."[30]

Of more importance, perhaps, than this reaction to overblown language was the post-war disillusionment with overblown philosophical attitudes. The modern writer had to find not only the words to express his beliefs but, in many cases, the beliefs themselves. Nothing could be assumed; life had become a series of unanswerable questions. As Wallace Fowlie summarizes in The Age of Surrealism,

> In his solitude, which is his inheritance, the modern artist has had to learn that the universe which he is going to write or paint is in himself. He has learned that this universe which he carries about in himself is singularly personal and unique

> as well as universal. To find in one's self what
> is original and at the same time what can be trans-
> lated into universal terms and transmitted, became
> the anxiety and the occupation of the modern art-
> ist.[31]

And Jay B. Hubbell sets all this artistic and philosophical
unrest in an even broader context, that of twentieth-century
change.[32]

While the post-war mood may have intensified the
need for this particular set of poetic techniques, artists are
usually motivated more by what is happening artistically than
by what has occurred sociologically or politically. The importance of Imagism, as an artistic force, seems incontrovertible. As Christian Stead points out, it first of all
"shook up the literary scene" and prepared readers for a
great many new things.[33] Perhaps Winifred Bryher's recollection of the impact of free verse is valuable here:

> The horror that the Imagist manifesto produced
> had to be lived through to be believed. Poetry had
> reached an incredibly low level in 1913 although it
> was fashionable to quote it continually in conversa-
> tion. Verse then was distinguished from prose be-
> cause each line began with a capital letter and it
> rhymed. It was improper to mention the modern
> world except in terms of horror; the writer should
> be down on his knees in clover (odorous was a bet-
> ter word than scented) waiting to be stung by a
> bee. It was also important to use poetic language,
> we 'quoted' rather than spoke. Naturally free
> verse was confused with 'free love'....[34]

More seriously, as Graham Hough summarized, Imagism was
an integral part of the "revolution in the literature of the
English language as momentous as the Romantic one of a century before."[35] According to Stanley Coffman, the most important facet of Imagism was its unyielding emphasis on technical concerns, of which the average reader would be scarcely aware, but with which the would-be writer would be fascinated:

> the principles were all technical, having to do with
> the form of expression rather than content ... the
> new concerns at least provided some excuse for a
> re-examination of the fundamentals of expression,

and this, in turn, gave them some excuse, which
they could not find in their 'message,' for continuing to write.... Imagism [like Futurism] [gave]
to modern poetry its experimental direction ... as
one manifestation of the new century's realization
of the need to make form once again meaningful
and expressive.[36]

Edmund Wilson recalls in The Shores of Light that young
writers wanted to create "something in which every word,
every cadence, every detail, should perform a definite function in producing an intense effect.... Ezra Pound and the
imagists, to be sure, had a good deal to do with this" (15).

And so the era of technical concern was launched.
But what of Hemingway and Faulkner in relation to these
theories, first expounded when they were schoolboys? The
period from 1913 on was one of terrific experimentation,
terrific publicity for literature and the other arts, and terrific artistic self-consciousness. In 1921 Malcolm Cowley
wrote that the "youngest generation" in literature was interested primarily in "form, simplification, strangeness, respect for literature as an art with traditions." (The fact
that the original 1913 essays on Imagism had mentioned
Sappho and Catullus as ancestors of merit had opened a
whole new search for "traditions.") And in 1922 Gorham
Munson described the young writers as being "preoccupied
with researches for new forms." The great division between the pre-Imagist writers and the form-conscious group
is illustrated poignantly in Munson's reminiscence that, at
Lola Ridge's party for Edgar Lee Masters, "The younger
people were as usual discussing the everlasting topic of
form, the older people aired their views on anti-religion."[37]

There is no question that to the writers of the early
twenties--both post-war and post-Imagist--innovation in technique was of primary interest; and Gertrude Stein and
James Joyce were then the most important prose writers in
English, largely and in some cases almost entirely because
of, their innovation. For Pound and his cohorts, Joyce became the genius of modern fiction: his writing was not only allusive and ironic; it also was economical, dependent for
much of its effect on the "Luminous Detail"; it also found
its larger meaning through the concrete epiphany.

The apparent correspondence between Pound's image-
vortex and Joyce's epiphany is suggested in Morris Beja's

definition of the latter:

> a sudden spiritual manifestation, whether from
> some object, scene, event, or memorable phase of
> the mind--the manifestation being out of proportion
> to the significance or strictly logical relevance of
> whatever produces it.[38]

The liberating sense stemming--or, better, bursting--from
the (usually) concrete thing which acts as the nucleus for the
writer's realization is very close to the catalytic image as
Pound described it in his 1914 essay on Vorticism:

> The image is not an idea. It is a radiant node or
> cluster; it is what I can, and must perforce, call
> a VORTEX, from which, and through which, and
> into which, ideas are constantly rushing [469].

A. Walton Litz, writing in The Art of James Joyce, uses the
term image itself to describe Joyce's fictional method: "At
the center of this experimentation lay the doctrine of the
'Image,' an aesthetic concept which illuminates Joyce's mature methods." He sees this reliance on image as contributing to Joyce's non-linear structures, and also leading to
what he terms Joyce's "expressive form" (organic form), the
direct correspondence between substance and style.[39] In
these several points, Pound found Joyce's aesthetic extremely compatible with his own.

Forrest Read points out in his Pound/Joyce that 1914
to 1924, for a variety of reasons, was the "Joyce decade."
In 1914 Joyce's Dubliners and Stein's Tender Buttons were
first published, although both had been written much earlier.
The Portrait of the Artist was being serialized in The Egoist. But 1914 also saw the appearance of Pound's Imagist
anthology, Des Imagistes, including poems by H. D., Flint,
Aldington, Amy Lowell, Williams, Kip Cannell, Allen Up-
ward, John Cournos, Joyce, Ford, and Pound. In the next
three years, Amy Lowell's three anthologies, Some Imagist
Poets, were published, including only H. D., Aldington,
Flint, and Miss Lowell, and adding D. H. Lawrence and
John Gould Fletcher. (The slap on the hand to Pound and
his friends was evident.)

1917 brought The Portrait of the Artist as well as the
nationalistic Seven Arts magazine; and The Little Review began
the serialization of Ulysses. 1919 saw two different kinds of

literary landmarks--Mencken's The American Language, which
in one sense justified a more native art, and Sherwood Anderson's impressionistic series of unified stories, Winesburg,
Ohio. The next year Pound's Hugh Selwyn Mauberly, his
brilliant satire of the proper British literary life, and Dos
Passos' One Man's Initiation were published.

Dos Passos' Three Soldiers (1921) gives another unfavorable picture of war, in a style again marked by montage and the use of national idiom; this was followed in 1922
by The Enormous Room, Cummings' war novel. But more
important in that year were the appearances of Ulysses in
book form and of Eliot's The Waste Land. Each book created immense controversy, both in terms of form and content; and has come to symbolize not only the best of modern
literature, but also man's concept of his modern civilization.
But innovative literary effort did not stop with these works.
In 1923 William Bird's Three Mountains Press series was
launched, including Hemingway's 3 Stories & 10 Poems, Williams' The Great American Novel, Ford's Men and Women,
and Pound's Indiscretions; these were to be prose writings
which would "tell the truth about moeurs contemporaines
without fake, melodrama, conventional ending."[40] A new era
in purposely revolutionary prose was also ready to dawn,
with many of the former Imagist poets now writing fiction in
both short and long forms.

Contemporary prose was to change not only because
poets began writing fiction, but also because many prose
writers were influenced by literary theory and criticism which
was, in this period, largely poetic. John McCormick points
out in The Middle Distance, his history of American literature from 1919 to 1932, that nearly all contemporary critical
attention during the 1920's was devoted to poetic experimentation, not prose. He cites Pound and Eliot's prolific writing
as well as the keen interest in Poetry, The Criterion, The
Dial, The Little Review, to conclude that

> The unquestioned veracity and propriety of poetic
> experiment in the 1920's, together with the publi-
> cation of a great variety of prose that seemed to
> derive from the same fountainhead as that of poetry,
> conspired to urge many writers to experiment.[41]

By 1924, when Hemingway published the vignettes of
in our time, one could see the direct influences of the juxtaposition and tone of The Waste Land and the compression of

Imagist poetry; Winesburg (in the unified impression, the stories shaped as need indicated, and the connecting hero); the sometimes objectionable subject matter, like that of Joyce; and the use of epiphany in characterization.

in our time does, of course, easily stand on its own merits (see Chapter Three). But in terms of technique, the story collection apparently owes thanks to something besides Hemingway's news stories in the Kansas City Star. To view Hemingway's writing career as a series of quick movements from news columns to novels is highly incorrect. Hemingway's news writing is quite limited in quantity, and idiosyncratic at that (there is little formula writing in any of his columns, and the only debt he ever acknowledged to the mode was the "one clear sentence" comment). More important than his journalism experience, which covered periods of only months before World War I and intermittent writing after that, were his associations from 1921 to 1927 with the literary figures of Paris--Anderson, Stein, Pound, Ford, Shipman, Fitzgerald, Joyce, and Lewis. As William Seward recalled, "A Moveable Feast proves beyond any doubt what some of us have known all along--that the real apprenticeship of Ernest Hemingway as a writer of fiction occurred not in the news rooms of Kansas City or Toronto but in Paris during the early 1920's."[42] Indeed, as Seward indicates, A Moveable Feast documents these relationships rather accurately, once one overlooks the rancor of Hemingway-the-man's view and concentrates on the more balanced judgment of Hemingway-the-artist.

Given the bluff yet nervous aspiring writer (Hemingway was barely 22 when he arrived in Paris), it is easy to see how impressionable he would be before the literary greats. Fitzgerald, with two successes already to his credit, was not so easily intimidated, but perhaps his tighter control in Gatsby, the evidence of more frequent revisions, results from the same kind of advice that Hemingway was getting. As George Wickes suggests,

> In the twenties Paris was certainly the center of the American literary world. Four of the most important writers of the older generation lived there, [Stein, Joyce, Pound, Ford] and almost all American writers felt compelled to make the pilgrimage....
> The young writer who learned most from these elders was unquestionably Ernest Hemingway. The

record of his years in Paris is one of extraordinarily rapid development to full maturity [160-161].

Wickes continues that Hemingway knew Sylvia Beach, Stein, and Pound well, "the relationship of a pupil to his masters."

From Sylvia Beach, Hemingway probably acquired much knowledge about avant-garde literature on a fairly broad base--as well, of course, as books, usually lent, and introductions to such people as Joyce. (Because Stein and Pound were both so firmly committed to their own admirations, the wide literary scene sometimes escaped them.)

The easy generalities of Gertrude Stein were admittedly helpful. "There is a great deal of description in this, she said, and not particularly good description. Begin over again and concentrate."[43] But as Stein herself somewhat defensively admits, also in The Autobiography of Alice B. Toklas,

> Gertrude Stein never corrects any detail of anybody's writing, she sticks strictly to general principles.... When the vision is not complete the words are flat, it is very simple (263).

Despite his later personal malice, Hemingway does grant his reliance on Stein and her opinions during his first years in Paris, a reliance clearly shown by his frequent visits, with and without Hadley; his turning to Stein when he was both personally and artistically troubled; his labor in getting The Making of Americans copied and published; and his request that she and Miss Toklas be Bumby's godmothers.

Yet, once he had given up the Toronto Star position (at Stein's repeated suggestion), he seemed to grow further and further away from her. There is the August 15, 1924, letter to Stein in which he writes, "I'm trying to do the country like Cézanne and having a hell of a time and sometimes getting it a little bit ... isn't writing a hard job though?"[44] But he soon became convinced that writing, for Stein, was not the "hard job" that it was for him, that her "one true sentence" was so clouded with repeated nouns and/or abstractions that revision was useless. As he wrote in A Moveable Feast,

> I thought of Miss Stein and Sherwood Anderson and egotism and mental laziness versus discipline and

I thought who is calling who a lost generation?
[30].

In 1927, should one be tempted to dismiss Hemingway's last recollections as too highly colored, he had already ironically written of his "break" with her:

> I tried to talk about literature to Miss Stein. 'I am trying to form my style on yours, Miss Stein,' I said one rainy afternoon. 'I want to write like you, like Henry James, like the Old Testament and--' I added, 'like that great Irishman, James Joyce.'
> 'All you young men are alike,' Miss Stein said. Frankly, I was hurt. As I left, three young Russian painters entered. 'All you young men are alike,' Miss Stein greeted them. The young Russians broke into eager chatters. It was an exciting statement. They hoped it was true. What times we would all have then.[45]

The bitterness here as Stein reacts to the young writer's highest praise with an easy cliché needs no other explication. Her meaningless repetition is also used against her, as the vignette takes on homosexual tones and one thinks of Hemingway's supposed objection to Stein's own sexual relationships; and of his story of Stein's dislike of both "Up in Michigan" and Ulysses on the grounds that they were "inaccrochable." (Hemingway's defense of his vocabulary--"you are trying to use words that people would actually use ... the only words that can make the story come true"--brought only "It's wrong and it's silly" from Stein.)[46] Again, the heart of even this crude parody lies in Hemingway's disappointment with Stein as teacher in the all-important literary world.

Hemingway's disappointment with Sherwood Anderson also began several years before his reading of Dark Laughter, the 1925 novel that triggered his tasteless parody novel, The Torrents of Spring. In 1923 he wrote that Anderson once had seemed headed for the Nobel prize, but concluded that the older writer "has swerved a long way off now."[47] Nicholas Joost also sees the widening gulf between Hemingway and the Stein-Anderson contingent as reason for his vindictive Torrents. Joost summarizes,

> First, his difference with Gertrude Stein and Sherwood Anderson had to do with his dislike of their writing techniques as well as with their personal

self-indulgences and foibles. They did not subdue
themselves as craftsmen to the demands of the
craft of writing, because of ... their lack of discipline. And to Hemingway, that discipline was remarkably the same that it was for Pound; the
Imagist exploitation of the sensory datum, the
keenly sensed image. [48]

It is true that a writer soon outgrows generalities, if
he is practicing his art, and Hemingway was tirelessly practicing his. And then came Pound, who made pronouncements
it is true, but also worked in specifics and ample illustra-
tions--and the same blue pencil that worked so diligently on
The Waste Land. Because many of Hemingway's early stories were lost, and because the other early manuscripts are
not now accessible, we can only surmise what editing Pound
did. But working from such manuscripts as The Waste Land
and Ulysses, and considering that Pound's relationship with
Hemingway was as close in the mid-twenties as the poet's
ties with Eliot and Joyce had been somewhat earlier, [49] there
is strong evidence to suggest that Pound did work with Hemingway on at least some of his early writing. George
Wickes quotes John Peale Bishop as offering more than cir-
cumstantial evidence. In Bishop's words,

> In Paris, Hemingway submitted much of his ap-
> prentice work in fiction to Pound. It came back to
> him blue-penciled, most of the adjectives gone.
> The comments were unsparing [Americans in Paris,
> 162].

In his study of Pound's influence, K. L. Goodwin also describes the Pound-Hemingway relationship as being extremely
close:

> Pound's early relationship with Ernest Heming-
> way in Paris was similar to his early relationship
> with Eliot in London.... Pound used to look over
> Hemingway's early manuscripts, and to return
> them with suggestions for dispensing with many of
> the adjectives. Hemingway possibly had the same
> sort of advice from Gertrude Stein, but almost cer-
> tainly not with the same intensity. Pound's imagis-
> tic dictum to 'Use no superfluous word, no adjec-
> tive which does not reveal something' was one that
> he was still applying to both verse and prose. It
> obviously had some effect in forming Hemingway's
> characteristic spareness [43].

Then, too, there is the strange debt Hemingway paid
to Pound. Not only did he never criticize Pound, he had only praise for him as mentor throughout his life. In 1923,
in a Toronto Star column praising Yeats for having won the
Nobel prize, Hemingway shows his admiration for Pound's
poetry.[50] More explicitly, in 1925 Hemingway wrote "Homage to Ezra" for inclusion in This Quarter:

> So far, we have Pound the major poet devoting,
> say, one fifth of his time to poetry. With the
> rest of his time he tries to advance the fortunes,
> both material and artistic, of his friends. He de-
> fends them when they are attacked, he gets them
> into magazines and out of jail. He loans them
> money. He sells their pictures. He arranges con-
> certs for them. He writes articles about them.
> He introduces them to wealthy women. He gets
> publishers to take their books. He sits up all
> night with them when they claim to be dying and he
> witnesses their wills. He advances them hospital
> expenses and dissuades them from suicide. And
> in the end few of them refrain from knifing him at
> the first opportunity.[51]

Baker quotes Hemingway's 1932 remarks about Pound to Ford
Madox Ford, "any poet born in this century or in the last ten
years of the preceding century who can honestly say that he
has not been influenced by or learned greatly from the work
of Ezra Pound deserves to be pitied rather than rebuked. It
is as if a prose writer born in that time should not have
learned from or been influenced by James Joyce.... The
best of Pound's writing--and it is in the Cantos--will last as
long as there is any literature" (236).

Hemingway's fullest expression of his feeling for Pound
occurs throughout A Moveable Feast, and these spots of gentle praise are all the more striking for being set in the
midst of the other more bitter portraits. The memoir itself,
like The Torrents of Spring, is ample proof of Hemingway's
romantic tendency to create gods for himself; his terrible defeat whenever he ran into either a "damned phoney" or a
writer whose feet were partly of clay always comes through
in the same untempered sarcasm. Hemingway's own artistic
standards were so compelling that it was, unfortunately, easy
for other writers--even himself--to miss the mark he had
set. But his praise for Pound, as a "great poet and a gentle
and generous man" (28), is whole:

Ezra was the most generous writer I have ever
known and the most disinterested. He helped poets, painters, sculptors and prose writers that he
believed in and he would help anyone whether he
believed in them or not if they were in trouble.
He worried about everyone [110].

Again, he describes Pound as "the man I liked and trusted
the most as a critic then, the man who believed in the mot
juste--the one and only correct word to use--the man who
had taught me to distrust adjectives" (134).

One central difference between Hemingway's feeling for
Pound and that for Stein seems to lie in the younger writer's
appreciation of the work each actually did. He says of
Pound, "His own writing, when he would hit it right, was so
perfect, and he was so sincere in his mistakes and so enamored of his errors, and so kind to people that I always
thought of him as a sort of saint" (108). Even Hemingway's
mocking portraits in A Moveable Feast of Eliot and Ford Madox Ford are tempered because of Pound's sympathetic role
in connection with them. Pound is, as it were, even here
interceding for them.

After Hemingway won the Nobel prize in 1954, he considered sending Pound the prize medal; several years later,
in 1956, he did send Pound a check for $1000. It seems
evident that, along with the legendary boxing-fencing relationship, Hemingway and Pound also maintained a strong artistic
bond. As Jackson Benson also points out, there is a "close
connection" between Hemingway's concept of the writer and
"Pound's conception of the poet as maker.... [B]oth Hemingway and Pound attempt to produce a primary, rather than
a secondary document."52

For the young and relatively untutored writer, there
was also the personal fascination of the domineering Pound
--witness Hugh Kenner's recent book, The Pound Era.
Charles Norman reminisces,

No one who was not young in Paris in the Twenties will be able to understand the excitement
which the mere mention of Pound's name aroused
.... The whole modern movement in art and literature seemed to be embodied in that tall, handsome, strenuous and ungainly figure, that innova-
tor to whom all innovators paid homage, that

> bearded adventurer who dealt in masterpieces....
> [T]o that generation Pound's books, aside from his
> verse, were an academy [239-240].

Morley Callaghan, too, relates, "to young writers in English,
whether they lived in New York, Paris, or London, he was
the prophet, the great discoverer, the man of impeccable
taste." Glenway Westcott recalls that "All of us at the University [of Chicago] ... respected Pound as a poet; and
yielded enthusiastically to his every critical recommenda-
tion."[53] And Pound had said that Hemingway's writing was
"the best prose he had read in forty years."[54]

The tributes to Pound's genius and helpfulness are
nearly inexhaustible, ranging from the twenties to the present. One of the most interesting is this given by Katherine
Anne Porter, a writer on the periphery of the Pound circle,
when she in 1963 calls Pound the "critic who helped a whole
generation of writers to find out what they were doing." In
1950 she wrote,

> there's nobody like him, nobody to take his place
> .... This was the truth for us ... who came up,
> were educated, you might say, in contemporary
> literature, not at schools at all but by five writers:
> Henry James, James Joyce, W. B. Yeats, T. S.
> Eliot, and Ezra Pound. The beginning artist is
> educated by whoever helps him to learn how to work
> his own vein, who helps him fix his standards, and
> who gives him courage.[55]

In all three of these ways, Pound was an important influence
on the young Hemingway.

In his consistent allegiance to Pound, Hemingway may
have felt some compulsion to withdraw from the Stein circle,
for the enmity between Pound and Stein is also legendary. It
was Pound who landed his job on the transatlantic review
(and who made Ford at all bearable, according to Hemingway). It was Pound who introduced him to Ford, Williams,
H. D., Aldington, and many other writers he longed to know.
It was Pound who found a publisher for the first book, 3 Stories & 10 Poems. But most important of all, it was Pound
who gave him the hours and hours of conversation that
helped him formulate his own artistic theory.

Chapter Two

HEMINGWAY AS IMAGIST

In 1972, Ezra Pound made one of his rare comments, that "Hem did not disappoint."[1] Craftsman that Pound had consistently been, his admiration for Hemingway grew at least partly from the younger writer's accomplishments in his writing. Forty-two years earlier, in 1930, Pound had himself classified Hemingway's writing style as "Imagist," describing the younger man as

> accepting the principles of good writing that had been contained in the earliest imagist document, and applying the stricture against superfluous words to his prose, polishing, repolishing, and eliminating, as can be seen in the clean hard paragraphs of the first brief In Our Time, in They All Made Peace, in The Torrents of Spring, and in the best pages of his later novels.[2]

Of all Hemingway's critical statements, the most adamant do relate to this "stricture against superfluous words." From his iceberg theory[3] through his explanation for the brevity of The Old Man and the Sea[4], Hemingway preaches concision. "I take great pains with my work, pruning and revising with a tireless hand," he writes late in life.[5] The good writer, according to Hemingway, is seldom satisfied; surrounded by the myriad details of life, only the great writer can choose the unerring detail--and the single, usually simple word to convey that detail. "Good writers know how to excavate significant facts from masses of information," Hemingway states. And on the choice of the single word, Baker quotes Hemingway as remarking in 1939, "One misplaced word ... could be the tiny flaw that might open into a chasm five chapters later" (344). One again hears Pound, and as if in chorus, Ford Madox Ford, "Every word set on paper--every word set on paper--must carry the story forward."[6]

Some of Pound's critical principles have been

35

mentioned in Chapter One, and others will follow, particularly in the analysis of The Sun Also Rises. Generally, however, Pound's prolegomena were riddled with his admonitions
that the artist be in control at all times. "I believe in technique as the test of a man's sincerity," he wrote in 1917;
and technique included the selection of single words as well
as the arrangement of the whole, and the construction of
thematic motifs as surely as technical devices. Hemingway,
writing again of Roger in Islands in the Stream, describes
the genuine artist's obligation to his craft in this manner.

> Roger had thrown away and abused and spent his
> talent.... To say nothing of his métier, he
> thought. How can anyone think that you can neg-
> lect and despise, or have contempt for craftsman-
> ship, however feigned the contempt may be, and
> then expect it to be at the service of your hands
> and of your brain.... There is no substitute for
> it, Thomas Hudson thought. There is no substi-
> tute for talent either.... The one is inside you.
> It is in your heart and in your head and in every
> part of you. So is the other, he thought. It is
> not just a set of tools that you have learned to
> work with [103].

Talent and craft as inseparable, as two halves of the creative impulse--this too is a reflection of Pound's insistence
on the artist's education. The whole man must be creator,
and whether he is choosing a detail or a moral alternative,
he must bring all his skills into play. "The mastery of
any art is the work of a lifetime," Pound stated[7] and Hemingway, in The Green Hills of Africa, outlined the reasons
why writing--this "damned serious subject"--was "so difficult." Primarily because, says Hemingway, "too many fac-
tors must combine to make it possible."

> First, there must be talent, much talent. Talent
> such as Kipling had. Then there must be disci-
> pline. The discipline of Flaubert. Then there
> must be the conception of what it can be and an
> absolute conscience as unchanging as the standard
> meter in Paris, to prevent faking. Then the
> writer must be intelligent and disinterested and
> above all he must survive. Try to get all these
> in one person and have him come through all the
> influences that press on a writer. The hardest
> thing, because time is so short, is for him to
> survive and get his work done.[8]

Hemingway's tone here echoes Pound's in its seriousness. The period of aesthetics become religion was at its height (Ford in 1924 spoke of "the religion of English prose"[9]); and the way a man worked came to have real moral significance. "A good writer is a conscientious craftsman," Hemingway continued--and, further, "A characteristic of great writers is their intense earnestness. Their lives are often sad or cheerless, but they are never idle."[10]

As Hemingway in these statements moves from writing as craft of words to writing as craft of life, we can perhaps better understand the near-obsession with the process of writing that figures throughout his own life. The right way to do a thing--whether it be bullfighting, fishing, making love, or writing--is frequently Hemingway's objective correlative, his means of characterization. We know a man better from the way he ties a fly or drinks from a wine skin than we do from what he says or from the things others say about him. Aside from being an important fictional method, this practice also gives us insight into Hemingway's own strangely compulsive and competitive behavior. Notice his very real pathetic urgency in these comments from his Paris Review interview:

> The further you go in writing the more alone
> you are. Most of your best and oldest friends die.
> Others move away.... [Y]ou are more alone be-
> cause that is how you must work and the time to
> work is shorter all the time and if you waste it
> you feel you have committed a sin for which there
> is no forgiveness.[11]

While most of Hemingway's sense of obligation surely stems from his own personality, the high seriousness in which Pound (and Ford and Joyce) held the writer's mission was undoubtedly a difficult attitude to erase. As Pound had written in 1917,

> 'The lyf so short, the craft so long to lerne.'
> It is a foolish thing for a man to begin his work
> on a too narrow foundation, it is a disgraceful
> thing for a man's work not to show steady growth
> and increasing fineness from first to last [10].

Perhaps Hemingway's compulsion to write better than everyone--and his own ultimately defeating insistence on outdoing himself--had its roots in Pound's convictions described here.

Of all the tenets of Pound and/or Imagism, it is likely that the most influential to Hemingway were those regarding the language suitable for contemporary writing and those describing the fluid forms modern art utilized. Pound wrote often about boiling away the "perdamnable rhetoric" of English, getting to a pliable simplicity, "a speech without inversions" (11-12). And Ford had early described various levels of simplicity:

> Differing subjects bear differing degrees of simplicity: To apply exactly the same timbre of language to a dreadful interview between a father and daughter as to the description of a child's bedroom at night is impracticable because it is unnatural
> ....
> Our vocabulary, then, was as simple as was practicable. But there are degrees of simplicity. 12

Pound too had explained in 1924 that style "should be as clear and simple as is consonant with the subject being treated."13

Hemingway was usually somewhat defensive about this area of his art, since his simplicity had been turned against him more often than he liked; but he did make pronouncements along these lines also: "The indispensable characteristic of a good writer is ... lucidity." "Writing plain English is hard work"; "writing with straightforward simplicity is more difficult than writing with deliberate complexity.... A writer's style should be direct and personal, his imagery rich and earthy, and his words simple and vigorous. The greatest writers have the gift of brilliant brevity."14

The younger writer also mirrors Ford's realization that "there are degrees of simplicity." Hemingway's "one true sentence" maxim is often quoted, but it was not long after he had begun writing fiction that he qualified that insistence. As he wrote in A Moveable Feast,

> I was learning something from the painting of Cézanne that made writing simple true sentences far from enough to make the stories have the dimensions that I was trying to put in them [13].

This multi-dimensional effect of the seemingly clear and simple writing was a structural matter as well as a verbal

one. Hemingway's interest in counterpoint and harmony, like
his interest in the techniques of graphic art, reflects his
concern with the shape of writing. Given words as his medium, his skill in arranging those words lay at the heart of
his craft. Such an interest can be seen to stem logically
from Pound's own fascination with the "absolute rhythm"
which every piece of writing must have, "a rhythm which
corresponds exactly to the emotion or shade of emotion to be
expressed."[15] (Pound's own very genuine contribution to contemporary music has recently been traced by William W.
Hoffa, who calls attention to many of Pound's writings dealing with Arnold Dolmetsch and George Antheil, as well as
more theoretical matters in music.[16] Pound's 1924 "Trea-
tise on Harmony" was especially important for its emphasis
on the significance of interval and silence in composition.)

Pound's emphasis on a kind of "organ base" for each
piece of writing was a progression from "Compose in the
sequence of the musical phrase"; it is closer to the more
contemporary concept of organic form--shape and pace
unique to each thing composed. Vers libre appealed to Pound
not because of its unrestrained freedom, but because of its
usefulness as a means of achieving the perfectly-realized
whole. "Poetry is a composition of words set to music. . . .
It is too late to prevent vers libre," Pound wrote in 1918.
"But, conceivably, one might improve it" (Literary Essays,
437). As always, the artist must be in control, working to
achieve multiple effects in his poem. As he had commented
in his praise of Ulysses, Joyce was a great artist because
of his ability to, first, select and, then, to arrange:

> We return to the value of arrangements, to the val-
> ue of clear definitions, and to the value of design
> in composition.
>   The Stream of consciousness in Ulysses is as
> different from any stream of consciousness that has
> actually occurred as is a plot of Racine's. It is
> equally a composition and a condensation. After
> the principle of "conscious flow" has been mani-
> fested, the relative value of presentations of such
> imagined streams will depend, as writing in the
> past has depended, on the richness of content and
> on the author's skill in arranging it.[17]

Pound has often mentioned juxtaposition, the imping-
ing of separate images with no apparent verbal transition,
and the sharp, hard effects gained from that sudden, almost

visual relationship among the words (he sometimes referred to this as the "ideogrammic method"). [18] And Hemingway's echoes of "counterpoint" and "harmony" show as clearly as his practice both in poetry (see Appendix I) and fiction that he too was convinced of the significance of the writer's arrangement. The artist had a responsibility beyond the mere accumulation of detail, as Hemingway says in comparing Zola with Stendhal, the great "selector." To Hemingway, Zola's "piled on detail ... is as dead and unconvincing as a steel engraving."[19]

There is much intrinsic evidence, I think, that Hemingway was influenced a great deal by Joyce. Although most critics do not apply the word epiphany to Hemingway's fiction, his reliance on letting a concrete object, act, or gesture signify much more than its physical limitations would suggest is clearly in the same tradition. Hemingway's own mistrust of the "philosophical" is not unlike the pose of Stephen Daedalus in places; Morley Callaghan recalls that Hemingway "distrusted physics, all abstract thought. The job of the writer was to deal in what was concrete, what a character could feel, and taste and touch."[20] Joyce's own intricate use of balance and juxtaposition would also give Hemingway actual patterns for his writing, whereas Pound's poems would have provided more oblique examples. And Joyce's attitude about non-essentials in prose was surely compatible with Pound's and Hemingway's; Chester Anderson quotes Joyce saying proudly to Beckett, of Finnegans Wake, " 'I can justify every line of my book.' "[21] As Hemingway said in his Paris Review remarks, he had learned from "Joyce, Ezra, the good of Stein."[22]

That one begins with the concrete, with the image, is a given in the aesthetics of Joyce, Pound, Stein, and Hemingway: "A writer, if he is any good, does not describe. He invents or makes."[23] And their reliance on the natural image rather than on a difficult or tenuous symbolism also becomes basic. Hemingway repeatedly stressed his distrust of symbolism, often in sarcastic attacks; but his most convincing comment about his feeling toward symbols in The Old Man and the Sea is quoted by Baker in A Life Story:

> The secret about the novel, Ernest explained, was that there wasn't any symbolism. Sea equaled sea, old man was old man, the boy was a boy, the marlin was itself, and the sharks were no better and no worse than other sharks [505].

More important than any single principle, however, was the total effect: "the aim of technique is that it establish the totality of the whole."[24] The best illustration of Hemingway's prose as product of the theories of Imagism/Vorticism would appear to be his actual writing.

Influence studies are impractical unless intrinsic evidence exists in quantity. The montage effect of the highly compressed In Our Time is the young writer's most obvious tribute to Imagism. (It has been noted by several critics[25] and will be discussed in Chapter Three as well.) But perhaps the most sustained example of the Imagist method transferred to prose is that maligned Hemingway novel, The Sun Also Rises, 1926. In transferring the methods of suggestion, compression, and speed to the novel form, Hemingway achieved a lyric evocation of one segment of life in the twenties.

Perhaps one should remember that Hemingway was disappointed throughout his life because this was the book most often misread; it was the "naturalistic" Hemingway, or at any rate, the "realistic" novel. As he recalled much later, "I sometimes think my style is suggestive rather than direct. The reader must often use his imagination or lose the most subtle part of my thought."[26]

The Sun Also Rises is not, of course, a picture of the "lost generation." Hemingway's poetic method of telling the reader that, however, has caused some confusion. His two epigraphs and the final affirmative title (the book was called Fiesta in its earlier European publication) prove that to him the Stein comment is indeed only "splendid bombast."[27] He uses her remark about the "lost generation" as the first epigraph for the novel, but the second--the quotation from Ecclesiastes--follows it, as if in contradiction:

> One generation passeth away, and another generation cometh; but the earth abideth forever.... The sun also ariseth, and the sun goeth down, and hasteth to the place where he arose.... All the rivers run into the sea; yet the sea is not full; unto the place from whence the rivers come, thither they return again.[28]

By choosing the affirmative phrase from Ecclesiastes as title, Hemingway further reinforces his view, that these characters are not "lost," but merely "beat up." More important, they still have the strength to act against wornout social forms and find truth for themselves. Jake does, when he gives Brett to Romero in order to make her happy; and Brett does when she sends Romero away. But, because society's arbitrary evaluations of these acts would be unsympathetic, Hemingway has to create the organic whole of the novel so that the acts in themselves convey the proper nobility. It is a difficult task, bucking conventional morality; but Hemingway made it even more difficult by using techniques that could easily be called "poetic," at least in relation to Pound's terminology.

One of the most troublesome of Heminway's techniques was his use of the strict first person narration, a practice certainly in keeping with Pound's view of the author as one who renders or presents rather than reporting. Jake Barnes, with his self-effacing terseness, gives us only skeletal action and characterization. We know very little about Bill and Mike, for example, though everything Hemingway tells us about Bill is positive. But interpreting Mike's dialogue is sometimes hard; we seldom know enough. The same kind of ambivalence surrounds both Brett and Jake. Obviously they are the protagonists, but some of the circumstances surrounding them could stand a more sympathetic explanation--or at least a fuller one--than Jake with his assumed stoicism can realistically give them. Hemingway tried rewriting this novel in third person, so that his 1926 audience would have help with the somewhat unconventional characters; but he evidently liked that effect less well. So he returned to the strictly "objective" presentation of Jake's telling his own story, as it occurred, rather than in a past tense, which would also have allowed for more reflection. This turning loose a character on an audience, reminiscent as it was of Pirandello, was also a manifestation of Pound's principle, "Direct treatment of the 'thing' concerned," with little ostensible interference from the author. How different Jake Barnes' version of "his" story was from Carrie Meeker's account of "hers."

When Pound directed writers to "Use absolutely no word that does not contribute to the presentation," he is implying a sharp selection of detail. Because Hemingway's selection of detail was so accurate, even skeletal presentations are usually convincing. Brett's bowed head as Mike and Robert argue shows well her tired submission to the present situation, just as Jake's drinking too much after Brett leaves with Romero tells us clearly his emotional state. The repetition of mealtime and drinking scenes in the novel is particularly good for showing the slight but telling changes in a few recurring details. It is these changes in the existing relationships that are the real center of the novel, rather than any linear plot.

Hemingway also used somewhat oblique characterization of his protagonists. Jake and Brett are not always present. Jake as narrator usually speaks about others rather than himself, and when he does think about his own dilemma, it is again in the laconic phrases that leave much to the reader's own empathy. Even though Hemingway introduces Jake in the opening chapter, his focus seemingly falls on Robert Cohn. He tells us innocently enough that Cohn was a college boxing champ, although "he cared nothing for boxing, in fact he disliked it." Then Hemingway begins to accumulate related details: later we see that Romero loves his bullfighting, just as Bill and Jake love fishing. We must then, in retrospect, suspect a man who devotes himself to something he dislikes. Subsequent chapters continue the parallel descriptions of Jake and Cohn, and less apparently of Frances Clyne and Brett. It is a stroke of genius that Hemingway waits until we have clearly seen what Jake and Brett are not in order to present them for what they are-- sad but honest people--together, in a would-be love scene.

The Sun Also Rises is also filled with passages that could easily be considered images if they were isolated from their context. An image to Pound was to be more than just a picture: "an image presents an intellectual and emotional complex in an instant of time." The brief moment when Brett enters the cafe in the company of homosexuals combines a good set of graphic details with the evocation of Jake's sad excitement and anger as he sees her:

> A crowd of young men, some in jerseys and some in their shirt-sleeves, got out. I could see their hands and newly washed, wavy hair in the light of the door. The policeman standing by the door looked at me and smiled. They came in. As they went in, under the light I saw white hands, wavy hair, white faces, grimacing, gesturing, talking. With them was Brett. She looked very lovely and she was very much with them.
> One of them saw Georgette and said: 'I do declare. There is an actual harlot. I'm going to dance with her, Lett. You watch me.'

The tall dark one, called Lett, said: 'Don't you
be rash.'
The wavy blond one answered: 'Don't you worry,
dear.' And with them was Brett.

The policeman's smile, the grimacing, the dancing--Heming-
way often worked through actions to reveal character and specific mood. But the touchstone here, as often throughout the
book, is Jake's own mood, his astonished sadness, caught in
the simple refrain line, "And with them was Brett."

Not only does Hemingway use concentrated descriptive
passages, he also employs juxtaposition, an arrangement of
images and scenes that lets him move quickly from one passage to another, sometimes without logical transition. Near
the end of the novel, when the reader's attention should be
on Brett and Romero as lovers, or on Jake's anguish, Hemingway instead gives us the account of a young man killed in
the morning bull run. "A big horn wound. All for fun.
Just for fun," says the surly bartender, picking up one of
the repeated key words in the book--fun, luck, values. The
bartender's emphasis on the unreasoning fun ends with Hemingway's objective report of the younger man's death, his
funeral, and the subsequent death of the bull.

The coffin was loaded into the baggage-car of the
train, and the widow and the two children rode,
sitting, all three together, in an open third-class
railway-carriage. The train started with a jerk,
and then ran smoothly, going down grade around
the edge of the plateau and out into the fields of
grain that blew in the wind on the plain on the way
to Tafalla. The train started with a jerk,
The bull who killed Vicente Girones was named
Bocanegra, was Number 118 of the bull-breeding
establishment, of Sanchez Taberno, and was killed
by Pedro Romero as the third bull of that same
afternoon. His ear was cut by popular acclama-
tion and given to Pedro Romero, who in turn, gave
it to Brett, who wrapped it in a handkerchief belonging to myself, and left both ear and handkerchief, along with a number of Muratti cigarette-
stubs, shoved far back in the drawer of the bed-
table that stood beside her bed in the Hotel Montoya, in Pamplona [198-99].

Hemingway follows this already wide-reaching image with the

suggestion of Cohn's "death" as Brett leaves with Romero. This brief descriptive sequence, then, has established the deaths of man, bull, man--all at the whim of the fiesta and its larger-than-life hero, the matador. [29]

Another device used frequently in the book is Hemingway's re-creation of natural idiom--in both dialogue and introspective passages--and perhaps more importantly his use of prose rhythms appropriate to the effect of the writing desired. Although the Imagist axiom, "Compose in the sequence of the musical phrase, not that of the metronome," was more liberating to poetry than it was to prose, it also spoke for a kind of freedom in prose--sentences unrestricted in tone, diction, or length because of formal English standards. In passages like this opening to Part III, Hemingway arranges sentences of varying lengths and compositions to create the tone he wants (here, a melancholic nostalgia), a tone which may be at odds with the ostensible facts of such a passage.

> In the morning it was all over. The fiesta was finished. I woke about nine o'clock, had a bath, dressed, and went down-stairs. The square was empty and there were no people on the streets. A few children were picking up rocket-sticks in the square. The cafes were just opening and the waiters were carrying out the comfortable white wicker chairs and arranging them around the marble-topped tables in the shade of the arcade. They were sweeping the streets and sprinkling them with a hose.
> I sat in one of the wicker chairs and leaned back comfortably. The waiter was in no hurry to come. The white-paper announcements of the unloading of the bulls and the big schedules of special trains were still up on the pillars of the arcade. A waiter wearing a blue apron came out with a bucket of water and a cloth, and commenced to tear down the notices, pulling the paper off in strips and washing and rubbing away the paper that stuck to the stone. The fiesta was over [227].

In these two paragraphs Hemingway moves from an emphasis on Jake's feelings and actions to the specific details of his locale, using those details to complete his sketch of Jake --alone, and now numbly realizing only that "it was all over." To open the second section with more description

of Jake helps the reader keep his focus on the protagonist.
The observable details are significant to the story (here and
usually throughout the novel) primarily because they help
identify an emotional state. Even the movement within this
passage, building from the short rhythms of the opening to
the longer phrases of the penultimate sentence, and coming
back to the restrained "refrain," suggests a crescendo in
Jake's feeling.

"The fiesta was over," repeated as it is in varying
contexts, is an example of Pound's organ base, which term
he described as "a sort of residue of sound which remains
in the ear" and acts to establish mood.[30] That Hemingway
was cognizant of the effects single repeated words or phrases
might have is evident not only in his fictional techniques but
in his comments about this repetition. Lillian Ross, for one,
quotes his saying, "In the first paragraph of Farewell, I
used the word and consciously over and over the way Mr.
Johann Sebastian Bach used a note in music when he was
emitting counterpoint."[31] It seems unlikely that Hemingway
would have missed Pound's later enthusiasms about the
"prose tradition in verse." As Pound had explained,

> Good writing is writing that is perfectly con-
> trolled, the writer says just what he means. He
> says it with complete clarity and simplicity. He
> uses the smallest number of words.... Also there
> are various kinds of clarity. There is the clarity
> of the request: Send me four pounds of. ten-penny
> nails. And there is the syntactical simplicity of
> the request: Buy me the kind of Rembrandt I like.
> This last is an utter cryptogram. It presupposes
> a more complex and intimate understanding of the
> speaker than most of us ever acquire of anyone.
> It has as many meanings, almost, as there are per-
> sons who might speak it....
> It is the almost constant labour of the prose art-
> ist to translate this latter kind of clarity into the
> former; to say 'Send me the kind of Rembrandt I
> like' in the terms of 'Send me four pounds of ten-
> penny nails.'[32]

Hemingway's emphasis on clarity and seemingly simple diction certainly reflects these kinds of distinctions.

The passage describing the fiesta also provides a good
example of Hemingway's failure to use overt symbols (a

failure which troubled many critics enough that they began inventing parallels between bulls, steers, and men). In repeating "The fiesta was over," Hemingway suggests broader implications for "fiesta"--a natural expectation of gaiety and freedom, here ironically doomed because of the circumstances of the characters. Through the description, we easily feel Jake's nostalgia, but not because fiesta is a true symbol; it never assumes any existence other than its apparent one. As Pound, again, had phrased the definition, "the natural object is always the adequate symbol ... if a man use 'symbols' he must use them that their symbolic function does not obtrude."[33] In one sense, in The Sun Also Rises, the amount of liquor a person drinks is symbolic--of both the kind of person he is, and the emotional condition he is in. So too is anger, and various stages of it. But the purely literary symbol--which the unsuccessful fireworks exhibition might suggest--is rare. Even the fireworks sequence is used more to show various characters' reaction to the failure than it is to represent another object or state of being per se. That Brett does not want to watch the failure is as significant for her character as the fact that she enjoys the artistry of the bullfights.

A corollary to the principle about symbolism is Pound's warning that the writer "Go in fear of abstractions." Love, hate, grief, religion, death, fear--these are the prime movers of the novel, yet the words scarcely appear. The Sun Also Rises is essentially a study of various kinds of love, yet no character ever discusses that passion. We are forewarned of Hemingway's definition to come in Death in the Afternoon, that "obscenity" is "unsoundness in abstract conversation or, indeed, any other metaphysical tendency in speech" (95). As Floyd Watkins has capably pointed out, Hemingway characters are nearly always to be mistrusted when they speak in abstract terms, whereas Hemingway heroes identify themselves by their preference for the concrete.[34]

Perhaps more than being a study of kinds of love, The Sun Also Rises is the paradigm of Jake's initiation into the fullest kind of that emotion. Jake's self-abnegation is not martyrdom; he knows he can not benefit from Brett's affair with Romero. But his education throughout the book consists in learning just how much his love--and hers--can bear. In Part I, it is Jake who wishes they could marry. By Part III he has learned that any fulfillment of their relationship is impossible. There is no question that he still loves Brett, perhaps even more in her new-found and convincing nobility.[35]

The novel in its three-part division is also the story of Brett's coming to maturity. Although in Part I she considers herself one with the Count and Jake, the men share satisfactions she does not understand. By the end of the novel she has lost the coy femininity that makes her somewhat cloying. She has thought of someone else--Romero-- and she continues thinking, of Mike and--always--of Jake. Stanley Edgar Hyman suggests, "The key action of the book is Brett's renunciation of Romero for the boy's own good, the first truly unselfish act of her life."[36] It could well be that her separation from the church is stressed throughout the novel to help build toward the ending, with her turn to Jake. Brett has no suprahuman comforts; she must call Jake, and the reader must see her telegram to him, as he does, as completely natural.

In his first novel, Hemingway appears to have drawn a little on a Hamlet-like situation. The many male characters act as either complements or foils to Jake, and the inevitable comparisons serve to keep Jake before us at all times, whether he is or not. By making him physically less than a competitor, however, Hemingway allows Jake as person rather than as male to occupy the center of these relationships, even the peripheral ones with Krum and Woolsey, the Britisher Harris, and the Basques. All of these masculine ties help to substantiate Jake's real if injured manliness (see Hemingway's Paris Review comments), and add pathos to his love affair with Brett. Jake's wound is his ironic gift from life, and he has no choice but to live with it--gracefully. Never again will Hemingway create such a sensational wound for a protagonist, even in the more obviously war-oriented novels, but it does serve a powerfully dramatic function in keeping the otherwise normal Jake out of the all too normal rivalry for Brett's affections.

Yet, for all his anguish, what does Jake say? Hemingway's choice of idiom for his hero could well have been autobiographical, but it also bears the trace of Pound's ideal character, who speaks in his own unliterary voice, often in cryptic suggestion. "I've got a rotten headache," when he can no longer bear seeing Brett; "I wanted to get home." The leavetaking scene with Brett after the dialogue with Count Mippipopolous has Jake vacillating between "Don't be sentimental" and then, after a kiss, "You don't have to go."

But after Brett does go, Hemingway gives us some brief introspection so that we understand the depth of Jake's feelings. When he comes to the more important good-byes at the end of Part I, as Brett is going to San Sebastian, Hemingway relies on our earlier knowledge, and gives us Jake as only an objective sketch: "The door opened and I went upstairs and went to bed." We can presumably re-create the rest for ourselves.

Hemingway frequently relies on Jake's silence or near-silence not only in the love scenes. Jake says only "Wasn't the town nice at night?" trying to reach Cohn through his own foggy bombast. (Jake's method here is Imagist also, bringing Cohn back to one specific experience, one night, one town; and having Cohn react like the most literal-minded of men.) Instead of dialectics, Hemingway here gives us suggestion.

Even Jake's wound is given in a simple declarative sentence, the poignancy of its terseness aided by the opening modifier: "Undressing, I looked at myself in the mirror of the big armoire beside the bed." The only adjective in the sentence describes a piece of furniture; the situation itself needs no description. Hemingway is, graphically, and in mirror image, "presenting," as Pound had edicted. The mention of bed also adds pathos to the brief line. The concentration on the furniture offers a moment of deflection also, before Hemingway brings us back to more understatement:

> Undressing, I looked at myself in the mirror of the big armoire beside the bed. That was a typically French way to furnish a room. Practical, too, I suppose. Of all the ways to be wounded. I suppose it was funny [303].

The climactic act of the novel--for Jake, his giving Brett to Romero--is another model of suggestive gesture instead of speech: "He looked at me. It was a final look to ask if it were understood. It was understood all right."

The chief danger in reading Hemingway is, I think, to overlook the rather apparent origin of many of his stylistic traits. Simplicity has too often become simple-mindedness, just as Williams' "No ideas but in things" became "No ideas." For instance, a recent essay by Ihab Hassan equates Hemingway's style with the character of Jake Barnes. I

agree with Hassan's summary of Hemingway's remarkable
tightness in writing, "Its rigor, terseness, and repetitions,
its intractable concreteness and vast omissions, resist rhetoric, resist even statement, and discourage the mind from
habitual closure." We cannot read Hemingway with any sense
of complacence because we are thrown too much on our own,
and the old patterns of expectation do not work. But Hassan
goes on to move from seeing style, somehow separated, to
seeing style as the only possible means of re-creating any
Hemingway hero, any Hemingway theme, because he finds
Hemingway very close to a contemporary "blankness and
rage.... Indeed, Hemingway's fiction makes for itself a
place in the tradition of silence that extends from Sade,
through Kafka, Genet, and Beckett, to the inverted literary
imagination of our own day."37 He continues,

> the ethic of Hemingway's characters is not only re-
> ductive but also solitary. What they endure, they
> can never share with others. Existentially, they
> remain alone; they find momentary communion on-
> ly in a dangerous ritual. Always they disengage
> themselves from the complexities of human rela-
> tions, and simplify their social existence to the
> primary functions of the body. 'The only thing that
> could spoil a day was people...,' Hemingway
> writes. 'People were always the limiters of happi-
> ness except for the very few that were as good as
> spring itself' [91].

Hassan's thesis in the complete essay would be almost convincing, were it not for his tendency to over-state.
There is a tone of pride here that is misleading; an attitude
of "my-knowledge-is-so-dreadful-that-I-cannot-communicate-
it." Perhaps the Hemingway protagonist is "alone" in that
he is usually limited to a few confidants rather than a men-
age. But he does have intimates--Bill Gorton, the Count,
Montoya, in the sense Romero, and in another sense, Brett.
In fact, Jake seems much less isolated than the miserable
Cohn, who has literally no one to talk with. But yes, the
kind of idiom Hemingway uses is terse and cryptic, primarily because the emotions are too big to handle in abstract
words, not because no emotions exist, or because there is
no desire to communicate. The Sun Also Rises gives evidence, in its various set scenes, of a great deal of communi-
cation. Jake understands perfectly what he must do for
Brett, and Brett knows how little she has to say to reach
him (in contrast to Francis Clyne who takes an entire

chapter to do what Brett can do in three lines). "Let's not talk," Brett tells him. "Talking's all bilge" (25).

The tacit understanding that exists here is better evidence of the author's interest in love, it seems to me, than of his obsession with death. (The too-facile equation between death and silence need not shadow every cryptic idiom in American literature.) Neither is the prevalent mood in this novel one of terror, as Mr. Hassan later states. (Terror of what? In Jake's eyes, the worst has already happened.) It seems to be rather one of sorrow, of sorrow growing from the unfulfilled love of Jake and Brett which acts in turn as a graphic image for the loves of the many other characters --men with men as well as men with women--which comes so seldom to fruition. For those few relationships that had the warmth of the sun in his title, Hemingway was only too grateful. In fact, most of his fiction stands in tribute to just such slight moments.

In his eagerness to present rather than to tell, Hemingway erred only in following the Imagist doctrines perhaps too closely. <u>The Sun Also Rises</u> is a difficult book to read correctly, until the reader understands the way it works; then it becomes a masterpiece of concentration, with every detail conveying multiple impressions, and every speech creating both single character and complex interrelationships.

Chapter Three

THE DEVELOPMENT OF CRAFT

It is one of the ironies of literary criticism that The Sun Also Rises became known as the novel of the lost generation: that this book (the apex of what Hemingway called "fifth-dimension" prose) was categorized in sociocultural terms instead of artistic. Unfortunately for his work, Hemingway himself was then considered a bright, virile young American, rather than the serious and painstaking craftsman he was. And just as ironically, Paris during the early twenties came to be thought of as the rallying ground of dissatisfied liberal Americans instead of what it more importantly was, the mecca for innovative artists. As Emily Watts describes that real Paris:

> In the Paris of the last generation, creative minds in all areas of art met and exchanged ideas; all of art participated, ... so to speak, in a single art. It was a time when poets became librettists, painters became poets, musicians became painters .... Articles concerning music, the pictorial arts, and literature appeared in the same periodicals ... and these were read by writers, painters, and musicians.[1]

Hemingway, too, as his own statements imply, was eclectic. He was ready to draw from experiments in not only writing but also in music, painting, and sculpture (and, interestingly, in all these areas, his taste mirrors Pound's). Mrs. Watts also views Hemingway's prose as being written with a consciousness of the "single art" toward which the Dadaists had moved, as they fused separate art forms in order to "involve all the senses." This fusion gives Hemingway's prose what Watts calls its "visual and audile relevance," and makes more significant its reliance on colors and shadows, on planes and almost geometric structures.[2]

Contemporary interest in the "single art" was not

unique to Dadaism, of course, for as early as 1914 Pound had championed the same kind of unity through Vorticism, the movement that so quickly followed Imagism, and differed from it chiefly in being a combination of painting, music, sculpture, and literary art. Whatever its method of application, Vorticism was to be an intensive art: hard, clear, sharp, dependent on the concrete and on the artist's arrangement of that concrete. [3] Even more than Imagism, Vorticism stressed speed, ideas rushing through the image or vortex rather than assuming the static pictorial quality more often identified with Imagism. As a result, structure and what Pound called "the design of composition" became increasingly important.

By 1922, when Pound and Hemingway met, the quibbling about terminology was over, and Pound could use image and vortex simultaneously. What remained from the years of critical rankling was a more mature recognition of the basic principles of modernist writing: (1) reliance on the concrete; (2) selection and arrangement of detail; (3) concentration; (4) attainment of speed, often through juxtaposition or counterpoint; and (5) use of organic form, idiomatic language, objective presentation, and natural rather than symbolic images. Using these tenets, Hemingway had a firm basis on which to proceed; and his writing from 1922 to 1926 is convincing testimony of his adherence to those principles, whether one classifies them as Imagist or Vorticist. But Pound had another recurring dictum: "The artist is always beginning. Any work of art which is not a beginning, an invention, a discovery, is of little worth." [4] Pound's enthusiasm for the new--an enthusiasm that was both a reflection of current literary views and also a catalyst in their formation--was evident too in his listing kinds of artists, with inventors preceding masters (Literary Essays, 23).

With his usual foresight, however, Pound qualifies this insistence on innovation by also pointing out that "the new thing that is durable does not spring up without roots. Joyce did not begin as an eccentric." [5] Hemingway heeds the caution and repeatedly voices parallel beliefs. In 1932 he defines the great artist in terms of innovation, as one who "goes beyond what has been done or known and makes something of his own." [6] Somewhat earlier, in speaking of his contemporaries, he could already sense that "They weren't after what he [himself] was after." [7] In 1935 he states further that "Some writers are only born to help another writer to write one sentence." [8]

Hemingway's theorizing about a "new prose" suggests that same compulsion to write in new ways. Stressing the suggestive power of concentrated, highly-selected prose, Hemingway hypothesized that such prose "is much more difficult than poetry. It is a prose that has never been written .... There is a fourth and fifth dimension that can be gotten."[9] And much of Hemingway's interest in writing prose-- and hence, perhaps, some explanation for the way one would achieve these other dimensions--lay in his interest in structure, design, composition; in, as he phrased it in Death in the Afternoon, "the sequence of motion and fact" that created the emotion, the moment of insight. His emphasis here not only focuses on the concrete object or scene, but on the image in motion (p. 2).

For Hemingway, the parts must in themselves be perfect (no extraneous words, images working for ever-widening effects, rhythm consistent with the end result) but the whole must also be perfect. As he wrote in retrospect:

> The modern novelist ... must have sound judgment and an accurate sense of proportion to select and reject among ponderous masses of material, and to arrange all with due subordination of parts and with a true perspective.[10]

Once Hemingway began writing about writing, his emphasis was even clearer. His primary concern was with method, with the means the writer needed to effectively create his characters and, through them, his themes. I do not mean to imply that this preoccupation with method--both language and structure--weakened his thematic impact; more relevantly, much of the artistic excitement in Hemingway's work lies in the way he achieved his effects.

What complicated Hemingway's situation as writer was not his insistence on the new or his interest in his craft, but rather his primarily lyric stance toward his materials. The lyric poet traditionally writes to create a response in the reader, a response that echoes his own feeling. Usually the lyric poem is brief, poignant, and single-faceted. It is about love, or loneliness, or death, or joy. For Hemingway, too, the verities remained simple, and constant: love, honor, courage, death. And since the writer's aim is to instruct as well as to please,[11] Hemingway found it impossible to deviate from what were for him the most important themes; his subjects, accordingly, remained fairly constant.

A 1932 comment reveals the lyric impulse at work as Hemingway recalls that one of the hardest things for a beginning writer was knowing "what the actual things were which produced the emotion that you experienced."[12] His aim here is the recovery of the personal emotion, not the telling of stories--or at least not primarily the telling of stories. Hemingway's direction as writer, then, seems to have been determined by both this lyric propensity and by his restless search for the new. As the following discussion will show, Hemingway's experimentation in his art resulted in partial failure as well as success. Throughout his writing, the Imagist dicta remained at the center of his work, but his innovation in structure, point of view, and style gave shading and nuance to that primary effect.

IN OUR TIME

Hemingway's first collection of stories and vignette inter-chapters is perhaps his most striking work, both in terms of personal involvement and technical innovation. Thematically, all the later Hemingway writing is here in embryo --the fruitless if still polite marriages, the understated agony of war (both military and personal), veneration for the old but unbeaten, censure for the uncaring and unjust, and the fascination with the way man meets death. The Nick Adams/Hemingway persona, regardless of his fictional name, is as effective in these early stories as he is ever to be; and Malcolm Cowley, for one, thinks this collection may be Hemingway's best, most fully realized, work. [13]

Technically, too, the book is a masterpiece of that most intriguing device, juxtaposition. Brought to artistic attention early in the century through movies and graphic art, this practice of essentially omitting transition, of placing one concrete image against another, edge on edge, was also an outgrowth of Joyce's Ulysses and Pound's Cantos. The position of each story, and its relationship to what surrounds it, is crucial in creating the total effect of In Our Time, just as it had been in Hemingway's 1924 vignette collection, the lower case in our time. Situating his longer stories within the vignettes of this earlier book was effective partly because it placed the burden of association on the reader, and partly because the more formal stories--which usually concerned personal and relatively slight happenings --were thus coupled with the pieces which focused on war, honor, man against death. As Hemingway had explained to

Edmund Wilson, the arrangement was intended "to give the picture of the whole between examining it in detail. Like looking with your eyes at something, say a passing coast line, and then looking at it with 15x binoculars."[14]

Hemingway's progression in In Our Time combines a chronological arrangement (the stories) with a largely thematic one (the vignettes). The shorter sketches move from World War I to bullfighting, thus taking the reader from the question of man's honor as determined by the relatively impersonal forces of war, to man's honor as self-determined. The order of the vignettes varies somewhat from their sequence in the earlier in our time; Chapter IX for example, originally appeared as Chapter II, as bullfighting was paired with war in order to give what were presumably the author's first views of each: war, in Chapter I, appears at first to be a huge, unruly drunk to the new kitchen corporal; bullfighting, conversely, seems to be an unpleasant blood ritual.[15] Successive glimpses of each, however, educate the observer more fully.

The studies of war emphasize death and the way men, including Nick, prepare to meet it. But another theme in the 1924 version is that of man's fear, stemming often from his ignorance--the soldier's fear during the shelling, Sam Cardinelli's and the typhoid victim's, the Chicago policeman's fear of the very "wops" Hemingway admired so greatly.[16] And a further connecting theme is that of man's responsibility. It is the bull that gores Maera, but men let him die. All the deaths that Hemingway records in the vignettes occur because of men, whether they are performing under the guise of patriotism or justice.

In the 1925 work, the stories trace these same themes but more obliquely. The first stories reflect Nick's boyhood reaction to his parents, then his broken romance; Hemingway takes us briefly to war, then to a marriage, and finally to Nick's trying in "Big, Two-Hearted River" to reestablish himself, ostensibly after his war experience but perhaps too after his years of battering loves. At the end of the book, Nick is alone, happily alone. And it is this essential tranquility that in retrospect heightens the tension and sorrow of the preceding pieces. By finally seeing what is possible for Nick, we can better understand the real torment of Krebs, Nick, or Maera. The calm of "River" would be much less moving were it not surrounded by the deaths of Maera and Sam Cardinelli: Nick is managing to save himself; other men--for various reasons--could not. A further dimension to Nick's endurance in this two-part story is given in the recently-published section "On Writing," which was once included as the ending of "River," Part II. Here Nick speaks movingly of his future life as writer and we see that as much of his composure comes from his belief in his writing as in his pleasure from fishing.

What occurs in In Our Time, as in the best collections of fiction, is that the powerful cumulative effect of the prose obscures the force of many single pieces. The book is unified, finally, by its organ base of tone--a mood of unrelieved somberness if not outright horror. The mood is even more striking because it is given the reader so objectively, with such control that he is caught in the tension resulting from the discrepancy between what is said and how it is said. The short reportorial nature of the prose in the vignettes is particularly effective in creating the objective tone.

Throughout the collection, Hemingway's arrangement contributes a great deal to the creation of this mood. "On the Quai at Smyrna," the preface vignette which was added in the 1930 edition, makes explicit both the devastation of war/life and man's protective coldness toward it. This detached recounting of incredible human misery during evacuation intensifies the tragedy, once the reader realizes the gap between what is meant and the understatement of the narrator. Here Hemingway doubles on his irony; the speaker is not one of Hemingway's heroes but a refined dolt--British, as in Chapter 5--who may not really see the horror. His detachment is consequently open to question, unlike the self-protective attitudes of Krebs or Nick later.

> You couldn't get the women to give up their dead
> babies. They'd have babies dead for six days.
> Wouldn't give them up. Nothing you could do about
> it.[17]

The effect here of death and bereavement en masse prepares the reader for the close-up stories to follow, and for their parallel tone.

While the vignettes deal with death, and subconsciously make us search for our joys, most of the stories proper deal with kinds of love--yet, because their outlook is often so bleak, we realize that the stories too are studies of

death. In "Indian Camp" and "The Doctor and the Doctor's
Wife," the opening stories, Hemingway portrays the death of
Nick's feeling for his parents. The pompous answers of the
doctor--who should understand men but doesn't--are played
against the Indian husband's unspoken act of contrition, and
Uncle George's unspoken hatred. Nick's mock delusion at
the end of the story (knowing he will never die) is modified
in the next tale when he comes to understand the fantasy
worlds of both his parents, working against each other and
making him their only point of contact, and contest.

After this introduction, Nick comes of age. The next
two stories, "The End of Something" and "The Three-Day
Blow," recount his broken romance, his chagrin at not being
his own man, and his subsequent drunk. Slight stories, they
reinforce Nick's isolation, and prepare for stories like "The
Battler" and the sequence of four marriage stories where
Hemingway observes what can happen to people who live without real love. Ad Francis, "the battler," lives in delusion
not because he's been beaten so much, but because his wife
has left him ("He was busting people all the time after she
went away"). The Elliots' perversion occurs seemingly because they are too selfish to care about each other, as are
many of the characters in the more suggestive love stories.
The Marjorie stories also, ironically, prepare the reader
for the haunting sense of disbelief in "Cat in the Rain," "Out
of Season," and "Cross-Country Snow" as the hero grows out
of his earlier illusions about love and marriage just as he
had earlier grown out of his illusions about his parents and
Bill. As Nick was to say in analyzing the problems of the
people around him, "You had this fake ideal planted in you
and then you lived your life to it."[18]

Fittingly, at the very center of the book Hemingway
has placed "Soldier's Home," the powerful story that so well
summarizes his primary theme in In Our Time, one man's
alienation from his culture, even from--or especially from--
those who love him. Yet the story is not a romantic hero-
against-society indictment; the values of the parents and the
culture are not entirely to blame for his isolation. Krebs
is himself bewildered; it is too soon after his war experience; he recognizes the games he will have to play, but he
is not yet ready to play them. Krebs needs time. And Hem
ingway gives him time by placing Nick's resolution in "River" as far away as possible, at the end of the book. What
Krebs sees as tentative--that he will someday have to find a
job and a girl and a place in this world--Nick has accepted.

(He <u>will</u> carry those heavy cans of spaghetti and beans so that he can enjoy them for supper, knowing he has paid the price.)

"Soldier's Home" is a central story too in that Hemingway here first expresses his ethic of virtue:

> All of the times that had been able to make him feel cool and clear inside himself when he thought of them; the times so long back when he had done the one thing, the only thing for a man to do, easily and naturally, when he might have done something else ... [69-70].

Most of his later characters will rise or fall on the basis of that ethic. So long as man had choice, his heroism had to depend on his resolution of that choice--thus, Jake's decision to introduce Brett to Pedro; Jordan's decision to blow the bridge, even with its great risks to the people he loved; Morgan's decision to turn in the bank robbers; Santiago's decision to stay with the marlin--each man has choice. Each man acts as he needs.

Similarly, Hemingway uses the idea of choice to draw negative characters. In "Cat in the Rain," George goes back to his book, instead of giving his wife the love she so apparently needs; Nick breaks up with Marjorie, but because Bill wants him to, not because he wants to; Robert Cohn does not leave when he should; Pablo sabotages the bridge effort (but redeems himself by reversing that choice). It is interesting that Hemingway's characterization grows more positive in the later writing: he spends less time and effort drawing characters who are not in some way valuable.

Even in this tendency to interrelate characters, Hemingway shows an awareness of the cumulative effects of his writing. Knowing one novel prepares us to understand another, just as we can more fully understand a single story in In Our Time by seeing the way it fits into, and participates in, the whole.

Yet, the collection is a whole, and not merely a collection, and like any novel, it gains strength from apt beginnings and endings. Just as Hemingway used epigraphs as a means of clarifying his intention in his novels, and as he used "On the Quai" as preface piece to this book, so he closed it with another purposeful vignette. "L'Envoi"

completes the emptiness of the collection for, even though
Hemingway has seemingly ended on a positive note with
"River," the victory that exists there is only a victory for
Nick--and a partial one at that. The victory is meaningless
for the culture, the times, or for any other character in
Hemingway's fiction. "L'Envoi" repeats the limitation, with
a more ironic slant: the king finds his happiness on a very
limited basis (physically limited as well as emotionally),
resting on his fallacious dream to retain his optimism and
contentment. The last lines suggest that delusions are all we
have, but perhaps they are better than nothing. That this
"meaning" is itself irony, and that Hemingway disagrees with
the king's outlook, is clear only when the stories are read as
a unit: neither Krebs nor Nick deludes himself. Krebs will
not say the right things to his mother, just as Nick will not
yet try the swamp. (Their attitudes in turn prepare us for
Jake Barnes' final resolution in The Sun Also Rises, his
"Isn't it pretty to think so?")

  Crucial as juxtaposition is in creating the whole of In
Our Time, it is perhaps even more important as a device
within each story, particularly in achieving the suggestive
quality Hemingway admired. In "Indian Camp," for example,
he uses only a single passage of juxtaposition to tell the
reader, with no direct statement, why the Indian husband was
superior to the white doctor:

> Just then the woman cried out.
> 'Oh, Daddy, can't you give her something to
> make her stop screaming?' asked Nick.
> 'No. I haven't any anaesthetic,' his father said.
> 'But her screams are not important. I don't hear
> them because they are not important.'
> The husband in the upper bunk rolled over
> against the wall [16].

Carefully, as in all his writing, Hemingway has prepared us
for this effect: we have seen Nick's earlier more objective
reaction to the woman suddenly changed when she screams.
We have been convinced with the doctor's scientific explana-
tions for everything; now the question of "Why no anaesthetic?"
rears its head, and we are no longer reassured even though
he repeats, as if to mesmerize Nick, that her screams are
not important. In the next passage Hemingway is to blacken
the doctor further with his seemingly justifiable attention to
washing his hands. Because he describes the washing operation three times, our suspicions are aroused, only to be

confirmed when he tells us, in another masterful juxtaposition, both how dirty the surroundings are and that his father's cleanliness is more obsessive than practical:

> When he was satisfied with his hands he went in
> and went to work.
> 'Pull back that quilt, will you, George?' he
> said. 'I'd rather not touch it' [17].

The reactions of the other men in the story--Uncle George's distance from the doctor, the husband's rolling silently in his anguishing--are necessary to the story so that we can more clearly understand the rightness of Nick's instinctive responses and the weakness of his father's. Through juxtaposition, Hemingway compares the reactions of these four characters even before the more definite resolution of the story.

Similarly, in "Cat in the Rain," Hemingway uses the kindly old hotel padrone as a contrast to the young husband, George. This story has a less apparent resolution, Hemingway working almost entirely through juxtaposition:

> They went back along the gravel path and passed
> in the door. The maid stayed outside to close the
> umbrella. As the American girl passed the office,
> the padrone bowed from his desk. Something felt
> very small and tight inside the girl. The padrone
> made her feel very small and at the same time
> really important. She had a momentary feeling of
> being of supreme importance. She went on up the
> stairs. She opened the door of the room. George
> was on the bed, reading [93].

In six words, Hemingway tellingly dims the warm glow he has worked so hard to establish. The rest of the story only reinforces our knowledge of the dulling relationship between husband and wife.

"Cat in the Rain," "The End of Something"--many of the stories in In Our Time are sometimes maligned because of their lack of "plot," of resolution. The problem again seems to be one of terminology. Plot to mean prescriptive action, action that points a moral, was too artificial to appeal to either Pound or Hemingway. As Pound had written,

> Life for the most part does not happen in neat

> little diagrams and nothing is more tiresome than
> the continual pretence that it does [Literary Es-
> says, 400].

Hemingway would favor using plot to mean motion.   He seldom wrote a static story.   Its movement might be circular,
might bring the reader back--or at least close to--its initial
mood, but the very motion would be the means of telling the
story, just as the fact that the story did circle would be integral to its "meaning."   The exhilaration of skiing in
"Cross-Country Snow" both opens and closes the story, yet
within its brief compass Hemingway has conveyed the tension in the young marriage because of the coming of the
child (a situation so expertly foreshadowed in the behavior of
the pregnant waitress).   The story suggests the change in
life style, the change in the marriage and the change in Nick
and George's friendship, all through the objective correlative
of skiing.   That act itself is described by Hemingway as the
epitome of physical freedom in its "rush and sudden swoop,"
the very freedom that in other ways forms the theme of the
story.   In 1955 Hemingway described his concept of movement in fiction:

> Everything changes as it moves.   That is what
> makes the movement which makes the story.
> Sometimes the movement is so slow it does not
> seem to be moving.   But there is always change
> and always movement.[19]

With Hemingway, there is also always a reason for
his inclusion--as, above, the fact that the surly waitress
was pregnant, and that it was Nick in his sensitivity to the
situation who was aware of her pregnancy.   No character,
no scene, no line of description remains in a story without
some credible justification (the chief difference between his
fiction and non-fiction seems to be the discursiveness of the
latter).   He often complained about some modern writing as
being "crude and defective in art":

> Many of their novels are without unity of plot and
> action.   The story is at times tediously spun out,
> running on and on like the tale of a garrulous
> storyteller.   They seem to have little idea of what
> the next chapter of their novel will contain.   And
> sometimes they drag in strange and unnecessary
> scenes with no apparent reason whatever.[20]

Hemingway's insistence on justifying everything in the story can also be seen in his choice of titles. Titles are of two kinds: either they signal the objective focus of the fiction, or they contain definite and expressible irony, as with "The Revolutionist" who is shy and gentle or "The Battler," pathetic instead of fierce. With deepr irony, Hemingway chooses "Indian Camp" so that he can play on the connotations of the supposedly dirty and insensitive Indians in the opening of the story, and thus reverse our expectations of their behavior in the course of the action. That his father had no anaesthesia (as well as no sympathy) for the woman surely stemmed in part from his reaction to her race. And "Soldier's Home" with its echo of "old folks' home" or "veterans' home" catches the reader off-balance twice--first when he realizes that Krebs is in his own home, where people love him, and therefore better off than someone in a "home"; and again, when he realizes that his first take is wrong, and that in Krebs' home love is used--albeit unintentionally--to control instead of to protect.

Such separation in kinds of titles is, with Hemingway, arbitrary at best, for even the simpler titles carry double weight. "Three-Day Blow" and "Cross-Country Snow" refer to Nick's emotional state as well as to the weather, just as "The End of Something" describes three things, the mill, the love affair, and Nick's illusions; and "Cat in the Rain," both the woman and the animal.*

The result of this extremely tight writing is that the reader must value every word, every scene, every character in his reaction to the fiction. Hemingway's comment about his writing's being "suggestive" is, of course, helpful; so too is his remark to William Seward that his short stories were of two kinds, "tough" and "as delicate as they

---

*Hemingway's earliest story, "Up in Michigan," has the same kind of double play in its title, and the title is probably one of the reasons Stein objected to it as "inaccroachable" (and Hemingway did not include it in In Our Time). Still, paired as it is with "On the Quai" in The First Forty-Nine Stories, "Up in Michigan" would have been a helpful inclusion, for it presents one set of ground rules for the romantic love Hemingway studies in much of his fiction. In the lovemaking of Jim and Liz, Hemingway draws man's most intimate cruelty. He uses juxtaposition well, as Jim's sleep of satisfaction blankets Liz's sad and frustrated tears; and the story, reflecting its characters, seems purposely inarticulate ("She was cold and miserable and everything felt gone"). Considering this story with the war vignettes, the deaths from military action seem no less tragic than the death of Liz's romantic dream, and the cold soldier narrating "On the Quai" resembles Jim in his devastating lack of understanding.

come."[21]   What he meant by <u>tough</u> were stories like "The Light of the World," "Indian Camp," or the Paco story, "The Capital of the World," where the sensational characters or actions nearly obliterate any less pleasant philosophical meaning.   Hemingway always felt called to defend these "un-poetic" kinds of subjects, even though he was constantly us-ing them to capture the most basic of truths.

In contrast, the "delicate" stories are the relation-ship stories--"The End of Something," "The Doctor and the Doctor's Wife," "Out of Season"--and Hemingway is again accurate in his choice of term: <u>delicate</u> in the sense of sug-gestive (although even his tough stories are primarily sug-gestive); but <u>delicate</u> also in his approach to subject matter. What easier focus in stories of love and/or marriage than sex scenes, yet there is almost no sex anywhere in <u>In Our Time.</u>   What easier means of characterization than a con-flict between two characters, but Hemingway instead presents two characters' reactions to an outside force, as with George and the doctor to the Indians, or with Bill and Wemedge to literature and romance.   Such an approach is oblique per-haps, but it is also much closer to reality, where everyday events comprise the fabric of most lives.   Yet from mun-dane and trivial happenings, something dramatic does happen: lives are formed, as Hemingway's stories so expertly show. His selection of episodes in a way parallels his objective presentation.   What easier way to draw character than to tell a reader what a man is like?   Hemingway instead relies al-most entirely on dialogue and action.   The short dialogue be-tween Krebs and his "best" sister presents in miniature the story's theme of using love for one's own ends:

> 'Am I really your girl?'
> 'Sure.'
> 'Do you love me?'
> 'Uh, huh.'
> 'Will you love me always?'
> 'Sure.'
> 'Will you come over and watch me play indoor?'
> 'Maybe.'
> 'Aw, Hare, you don't love. If you loved me, you'd want to come over and watch me play in-door' [74].

With Hemingway, dialogue can convey information, establish character, present theme, and create tempo--even while it appears to be only repeating itself.

In "Cat in the Rain," the differences in the seemingly repetitious dialogue pattern signal the quickening pace of
the story. Early scenes used generally short speeches and
relatively polite responses; here the wife's longer, more impassioned sentences provoke George's more abrupt answers.

> 'I want to pull my hair back tight and smooth
> and make a big knot at the back that I can feel,'
> she said. 'I want to have a kitty to sit on my lap
> and purr when I stroke her.'
> 'Yeah?' George said from the bed.
> 'And I want to eat at a table with my own silver
> and I want candles. And I want it to be spring
> and I want to brush my hair out in front of a mir-
> ror and I want a kitty and I want some new
> clothes.'
> 'Oh, shut up and get something to read,' George
> said. He was reading again [93-94].

Like the varying pace of "Cat," the pace of In Our
Time as a whole slows as it progresses, moving as it has
from the war deaths and the shock of "Indian Camp" to these
relationship stories where very little happens, except under
the surface. Lest we miss the real tension, Hemingway employs his masterful juxtaposition; the stories occur amid bullfighting vignettes, which in themselves stress man's choice
of the life and death struggle. The bullfighter struggles to
live with honor; similarly, the marriage in question struggles
to live--also with honor. But the bullfighting sequence goes
on to an end with the great Maera dead, whereas Hemingway
spares us the end of this marriage and swings back to an
earlier period for the last three stories, "My Old Man" and
the two parts of "Big, Two-Hearted River." By ending with
these stories, Hemingway broadens his interest in romantic
love to include different kinds of love--one man's responsibility for another (man for son in "My Old Man" and for himself in "River" as Nick searches again to find his separate
peace). The stories also remind us of the opening and recurring motifs of death. That the deaths in this collection
are as often figurative ones, resulting from love as frequently as from war, foreshadows one part of the enduring Hemingway vision. And that Nick is able to find his life even after experiencing some of the inevitable dying foreshadows another side of his composite.

AND OTHER STORIES

Because of the apparent thematic concerns, In Our Time might well have borne the title of Hemingway's 1927 collection, Men Without Women. * There are no happy love stories in the earliest of the three. Neither are there in the second group, but there are brief glimpses of relationships that might once have been loving. Hemingway's emphasis here--judging from his arrangement of the fourteen stories--is on the ironic happening, on the senseless chance that shapes, and maims, men's lives.[22] And although the fictional techniques are basically similar, Hemingway is already experimenting with more types of stories and changes in point of view and inclusion. Flashbacks are used much more often in the stories of Men Without Women.

There are no vignettes here, but the stories seem to be paired in somewhat the same way as the pieces of In Our Time. The opening pair--"The Undefeated" and "In Another Country"--create the oppressively ironic tone of the entire book. In the ineffectual bullfighting of Manual Garcia, the "undefeated," Hemingway epitomizes the romantic man's view of life--doing what one wants rather than what he is suited for. By including Zurito, the older retired picador, as quasi-narrator, Hemingway provides a vehicle for his own attitudes. After the grotesque bullfight, Manuel escapes death, and in that sense remains undefeated, but to no purpose: the crowd throws insults and garbage at him; he is no matador even though he has repeatedly risked his life. The fickleness of the crowd parallels the fickleness of war in the second story, "In Another Country," where the irony occurs when the major must work to strengthen his wounded hand even though he has just lost his young and beautiful wife.

The first two stories emphasize lives lived against the current of their emotion and purpose, the next two--"Hills Like White Elephants" and "The Killers"--focus squarely on the issue of murder as an image for man's lovelessness. "Hills" continues the powerful dialogue of "Cat in the Rain" as the unnamed girl and her lover discuss the "perfectly simple" coming abortion. Again we meet the

---

*Indeed, the titles for all three early collections could have been interchanged. In Our Time, Men Without Women, and the 1933 Winner Take Nothing each share Hemingway's disillusionment with both love and war.

rational male view set against the less articulate but more emotional feminine view:

> 'You've got to realize,' he said, 'that I don't want you to do it if you don't want to. I'm perfectly willing to go through with it if it means anything to you.'
> 'Doesn't it mean anything to you? We could get along.'
> 'Of course it does. But I don't want anybody but you. I don't want any one else. And I know it's perfectly simple.'
> 'Yes, you know it's perfectly simple.'[23]

The impasse at the end of "Hills" parallels the lack of resolution of the primary action in "The Killers." We see neither abortion nor murder, but Hemingway lets us know they are inevitable, given the robot-like natures of Al and Max no less than that of the "realistic" lover. Nick's aversion to this cold-blooded killing, and to the town's equally cold-blooded apathy, reveals his still innocent philosophy. The stories that follow in Men Without Women give him further initiation: "Che Ti Dice La Patria?" shows the corruption of Italians under Mussolini; "Fifty Grand," that of the protagonist athlete Jack; with "A Simple Enquiry" and "Ten Indians" playing less directly with the then-controversial sexual initiation. In both this collection and Winner Take Nothing, many of the most fragmented stories have as their chief point this sexual frankness: the importance to Hemingway of these subjects is clear in his later praise of Joyce: "In those days when words we knew were barred to us, and we had to fight for a single word, the influence of his work was what changed everything, and made it possible for us to break away from restrictions."[24]

Two of the stories in Men Without Women most contrived to produce irony are, again, stories of marriage. "A Canary for One" has as refrain, "Americans make the best husbands," and concerns divorce between Americans. "An Alpine Idyll" is the macabre tale of the frozen wife whose jaw made such an able lantern hook through the long winter. Much the stronger story, "Canary" continues in the vein of the estranged lover story, whereas the non-idyll is another of the "someone-told-me-this" stories that were occurring more and more frequently in Hemingway's writing--usually to the detriment of a collective total effect. When Hemingway uses a second-hand story, his machinery for hearing the tale sometimes interferes with the story itself. The problem appears to be that of using the Nick or I persona in too much detail instead of only as a transmitter or narrator for the actual story.

Because of the fragmented or digressive effect of many of these retold stories, they are not usually so effective as Hemingway's later long stories. Increasingly, the strongest fiction seems to be that relating to the Nick Adams or I personae. Hemingway's concluding story for Men Without Women, "Now I Lay Me," is the most skillful story in the second half of the book. The title's suggestion of childhood prayer is apt introduction to the story of the sleepless lieutenant remembering his early experiences with family and fishing. Similar to the actions of Nick in "River," the meanderings in "Now I Lay Me" convey the same impressions of a boy alienated from his parents, searching to find some respite in nature. In reading Hemingway's flashbacks, one is reminded of Pound's insistence on selectivity, on the use of "luminous details" through which the writer can get at "the universal element beneath them,"[25] as in this scene of conflict between parents:

> About the new house I remember how my mother was always cleaning things out and making a good clearance. One time when my father was away on a hunting trip she made a good thorough cleaning out in the basement and burned everything that should not have been there. When my father came home and got down from his buggy and hitched the horse, the fire was still burning in the road beside the house. I went out to meet him. He handed me his shotgun and looked at the fire. 'What's this?' he asked.
> 'I've been cleaning out the basement dear,' my mother said from the porch. She was standing there smiling, to meet him. My father looked at the fire and kicked at something. Then he leaned over and picked something out of the ashes. 'Get a rake, Nick,' he said to me [365-66].

The reality of the scene is achieved partly through Hemingway's idiom ("making a good clearance"), and partly through the dramatic tension--his mother making her proper welcoming appearance and then retiring before anything "unpleasant" might be said.

Hemingway used this one scene from the hundreds he might have chosen to give the story its overall unity, for it too becomes a study of marriage. The ending section of "Now I Lay Me" is given as dialogue between the protagonist lieutenant and John, his simple Italian orderly. John's diagnosis of his lieutenant's sleeplessness is that he ought to get married: "Every man ought to be married.... You'll never regret it." Juxtaposed with what Hemingway has shown us of the marriage most familiar to the soldier, that of his parents', we can empathize with his rejection of that solution. His subsequent scathing comparison between girls and trout-streams only reinforces his rejection. The story ends--and so the collection--with the orderly's insistence on his "going back to America." He was "very certain about marriage and knew it would fix up everything." The resemblance between the irony here and that at the end of "L'Envoi" which concludes In Our Time is striking. Once again Hemingway has shown the futility of conventional answers, at least for a protagonist like Nick and his related heroes, who carry within themselves memories of not comfort, but torment. Nick's search is not for fulfillment, but rather for forgetfulness.

"A Way You'll Never Be," another Nick Adams story from the 1933 Winner Take Nothing, continues the depiction of Nick as alienated, this time actually labeled crazy or at least battle fatigued; but Hemingway here begins to work the strain of resentment against military authority that will pervade his Spanish Civil War writing. His stream of consciousness techniques in this story, largely flashback surveys, foreshadow most closely those used later in "Snows of Kilimanjaro." They have no vivid central focus episode as does that section on his mother's cleaning in "Now I Lay Me" or the passages of Nick's making love to Trudy in "Fathers and Sons": consequently they serve as summaries of moods rather than evocations of theme. That Hemingway was increasingly interested in flashback is evident in his several attempts to use it as the real backbone of these stories, and particularly of "Fathers and Sons," his widest-ranging attempt to depict his father and the effect of both his life and death on his son's (and grandson's) life. And that he liked its effects seems evident in the position he gives each of these stories--they are placed either at the end of the story collections or in the center.

Aside from "A Way You'll Never Be" and "Fathers and Sons," the other superior stories in Winner Take Nothing are "A Clean, Well-Lighted Place" and "The Light of

the World," both stories Hemingway had mentioned in his
list of favorites. (Also on the list were "In Another Country," "Hills Like White Elephants," "A Way You'll Never
Be," "Snows," and "Short Happy Life"--in addition to the
usual anthology pieces, "Killers," "River," "Indian
Camp").26 It is interesting that Hemingway himself preferred either the retrospective Nick Adams stories or the
more suggestive relationship tales. "A Clean, Well-Lighted
Place" is in the tradition of "Cat" and "Hills" in its emphasis on dialogue; its use of the two main characters' reacting
to a situation--the old man and his sorrow--instead of to
each other; and its somewhat circular progression. But this
story is also new to Hemingway because it is not an apparently lyric situation--there is no Nick or Nick prototype. Hemingway has consequently been able to achieve as real an effect using these characters as he had previously reached only through his identifiable protagonists.

In contrast to these stories of direct focus, "The Sea
Change," "The Mother of a Queen," "Homage to Switzer-
land," "A Day's Wait," and "God Rest You Merry, Gentlemen" are weak. These seemingly retold stories in Winner
Take Nothing disappoint both in the telling and in the author's
relation to them, particularly after the convincing effect of
In Our Time with its many lyric stories. The explanation
for this unevenness lies, I think, in the fact that in Winner
Take Nothing Hemingway was trying new things, experimenting with both point of view and format. His use of Clenden-
ing's letters in "God Rest You" and, more noticeably, "One
Reader Writes," shows his continued fascination with the re-
creation of actual speech--"a good ear in a writer is like a
good left hand in a fighter."27 "A Natural History of the
Dead" continues the social satire of the earlier "Banal
Story," using mixtures of elevated and sardonic diction to
make Hemingway's hardly hidden points. In all these stories,
Hemingway is playing with his means of narrating, locating
one level of diction to create a very different effect from
that of a different level. Just as he had in several of the
In Our Time pieces employed a haughty British diction, so
he experiments in nearly all these stories with different
voices (in "The Light of the World" he even helps make
Alice's speech more convincing by emphasizing what a lovely
voice she had). In "After the Storm" the first person narrator is a modern-day pirate, as ineffectual in his expression as in his pillaging. Part of the success of "A Clean
Well-Lighted Place" is also verbal, with the speech of the
older waiter and the younger clearly distinguishing each man,

and the use of Spanish pacing a finely-timed drama in the ostensible "plot" of the story. The stream of consciousness which Hemingway is trying in "Now I Lay Me," "A Way You'll Never Be," and "Fathers and Sons" is also, of course, new verbal experimentation.

Chapter Four

THE PLACE OF TO HAVE AND HAVE NOT

Like many of the stories in Winner Take Nothing, much of Hemingway's writing during the thirties can be viewed most sympathetically as technical experimentation. The move to ostensible non-fiction with Death in the Afternoon and Green Hills of Africa was another means of exploring still other areas of writing, and his defensive apology for that move[1] indicates again his own compulsion to find new ways of expressing his ideas. Continuing from the short story experiments, here Hemingway also uses dialogue (the mocking "little old lady"--narrator exchange) as well as stream of consciousness flashbacks. His recurring mention in these non-fiction writings of aesthetic matters and literary anecdote further reminds the reader that his own stance toward his occupation was here a questioning one. Yet, as he similarly had in A Farewell to Arms, Hemingway here again concentrates on presenting love of whatever absorbs a man's energies and spirit; a willingness to relinquish the merely personal for a meaningful ritual--fishing, bullfighting, hunting; and a readiness to die, if need be, well.

The subject matter of his writing during this period also shows his questioning. His recurring situation is man meeting death, or a possible death; or man involved in the moral and political dilemma of war. "I am interested in the goddam sad science of war,"[2] he told Lillian Ross. And in 1932 he had defended his interest in death: "I was trying to learn to write, commencing with the simplest things, and one of the simplest things of all and most fundamental is violent death."[3] To show Hemingway's own growth during this period, one might compare his attitude in 1932, when he was outraged by the abbreviated galley heading "Hemingways [sic] Death" on each sheet of proof for Death in the Afternoon, with his resolute statements a few years later in Green Hills that death now held no fears for him.[4] And as his fiction also showed, the Hemingway of "The Short Happy Life of Francis Macomber" and "The Snows of Kilimanjaro" is on his way toward a personal solution. By 1939, Hemingway is able to draw a convincing portrayal of Robert Jordan; and by 1942, when he edited the Men at War anthology, he used as epigraph the lines "By my troth, I care not: a man die but once; we owe God a death." He continued in this introduction to stress that since death was inevitable, man had control over only his manner of dying. It is this response that he investigated again and again in the stories of the thirties: whether obliquely in "A Clean, Well-Lighted Place," "A Day's Wait," or "The Gambler, the Nun, and the Radio" or more directly in "Snows," "Fathers and Sons," and To Have and Have Not. Indeed, it is the latter 1937 novel that gives him his widest canvas for his study of how men die.

Harry Morgan, his wife Marie and their three daughters live from his earnings as a guide fisherman in the waters off Cuba. Morgan is distinguished on three counts, each of which the novel works hard to both establish and support. He has integrity, as the opening scene shows. Morgan is approached by three young Puerto Ricans who will pay him $3000 to get them, illegally, into Cuba. He refuses, and unfortunately several pages later they are shot (the Machado revolt is the backdrop for much of the Cuban unrest). The second point Hemingway makes is that Morgan is a virile and handsome man, even after losing his arm; and his love for and with Maria is tender and compelling. Third, he is a loyal friend, as his many relationships with men throughout the novel show, but he is also a demanding one--his friends must know how to do things properly. In short, Morgan is the usual Hemingway man; yet he is not the usual "hero" for he has two handicaps--he is not particularly literate, as are Nick, Jake, and Robert Jordan; nor is he ambitious.* Morgan makes no plans for the future, and consequently what happens to him (in less than a year) is doubly pathetic. As Hemingway presents him, Morgan asked for nothing but a chance to work hard for a modest livelihood. Instead he was forced into murder and his own early death. There is no glamor or romance in the modern day pirate story; it is all too blatant that Harry (Henry) Morgan's turn to "piracy" (the smuggling of rum and aliens) came not from any love of adventure but from a dull, and dulling, economic necessity.

The description which Hemingway gave The Sun Also

---

*In this respect Morgan foreshadows Santiago, but because Santiago is so much older his lack of ambition seems more natural.

Rises, "A damn tragedy with the earth abiding forever as the hero," might well apply to this novel, but perhaps, as the last page suggests, with the sea abiding. Harry Morgan is not a tragic hero because his choice is so simply made; yet his circumstances are themselves tragic. He has slight recourse after Johnson, his customer, loses Morgan's fishing gear overboard, and then goes on to bilk him of the cost of the boat and guide for the eighteen-day trip. Morgan has to have money to get home, so he runs Chinese migrants, and murders the contact man rather than be killed himself. When the next step occurs and he loses an arm--and effectively loses his livelihood--he has little choice but to take on even more dangerous occupations. The very weakness of the quick characterization makes Hemingway's point: it did happen fast, from spring to summer to winter, and Harry Morgan was dead, another victim of a society that only used its maimed and deprived instead of helping them.

Ironically Morgan embodies the stable middle-class virtues. He loves his wife and children, he works hard and does his best, he trusts his fellow men--for a while. But society takes him, and gives him no opportunity to improve his condition. The irony of having even the debacle at the end go unexplained--so that he does die in vain, and Maria go penniless--is Hemingway's final word on the uncaring American system. We feel in the laconic presentation of it all the desperate need for a Horatio to tell Morgan's final, exonerating story. Instead, Hemingway gives us an obtuse novelist, a would-be spokesman for the people, who comes in contact several times with Morgan, and who thinks of writing about Maria, yet sees nothing of value in their episode.

The differences between this writer, Richard Gordon, and Morgan seem calculated to make the latter, with his inarticulate speech and his aim for the mediocre, a truly "average guy." Morgan is no spokesman for man in need; he is man in need. And the novel is certainly Hemingway's proletarian novel. The crux of the dramatic situation is economic; Morgan's only introspection centers on his financial dilemma. In the early thirties, when Hemingway actually began writing the story, there were no social agencies, no unemployment or disability aids;[5] even though the story is placed in Cuba, its implications are all too clear. As Morgan thinks to himself before he takes the job of transporting the bank robbers,

I could sell the house and we could rent until I

got some kind of work. What kind of work? No
kind of work. I could go down to the bank and
squeal now and what would I get? Thanks. Sure.
Thanks. One bunch of Cuban government bastards
cost me my arm shooting at me with a load when
they had no need to and another bunch of U.S. ones
took my boat. Now I can give up my home and get
thanks. No thanks. The hell with it, he thought.
I got no choice in it. [6]

When he is himself near death, trying to tell his friends
what really happened, Morgan finds only the same kind of ob-
tuseness the tourists show at the end of The Old Man and the
Sea. Even what he has died to learn is wasted.

So the story of man economically victimized by his society appears for the first time in a Hemingway novel, but
that theme does not stand alone. To Have and Have Not is
also concerned with Hemingway's constant search for purpose
in life (and death): nearly half the book deals with a writer
and his liberal crowd, these secondary characters juxtaposed
at sometimes awkward points with Harry and Marie Morgan.
Hemingway prepares us for including that unrelated story line
by shifts in his point of view. Part I (Chapters 1-5) is told
through Morgan's eyes, but in Part II (6-8) Hemingway has
used a mixed first and omniscient. Chapter 9 goes even further from Morgan's perspective. It has as subtitle, "Albert
Speaking," and presents the reflections of one of the starving
but uncomplaining Conches at whom Morgan marvels. Albert
says simply of Morgan, "he was changed now since he lost
his arm [and his boat].... When he was in a boat he always
felt good and without his boat he felt plenty bad" (97). Chapter 10 is Harry's crucial monologue: "What choice have I
got? They don't give you any choice now. I can let it go;
but what will the next thing be?" (105). Successive chapters
are handled through omniscient point of view, with the tone of
ironic understatement prevailing; Hemingway leaves this tactic only once, for Marie's soliloquy in the final chapter.
This shifting of narrative perspective is much better done a
few years later in For Whom the Bell Tolls, when stream of
consciousness passages appear within chapters instead of by
chapter. But the experimentation occurs for the first time
here, and as such--experimentation--is of interest.

Hemingway also foreshadows his technique in that
later novel with his emphasis on characters' effective uses
of language. Their speech indicates the differences between

Harry and his foil characters, writer Richard Gordon and professor John MacWalsey. Gordon especially serves as the contrast figure; he has talent, means, a beautiful wife; yet he is to lose love and purpose before the book ends. Again in preparation for For Whom the Bell Tolls, Hemingway here, from Chapter 18 on, alternates focus between Morgan slowly dying, alone, on the borrowed boat, and Gordon, losing his wife by talking at length with MacWalsey (his adversary) and the aimless men of the cafe. Gordon is the proud outsider, almost outside human experience, as his dialogues with his wife also show. Language for the writer, instead of being a vehicle, is only an obstacle.

That Gordon is ineffectual comes as no surprise, for Hemingway has damned him early: in one of the many contrived "crossing" scenes, Gordon glances at Marie Morgan, but dismisses her: " 'Look at that big ox,' he thought. 'What do you suppose a woman like that thinks about? What do you suppose she does in bed?' " Instead of admiring her, he uses her negatively in his current fiction,

> In today's chapter he was going to use the big woman with the tear-reddened eyes he had just seen on the way home. Her husband when he came home at night hated her, hated the way she had coarsened and grown heavy, was repelled by her bleached hair, her too big breasts, her lack of sympathy with his work as an organizer. He would compare her to the young, firm-breasted, full-lipped little Jewess that had spoken at the meeting that evening. It was good. It was, it could be easily, terrific, and it was true. He had seen, in a flash of perception, the whole inner life of that type of woman [177].

In Gordon's inability to know reality lies his failure either to write or to manage his own life. Yet he is a "have" and the Morgans are the "have-nots." Throughout the book Hemingway treats this irony crudely; and he gives the last chapter--in effect, the last word--to Marie's monologue of mourning for her beloved husband. An earthier Molly Bloom, Marie is never resigned to Harry's death; she is not complacent; she is bitter and blunt, and there is no mistaking the depth of her grief. The novel ends, as it began, with all attention on the Morgans.

As readers recognized, To Have and Have Not was

not one of Hemingway's smoothest novels. It was a groping book, similar in many ways to <u>Death in the Afternoon</u> and <u>Green Hills</u>, because Hemingway was questioning his life role, his presumption at setting himself up to judge people he could not hope to understand. It is true the novel is marred by bad writing, by including too much literary and academic gossip, and by emphasizing the secondary story overmuch; but that it holds more interest than many proletarian novels should also be acknowledged.

The same themes (aside from economic ones) appeared almost simultaneously in Hemingway's two long stories of 1936, both more representative stylistically. "The Snows of Kilimanjaro" took as its primary theme the writer's wasted potential, treating it almost as an objective correlative for the writer's wasted life. "The Short Happy Life of Francis Macomber" worked with a sub-theme of both "Snows" and <u>To Have and Have Not,</u> the possible relationship between husband and wife, here too used as an objective correlative for man's relationship with life. (This shift in his use of the relationship indicates a wider awareness, a different purpose in these stories. The relationship in "Out of Season," for example, was central in itself, not a means to view the protagonist's whole life.) In both stories Hemingway was utilizing the key situation of a man facing imminent death, with much of his character in suspension, depending upon his manner of meeting that death.

"Short Happy Life," a superbly toned story written in the spring of 1936, mines Hemingway's ironic vein, as Francis finds his courage, his manliness, only in the closing moments of his life. The fear that had earlier driven him to cowardice has now driven Margot, the gentler sex, to murder. Drawing partly on his own safari experiences, Hemingway swathed the story in the caustic banter the "society" spoke and even structured it to maintain the semblance of decorum so important to the Macombers. The opening scene is luncheon, with "Will you have lime juice or lemon squash?" as initial dialogue. Not for two pages does the objective narrator explain Francis' disgrace, and he does so then in one of his misleading compounded sentences, aligning elements that are certainly of unequal importance:

> He was dressed in the same sort of safari clothes that Wilson wore except that his were new, he was thirty-five years old, kept himself very fit, was good at court games, had a number of big-game

fishing records, and had just shown himself, very publicly, to be a coward. 7

Margot's murder of her husband is also casually played. The reader's interest is all on Macomber's "coming of age" for Wilson too is involved in that; both Wilson and the reader underestimate Margot's fear. Hemingway devotes an entire paragraph to the exciting details of the buffalo's charge, ending--in a pattern somewhat like that of the above quotation--with Macomber's death.

"The Snows of Kilimanjaro" is a more explicit study of these same "haves" that were to figure in To Have and Have Not, but the social study again is only a sub-theme. Here Hemingway comes more fully to grips with his self conscious quest for purpose in life, and answers his doubts about the occupation of writer. Like the leopard found in the snows of the mountain, men too eternally seek satisfaction and purpose; and some dare to go so far beyond their peers that they die in isolation. The unique qualities in this story --probably one of the most mature of Hemingway's statements about the dilemma of art and its responsibilities--are his poetic reliance on images and the juxtaposition of the italicized flashbacks. Rather than the understatement of style and structure in "Short Happy Life," Hemingway here expands and embroiders the basic theme of dying man facing himself. This is a much more introspective story than most Hemingway had written (it may well lead directly to Across the River) and thus he is forced to use what were, for him, new techniques.

The first series of flashbacks all relate somehow to the theme of snow; the second, to love and/or death--death in war, and death of love; the later series to death alone-- yet all serve to reinforce Harry's alienation, his disunion from his wife and her life, the life he had chosen for himself to the detriment of his art. Like the flashbacks, every image in the story gives us deeper understanding of the protagonist, and it is only against the image patterns that the ostensible plot, as recited in the dialogue, "works." Consequently the ending, which on one level matter-of-factly depicts Harry's death outside the tent, and Helen's later realization of it; and on another has him, in a sense, rescued from the living death which his life had become (the same kind of living that Macomber experienced before his "short happy life" began) and carried, imaginatively, to the bleak proud snows that imaged so many of his happier memories.

Given the progress of the story, it is entirely plausible that both endings are intentionally real, and that the reader need not choose between them.

As the story moves toward his death, Harry's self-destroying bitterness does ameliorate, and he manages to re-capture it all. The sense of loss merges into the tranquility that pervades the ending (it is this tone that lures the reader into at first believing the "escape" to the mountain). The scene is not unlike that of Harry Morgan, so slowly dying on board the boat, holding on to his life only to help Marie. The scenes are almost unbearably slow.

That his later fiction all deals with this same dramatic situation is clearly evident. Santiago's readiness to accept death, if need be, as of little consequence in relation to his mysteriously beautiful quest is as convincing as Robert Jordan's disdain for thinking of himself as he tries to gain time for Pablo's escaping band. Perhaps Hemingway's choices here--to leave Jordan before his actual death, and to spare Santiago his--were wise; for these novels are triumphs. The death scenes in Islands in the Stream and Across the River and Into the Trees (as well as in To Have and Have Not) are ultimately disappointing, although these books are perhaps more directly built around the issue of how men die. (Indeed, one critic has described Across the River as "a gentle story, intended to give a procedure for dying."8)

Paradoxical as it seems, the result of all this presentation of characters nearing the moment of death is affirmative. Those who lived well, fully and humanely, died well too; in fact, those who lived less than nobly usually ended better than one might have thought. Death for Hemingway--once his own critical years had passed--seemed to take on more qualities of panacea than of mystery.

PROGRESSION TOWARD
FOR WHOM THE BELL TOLLS

During the thirties, much of Hemingway's writing effort was directed toward trying new methods of fiction; exploring the subjects of hunting, fishing, bullfighting, and Cuban living; and approaching from different directions the theme of man meeting his death.

In one way Hemingway was lucky that, at the point of

his consuming interest in the way a man lives and dies, the Spanish Civil War presented a dramatic vehicle for his philosophy. By capitalizing on the high social interest in the Fascist-Loyalist conflict, he insured a market for his war novel, and markets--as well as critical opinions--were of consequence to Hemingway. But more important than the obvious commercial value of the war was what Hemingway viewed as its ambivalence. Neither side was completely trustworthy; few men were noble; there was the usual political chicanery moving at the expense of men's lives. And because the conflict was geographically removed, any writing about it could be free of propaganda without hamstringing the author.

Writing about war immediately freed Hemingway of the kinds of problems he had had in making Jake Barnes an heroic figure--when he has no bridges to blow; indeed, when he has nothing more to organize than Brett's love affairs and nothing more to do than keep peace among his friends. It is difficult for some readers reared on situation thrillers to find the drama in Jake and Brett's situation. But a war setting, a lesson in isolated-man heroics, a beautiful girl to love--the outlines, at least, were much more conventionally heroic. The artistry of For Whom the Bell Tolls, of course, is that it is not only a good story but that it brings to a resolution many of the questions and themes that had been bothering Hemingway for at least a decade, and possibly for two.

I suppose it begins with A Farewell to Arms, the novel Hemingway had been trying to write for ten years, at least partially the account of his own war experience in Italy, and of his own love for his Catherine. In many ways it is an early novel: the war setting and the love-against-all-odds situation are easily dramatized; and Frederic Henry's defection and resulting "knowledge" are easy reflections of postwar disillusionment. (Carlos Baker suggests too that Farewell "might have been Hemingway's first novel rather than his second. More than four years before he brought out his first novel, The Sun Also Rises, 1926, he had already begun to write a story about a young American ambulance driver on the Italian-Austrian front ... 1922. Nobody except his first wife ever saw this story, but it seems to have been, according to her, highly romantic in manner and conception."9) A Farewell to Arms does give Hemingway his chance to write a Tietjens story; it also gave him a chance to try alternating "treble and bass"10 as he juxtaposed war scenes with the lyric love scenes; but in several ways (transition within scenes, dialogue, both in pace and content; and too easily symbolic weather) the work is less well written than Hemingway's first fiction.

Thematically, too, the despairing attitudes of Frederic Henry are not the usual Hemingway responses (Robert Jordan does not run out, nor does Santiago or even Cantwell), as is Catherine in her passivity not the usual Hemingway heroine.[11] The novel seems to be pre-<u>Sun Also Rises</u>, in fact, because the resignation Henry learns at the end of the novel has already been the basis of Jake Barnes' usual behavior. Perhaps that was Hemingway's intention, and perhaps more of the novel than just the beautiful American nurse is autobiographical. Perhaps this is the story of one man's initiation. But being published after <u>The Sun Also Rises</u> as it was, <u>Farewell</u> was viewed as a progression. Perhaps Hemingway--in the next years of self-exploration--regretted some of that impression; perhaps part of his desire to write another war novel was to correct it--or, if not exactly to correct it, to strengthen it in terms of his more mature perspective. He had explained in the Ross profile that <u>Across the River</u> was a better novel than <u>A Farewell to Arms</u> because "It hasn't got the youth and the ignorance" (43). And he wrote in his 1942 introduction to <u>Men at War</u>,

> The editor of this anthology [himself], who took part and was wounded in the last war to end war, hates war and hates all the politicians whose mismanagement, gullibility, cupidity, selfishness and ambition brought on this present war and made it inevitable. But once we have a war there is only one thing to do. It must be won. For defeat brings worse things than any that can ever happen in a war (5).

Like Frederic Henry, Hemingway echoes Clausewitz in viewing war as a political operation; but, unlike Henry, he assumes responsibility for its outcome. That war "must be won" or the culture will suffer is a newer outlook for Hemingway than Henry's. Or it could well be that the despair at the end of the book was designed to make the reader feel the futility in the lovers' choice. Had Henry stayed where he belonged, or found a niche where he could belong, he would have had at least that. As it is, he is a man without a wife, a man without a country.

Despite the important differences, Hemingway has very clearly drawn from <u>Farewell</u> some basic elements of <u>For Whom the Bell Tolls.</u> In the earlier work, Henry's puzzled rage during the retreat from Caporetto because a small bridge has been destroyed while the main bridge remains intact foreshadows the importance of Jordan's mission in the later work:

> 'Why isn't there somebody here to stop them?' I said. 'Why haven't they blown the bridge up? Why aren't there machine guns along this embankment?'
> 'You tell us, Tenente?' Bonello said. I was very angry.
> 'The whole bloody thing is crazy. Down below they blow up a little bridge. Here they leave a bridge on the main road. Where is everybody? Don't they try and stop them at all?'

Another detail that appears as, really, theme in <u>For Whom the Bell Tolls</u> is the sudden and arbitrary death of Aymo. The sharp-eyed Aymo first spots the German bicycle troops, yet it is he who is shot in the back in a place where there is apparently no danger, by not Germans but Italians. Robert Jordan's death, like Catherine's, shares the same arbitrariness, for his mission was itself successful, and his escape nearly so. Jordan's way of meeting his death was, to be sure, <u>not</u> arbitrary.

The many differences between <u>A Farewell to Arms</u> and <u>For Whom the Bell Tolls</u> may be attributable not so much to a change in Hemingway's political ideology, as Floyd Watkins attempts to prove in one of the weakest sections of his book,[12] but rather to a difference in the point of origin for each of the two novels. The earlier is admittedly Hemingway's most autobiographical work, and critics have often used this identification as a virtue. While finding familiar elements may comfort the reader, the writer is often working more truly when he is not bound by facts from a real experience. As Henry James wrote in 1884 when discussing the matter of young ladies trying to write about soldiers, understanding an emotion is more important in some cases than literally experiencing it:

> Experience is never limited, and it is never complete; it is an immense sensibility.... It is the very atmosphere of the mind; and when the mind

> is imaginative--much more when it happens to be
> that of a man of genius--it takes to itself the faint-
> est hints of life.... The power to guess the un-
> seen from the seen, to trace the implication of
> things, to judge the whole piece by the pattern ...
> --this cluster of gifts may almost be said to con-
> stitute experience. [13]

Particularly when an author is creating character, self-determination is essential. The writer must be comparatively
free to let the character direct his own way. In A Farewell,
Hemingway's portrayal of Catherine, probably his weakest
heroine, is a case in point; yet when Carlos Baker was questioned about the supposed unreality of Catherine, his answer
assumed the autobiographical fallacy--that because a character was modeled from living people, that character would be
a vital one:

> Catherine herself is a composite of not only Agnes
> von Kurowsky but also Hadley Richardson and Paul-
> ine Pfeiffer.... The very fact that they [Henry
> and Catherine] originate in real persons seems to
> me to give them some claim on credibility. [14]

Rather, the reverse would appear to be true, considering
that Pilar and Maria are Hemingway's best-drawn heroines,
and For Whom the Bell Tolls is his most imaginative novel.
(Very few characters from the book can be identified as real
persons by the critics.) However, in Hemingway's own view
of the way writers create best, perhaps that high imaginative quotient is the reason For Whom the Bell Tolls is such
a superb book:

> The only writing that was any good was what
> you made up, what you imagined. That made ev-
> erything come true. Like when he wrote 'My Old
> Man' he'd never seen a jockey killed and the next
> week Georges Parfrement was killed at that very
> jump and that was the way it looked. Everything
> good he'd ever written he'd made up. None of it
> had ever happened. Other things had happened.
> Better things, maybe. That was what the family
> couldn't understand. They thought it all was ex-
> perience.
> That was the weakness of Joyce. Daedalus in
> Ulysses was Joyce himself, so he was terrible.
> Joyce was so damn romantic and intellectual about

> him. He'd made Bloom up, Bloom was wonderful.
> He'd made Mrs. Bloom up. She was the greatest
> in the world.
>   That was the way with Mac [Robert McAlmon].
> Mac worked too close to life. You had to digest
> life and then create your own people....
>   Nick in the stories was never himself. He
> made him up. Of course he'd never seen an Indi-
> an woman having a baby. That was what made it
> good.[15]

And as Hemingway told Robert Manning,

> To invent out of knowledge means to produce in-
> ventions that are true.... In The Old Man and
> the Sea I knew two or three things about the situa-
> tion, but I didn't know the story. I didn't even
> know if that big fish was going to bite for the old
> man when it started smelling around the bait. I
> had to write on, inventing out of knowledge. You
> reject everything that is not or can't be completely
> true. I didn't know what was going to happen for
> sure in For Whom the Bell Tolls or A Farewell
> to Arms. I was inventing.

Hemingway's statements reveal once again his allegiance to
the Pound camp. For this trust in the writer's own imagination parallels Pound's conviction that "All poetic language
is the language of exploration,"[16] that the writer trusts his
work to take him into previously unknown areas, often in-
sightful ones. (See also Denise Levertov's prolegomena
about writing as a voyage of discovery,[17] and the way this
rationale relates to the entire aesthetic of organic form).
Pound continues to connect his idea that such exploration
(best shown in the Japanese art that proves "the beauty of
this sort of knowing") has viable translation into the role of
image: "The image is the word beyond formulated language."

> I once saw a small child go to an electric light
> switch and say, 'Mamma, can I open the light?'
> She was using the age-old language of exploration,
> the language of art. It was a sort of metaphor,
> but she was not using it as ornamentation.
>   One is tired of ornamentations, they are all a
> trick, and any sharp person can learn them.[18]

To Hemingway, too, the word <u>trick</u> as Pound used it here quickly became an anathema. So long as he wrote, he prided himself on never using any of the "tricks" possible.

The larger concept remains--the artist as maker, just as the root of the word <u>poet</u> suggests; and the role of the artist-maker to create meaningfully. As Pound had declared in 1915, "The essential thing in a poet is that he builds us his world"[19]--not <u>the</u> world, or a <u>fictional</u> world, or a world that teaches the great moral lessons, but the world of the writer, filled with both his strength and his limitations.

In many ways <u>For Whom the Bell Tolls</u> is the re-creation of Hemingway's world, as he presents the single man caught in an impossible situation, the resolution of which can only be satisfying once the hero understands himself. That Hemingway was able to complete the canvas with many characters that he loved, and to locate the situation in the midst of a provocative country and compelling politics only added to the brilliance of his "exploration."

Chapter Five

THE MARINATING OF
FOR WHOM THE BELL TOLLS

There is evidence that most of Hemingway's successful fiction has undergone not only serious and major revising, but long periods of pre-writing.[1] As early as 1936 Hemingway was planning to write Santiago's story; A Farewell to Arms grew from reactions covering at least ten years before the novel's 1929 publication. Contrastingly, To Have and Have Not began as a long short story and accidentally--and rapidly--grew into a novel, as did Across the River and Into the Trees. Hemingway's own amazement at the completion of the latter novel testifies to the very brief time between the story's inception and its finish. Max Perkins tells the story of asking Hemingway why he did not write about the life in the Cape Sable waters. " 'Maybe sometime,' said Ernest, pensively. 'I don't know enough about it yet'.... He did know, thought Perkins, but it would not emerge in written form until it had marinated a long time in the depths of his subconscious."[2] As this anecdote illustrates, Hemingway's usual approach was to have his story so well in mind--at least in character and intent, if not in plot--that the writing of it was almost always "right."

No major Hemingway novel so well reveals this process of gradual mastery of possible materials as For Whom the Bell Tolls, the book which was written only after Hemingway had explored its themes, and established prototypes for many of its characters, in much of the writing from A Farewell forward, but more particularly in his North American News Alliance columns, a movie scenario, The Fifth Column (his only play), and six short stories. The setting for each is the Spanish Civil War, but Hemingway uses numerous scenes and characters to convey the mood of that conflict. Because he in 1937 announced that he was planning to do a novel about these experiences, it is plausible to consider this writing--done from the fall of 1937 to the spring of 1939-- as very closely related to the novel.

Perhaps the most surprising point about the writing here considered is that it is not the novel in miniature. At the beginning of his Spanish Civil War experience, Hemingway had forgotten what war is like, and, as his dispatches so clearly show, his early impressions of the Spanish conflict were very different from his reactions two years later. The strongest consensus of the dispatch coverage, which begins in March of 1937, is that of understated surprise, replaced quickly by less understated horror. Then as he learns about the Loyalist methods of survival, his horror at war turns to admiration for the people involved, and that admiration deepens, and deepens. Finally comes the disillusionment with the politics of the cause, and with leaders and their lack of concern for the people.

In light of this progression in Hemingway's attitudes, it is interesting that The Fifth Column, his only play, was written when he had been in Madrid only six months. Some elements in the play suggest that war is still somewhat glamorous, and the flip attitudes and stock triangle situations seem appropriate to an almost romantic view of the conflict. Living in the Madrid Hotel Florida, with drinking buddies, girls, and the "fiesta" atmosphere[3] was hardly Robert Jordan's experience with Pablo's band. In fact the cast Hemingway has assembled is more nearly a continuation of the writers and society fops of To Have and Have Not than forerunners of the Loyalist peasants. (Indeed, the key to the tone of much of the play seems to lie in the dialogues about hoarded food and supplies, reminiscent of "home-front rationing" woes.)

Dorothy Bridges, "a bored Vassar bitch" and a magazine correspondent, calls everyone "Darling," and changes lovers in the course of the play to end up with Philip Rawlings, the counterspy posing as playboy. Although Hemingway presents her as heroine, Dorothy's vapid conversations and materialistic interests make her less than sympathetic. If this is the best Hemingway could do with an American girl as heroine, his choice of the Spanish Maria for For Whom the Bell Tolls was probably wise.

Rawlings is the embryonic Jordan, although--with less introspection possible in the dramatic format--not such a convincing hero. Rawlings too comes from living a selfish life to caring a great deal for Dorothy, but eventually he breaks with her because of his love. As he says bitterly to Max, "We're in for fifty years of undeclared wars and I've signed

up for the duration."[4] There is no place in his life for marriage; but before his renunciation of that possibility, he does
tell Dorothy, "I'd like to marry you, and go away, and get
out of all this" (58).

Rawlings' personal dilemma--facing a genuine love for
the first time in his life--is played against his professional
activity--capturing a civilian leader of the Fifth Column in
Madrid. When Hemingway gives full play to the successful
capture scene, however, he drains off that plot-oriented tension, and the play dwindles to its eventual close. The Fifth
Column lacks drama because the high point of the espionage
has passed, and we care relatively little about Rawlings' relationship with Dorothy. (In the novel, the plot is reversed:
Jordan's romance is successful, whereas his professional
endeavor brings him death.)

Pilar's account of the way the various men of the village met death at Pablo's hands is foreshadowed here when
Rawlings talks with the executioner about the ways men die.
Again, Hemingway's interest in man facing death is evident;
but he chooses not to have Rawlings meet his own. The
choice--dramatically--may well have been a mistake. The
essential conflict of romance vs. opposing duty is the basis
of both the play and the novel, yet because the materials
are used so differently, the effect is quite dissimilar. Once
Hemingway had opened the play with jokes by minor characters whose roles could only be comic (the hotel manager is
a stamp collector with a voraciously hungry mother-in-law),
building toward tragedy was almost impossible. Perhaps for
that reason he so clearly creates mood in the first chapter
of For Whom the Bell Tolls, placing Pilar's reading of Jordan's palm very early in the novel.

Other elements of the novel have their inception in the
six short stories written after the play. "The Denunciation"
treats of man's loyalty to his own code of conduct, a more
important concern than any political affiliation. Just as in
the novel, Jordan blows the bridge for the people of Spain--
and much more immediately for Maria, Pilar, and Pablo's
band--so Enrique in "The Denunciation" would overlook the
fact that one of Chicote's customers is a Fascist. Enrique
would not himself denounce Luis Delgado, but he gives the
proper phone number to the waiter who has talked with him
about such an act. Enrique's hypocrisy is the issue here:
at first he is angry because Delgado has returned to the bar
and thus put everyone in awkward positions, although he
also understands the reason for the man's return:

> All we old clients of Chicote's had a sort of
> feeling about the place. I knew that was why Luis
> Delgado had been such a fool as to go back there.
> He could have done his business some place else.
> But if he was in Madrid he had to go there. He
> had been a good client as the waiter had said and
> we had been friends.[5]

Then Hemingway uses flashback as Enrique remembers what
a good loser Delgado had been years before in a shooting
match. Realizing his own involvement, he sees that he could
have discouraged the old waiter instead of giving him the information he needed. And finally, with a rather strange
sense of exoneration, he calls the executioner and asks that
he, Enrique, be named as informer instead of the old waiter.
Unless one understands Hemingway's conviction that human
relationships are the most essential supports a man has--
and that those between man and man, man and chauffeur, and
man and waiter have particular intensity--Enrique's act has
little significance.[6] The gesture is similar to Jordan's al-
lowing Pablo to pretend that he has not killed his men at the
end of For Whom the Bell Tolls. Man has so little to believe in; other men should not take any dignity from him.

In "The Butterfly and the Tank" Hemingway relates a
simple but tragic incident he had already mentioned more
briefly in The Fifth Column. A half-drunk young civilian was
squirting people in Chicote's Bar with a cologne-filled flit gun,
and as tempers rose, he was himself killed. In the travesty
of justice that resulted, the man responsible for his death
walked out while the rest of the bar patrons were held long
hours for questioning. The incident prompts the narrator to
think about the political issues of the story; that is, would it
be maligning the Loyalist side to write about their mock-
justice? And, in a larger sense, he considers the death of
this Pedro as another senseless debt to the hysteria of war,
"the deadly seriousness that is here always," in the words of
the old waiter. Hence, the waiter's title for the story, as
he describes the young man: "His gaiety comes in contact
with the seriousness of the war like a butterfly ... and a
tank" (108-9).

The attitudes of the narrator in this story parallel Jordan's in the novel. Both men are already aware of the travesty of some war-time justice, and each has seen more than
once that the poor will do the suffering. It is Pedro who
pays for the edgy tempers of war, Pedro who wears no

undershirt and whose soles are worn through. The extension of this realization forms the theme for "Night Before Battle," the most powerful story of the six, in which Hemingway questions the military strategy of the Peoples' Army, and defames the authority which plans such wars. Written in October of 1938, just a few months before he began the novel, "Night Before Battle" is also Hemingway's tribute to the men he most admired, the tank drivers who did their best in Spain, but against frightening odds. 7

By centering on Al Wagner, the tank commander who knows that the coming attack will fail, Hemingway can use the vernacular to make Al's view of the debacle more readable ("Listen the whole thing is just as crazy as a bedbug. Why do they want to make a frontal attack against positions like those? Who in hell thought it up?") Throughout the evening, narrator Hank and Al mix with other soldiers and fliers who are playing craps in Hank's room, so that attention is always on the men who do the fighting, not on those who make the plans. Al is killing the night bit by bit, trying whatever will keep him from thinking. For, as he says,

> I don't mind dying a bit.... Only it's wasteful. The attack is wrong and it's wasteful.... If we had tanks that were a little bit faster the anti-tanks wouldn't bother them the way it does when you haven't got the mobility.

Al is concerned not only for himself. The other tank men know what he does, and his problem will be to make them attack. "I can make them start all right and I can take them up to where they will have to quit one at a time" (117).

As in For Whom the Bell Tolls, Hemingway establishes the conflict in the opening of the story as Al describes the impossibility of it all, and tells Hank that he thinks he will die during the attack. Because the story ends before daybreak, the plot line is unresolved, but it serves to color the other actions within the story: the gambling, the search for love, the drinking--all are more understandable in this desperate atmosphere. The real climax of the story occurs when the balding drunk riding the elevator with six bottles of champagne turns out to be a pilot-hero who has miraculously lived through the adventure he tells. The whole scene with Baldy Johnson changes the direction of the story by emphasizing that war is not rational, that chance plays a major role. 8 Underlying even this episode, however, is Al's tense recognition of his "duty" ("my duty is to do what I'm ordered to do"), and his thoughts about the coming "blood bath."

"Under the Ridge," the fourth story, is an expansion of Al Wagner's quandary about the recalcitrant soldiers. What should be done? Is a dead man good for anything, even encouraging discipline? Hemingway explores that problem here, and also gives the reader some insight into the feelings of the native Spaniards. Here the narrator Henry is also unaware of what has happened, and the story of Paco eventually comes from the bitter Extremaduran* who distrusts all foreigners, but especially the Russian battle police. (The fact that several of these stories were told to Hank, and the fact that throughout them the narrator has the same name, or is unnamed, suggests that the group might well have been intended for a unified collection, perhaps a Winesburg at war.)

The young soldier Paco had some months before shot himself in the hand in order to leave the front. After an amputation and recovery, he is brought back to his former brigade at mealtime and, summarily, to everyone's horror, shot in the head. This "lesson" occurs the evening before the battle now in progress, which the Loyalists have again lost because of inadequate arms and men, and poor strategy. As Hank watches the dying battle in progress, he sees a tall middle-aged Frenchman walk away from it, and soon sees him hunted down and shot--thirteen times--for his cowardice. But as Hemingway concludes, "The nearest any man was to victory that day was probably the Frenchman who came, with his head held high, walking out of the battle" (151).

The more complicated structure of this story, and the narrator's role in it, convey its ultimate meaning. Section I gives the somewhat humorous animosity of the Extremaduran to all foreigners. Section II presents the Frenchman's proud desertion and his execution. In some of his best writing in the story, Hemingway exonerates the Frenchman; but, although his sympathies are with the deserter, he tries to conclude that "In war it is necessary to have discipline" (147). The dour Extremaduran checks his glib assurance, however, by pointing out, "There is one kind of discipline

---

*In the early thirties Hemingway had hunted wild boar in Extremadura.

and another kind of discipline." And then he breaks his silence and tells the story of young Paco, reinforcing the apparent inhumanity of the Russian "bloodhounds" who serve as executioners. By ending with the pathos of this story, Hemingway has effectively undermined his own argument for "discipline."

It is evident that the novel contains many of the same attitudes and premises that have been operative in the play and the republished short stories. Hemingway's decision to make the novel one of people, one of human relationships, must have been made on the basis of his own loyalties during the two years he was in Spain. The political systems are rotten, but the people who believe in them are, or can be, magnificent. By making the work nearly apolitical, Hemingway created an image that would relate to all wars, all conflict.

Even Hemingway's text for The Spanish Earth, the propaganda movie designed to raise funds for the People's Army, had its moments of impartiality. Just as Hemingway shows the human side of the Fascists in For Whom the Bell Tolls, cameras focus on Italian dead during the film, and the text reads,

> These dead came from another country. They signed to work in Ethiopia, the prisoners said.... The Italians lost more killed, wounded and missing in this single battle of Brihuega than in all the Ethiopian war. [9]

This scene, besides emphasizing again the victimization of the common people, also creates sympathy by mentioning reading letters of the dead soldiers, "We took no statements from the dead but all the letters we read were sad."

Such inclusion is characteristic with the theme of the film, for The Spanish Earth does not censure political philosophy; it instead (nearly) ignores it. The film is a study in faces--soldiers', workers', women's, men's, children's; pained and happy; angry and sad; gaunt and prosperous--and the text opens with that emphasis,

> The Spanish earth is dry and hard and the faces of the men who work on that earth are hard and dry from the sun.

Centering on the right of people to own land, to improve that land by irrigation, the film shows the physical waste of land under an autocratic political system. The film is amazingly free of diatribe; the word fascist does not appear anywhere in the narration, and even the commentary about hired mercenaries is sympathetic to them, since war is their only means of earning a living.

"Old Man at the Bridge," the news dispatch published as a story in the spring of 1938, is a character sketch of "an old man with steel rimmed spectacles and very dusty clothes," too tired to go any further in an evacuation. Similar to his tactics in The Spanish Earth, Hemingway here tries to re-create the humanity of the old man, bereft of his pets and his hope, unwittingly the victim of the political war:

> 'I am without politics,' he said. 'I am seventy-six years old. I have come twelve kilometers now and I think now I can go no further.'[10]

Hemingway's last use of the Spanish Civil War before he began For Whom the Bell Tolls is another story which Mary Hemingway excluded from publication in The Fifth Column collection. "Nobody Ever Dies" is the story closest to the novel. Published in March, 1939 (written in the fall of 1938), it is the longest of the six stories and the least polished; but its roughness probably stems both from Hemingway's strong convictions about its theme and the wide range of material within the story. In it he creates the prototypes for both Robert Jordan and Maria, lovers persecuted by the Cuban secret police after their activities in Spain. Jordan is again named Enrique, and is described on the first page as "a young man of about 28, thin, dark, with circles under his eyes and a stubble of beard."[11] Horribly wounded in battle, he has a hole in the small of his back a man could put a fist through (Regler's wound). His greatest parallels with Jordan are his tough, intellectual response to life, and his amused shock at the way the Spanish people carry on and survive the war.

Jordan is also somewhat intellectual, but in the novel Hemingway puts the discussion of his "coldness" in Pilar's words ("The boy is smart.... Smart and cold. Very cold in the head"). Because we know that Pilar likes Jordan, the condemnation is not harsh--his intellect is more a foil to her own gypsy reliance on instinct, and even mysticism. Also, because we are given many monologues for Jordan, we know that much of what appears as coldness is really self-discipline. We are thus conditioned to think of Jordan's intellect as a positive force, especially when it is tempered by his very real love for Maria. But in "Nobody Ever Dies" we have only a brief dialogue between Enrique, the political machine, and Maria, who rather naturally loved Vincente, her brother. In this scene she has just discovered that Vincente has been killed, along with many other friends; and she is anguished by her grief. Enrique says coldly,

> It does no good to discuss it. They are dead.
> But it is not only that Vincente is my brother.
> I can give up my brother. It is the flower of our party.
> Yes. The flower of the party.
> It is not worth it. It has destroyed the best.
> Yes. It is worth it.
> How can you say that? That is criminal.
> No. It is worth it.
> She was crying now and Enrique went on eating.
> Don't cry, he said. The thing to do is to think how we can work to take their places.

The choppy, slow sentences; Enrique's eating; his complete political bias certainly load our reactions in Maria's favor. Unfortunately for our view of the hero, Hemingway later in this scene also has him deal in abstractions like "romanticism," "terrorism," and something labeled "revolutionary adventurism." We are with Maria as she screams, "You talk like a book ... not like a human being. You have a dry heart and I hate you."

One of the implausibilities of the story comes then, as Enrique, hurt by her words, shows her his wound; she begs forgiveness, and he melts. The character reversal is too fast--and too much--for us to accept. But, in terms of plot, the reversal is necessary because on the next page Enrique is shot, and Maria captured by the Cubans. Their threats of torture only bring out Maria's bravery as she gains strength from all the dead. Her promise that she will not talk, that she will live through the dead, gives Hemingway his title; it also gives him reason to picture this Maria as another Jeanne d'Arc. Since we have seen her only as a girl grieving for a brother, this concluding extension of her character is too melodramatic to be effective.

Hemingway often praised himself for knowing when to

revise and when to cut. In creating the metamorphosis of
Enrique into Robert Jordan, he has changed many traits to
make the young American less objectionable, but some basic
parallels remain. Jordan like Enrique believes in the cause,
but he has a sense of humor to go with his belief (as Jordan
mused, he fought so that "there should be no more danger
and so that the country should be a good place to live in.
That was true no matter how trite it sounded" [162]). And
their thoughts about a man's doing the impossible are almost
identical: Enrique says, "Some things we had to do were
impossible. Many that looked impossible we did." And Jordan questioned introspectively, "should a man carry out impossible orders knowing what they lead to? ... Yes. He
should carry them out because it is only in the performing
of them that they can prove to be impossible. How do you
know they are impossible until you have tried them?" (162).

In the short story, with Enrique's death on no field of
battle, Hemingway seems impressed with the irony of it all,
with the discrepancy between the glorious sound of the man's
words and his final act, crawling painfully through the dusty
weeds. The glory is reserved--though arbitrarily--for Maria, whose trial is yet to come (similarly in The Spanish
Earth, a recurring image is the "enduring bravery" of the
Spanish women). Maria's simplicity of both speech and action are admirable. While her saintliness may be an exaggeration, Hemingway tries to build the impression of her
aura of power through the use of the Negro informant who
rides with her, fingering his blue voodoo beads but still
afraid ("they could not help his fear because he was up
against an older magic now"). The primitive posed against
the saintly provides at least a colorful closing image and in
some ways suggests Hemingway's slight definition of "religion" as simply "love lived."[12]

This phrase--"love lived"--is an apt description of the
Maria of For Whom the Bell Tolls as well. Although she
has already had her torture at the hands of men, she is for-
giving enough to love one of them again. Maria embodies
all the qualities Hemingway considered virtues--she has a
great capacity to love, she is gentle and soft spoken, she
does not demand anything, and she has been tested and still
maintains a stable "perspective" with help from Pilar.[13]
With Pilar's obvious approval of Jordan, and with everyone's
recognition of the imminent danger ahead, Maria's love for
Jordan is quite plausible.

Hemingway was careful, however, to place the Jordan-Maria relationship in its proper context. It has been initiated and fostered by Pilar. Her anger in the forest as she speaks of her age and resultant ugliness, her immediate trust of and admiration for Jordan suggest that theirs is also an enduring bond. Pilar dominates the story partly because of her physical power, still in evidence with Pablo; she has gone through life as the mistress of some truly great men, and she responds to Jordan on these same quasi-sexual terms. Pilar's character must be a genuine amalgam, possibly growing from that of Marie Morgan in To Have and Have Not, enlivened by bits of the minor characters Anita in The Fifth Column and Manolita in "Night Before Battle," but surely one of Hemingway's more inventive and consistently-done women. She is the realization full blown of the enduring Spanish women from his film, and one of her best scenes is her introspective questioning of that very endurance: "Neither bull force nor bull courage lasted, she knew now, and what did last? I last, she thought. Yes, I have lasted. But for what?" (190). She is also, in a way, a tribute to Hemingway's own maturity.[14] In her struggle with Pablo, Pilar wins when she needs to win, but she always leaves the door open for Pablo. When he is ready to act like a man, she will give back his place, and assume her more culturally appropriate one. Maria is not the only woman in the novel who knows how--and when--to be submissive.

The character of Robert Jordan is the most predictable in the novel. A kind of dogged Al Wagner, with his real but realistic devotion to duty, Jordan also has the Extremaduran's humane convictions, Philip Rawlings' bravado and capacity for love, and Hank's respect for the simple verities. Like Jake Barnes, he eventually becomes the fully matured Hemingway hero--and, for a while, an uninjured one. He deserves the love he finds with Maria.

Jordan too understands Pablo. Consequently he does not kill him, either in the struggle for leadership or after his sabotage. Pablo has found something to love in the horses and resents being dragged into more danger; he has been too long in the war. In the character of Pablo Hemingway makes his strongest condemnation of the war itself, for he presents Pablo as sympathetic. The war has made him what he is, and what he is now is not good; but Pilar stays with him, as does the band, because of the man he once was.

Making Pablo a strong person has the same effect as making the scenes at Gaylord's more than just local color. Because Jordan is not the non-intellectual he would like to be, he has to remember how this all began: his conversation with General Golz in Chapter 1 gives us a perfect reading of the situation, and subsequent references to Gaylord's and headquarters only reinforce that dismal opening. Most masterful touch of all is the last headquarters scene (Chapter 42) when we see the powerful but insane André Marty pocketing the crucial message from Jordan. Marty's confrontation with Karkov brings to a head all the cryptic statements scattered throughout the novel. The attack will be a blood bath, and very few at Gaylord's will care. This kind of structured, insistent emphasis reminds one of the opposite effect an outright diatribe would have had. As Hemingway wrote in 1942, "Screaming, necessary though it may be to attract attention at the time, reads badly in later years."[15]

STRUCTURE IN
FOR WHOM THE BELL TOLLS

That Hemingway did know this--and did know why his characterization in the novel was more effective than that in The Fifth Column and the intervening short stories--is all part of the great writer's equipment. Since every novel, every piece of writing, is a new experience, there are times when the writer cannot follow precedent but must eventually trust his intuition. Former practices, like logic and "rules," are sometimes inadequate. With For Whom the Bell Tolls, or more generally, with all the Spanish Civil War materials, Hemingway had admitted that the scope of the subject baffled him.

> In stories about the war I try to show all the different sides of it, taking it slowly and honestly and examining it from many ways. So never think one story represents my viewpoint because it is much too complicated for that.[16]

As this summary of these separate stories has indicated, Hemingway was obviously interested in several themes: (1) the qualities of the common soldier, and of the Spanish peasant; (2) the relationship of the soldier to the military powers, and the peasant to his rulers; (3) the milieu of war, and the acts it provokes; (4) the conflict between private lives and public duty; and (5) Hemingway's most enduring theme, that of love, whether it be for person or for country.

Given this variety of thematic interests, it comes as no surprise that there are several stories within the novel. Some critics, however, have objected to the epic nature of the novel; most recently, Chaman Nahal writes,

> There are three distinct stories in For Whom the Bell Tolls which have no true bearing on each other. First, there is the story of Robert Jordan and Maria. Then we have the story of Pilar and Pablo. Last, there is the story of the Russians, which includes men like Golz, Kleber, Hans, André Marty and Karkov.[17]

Perhaps the thematic issues are clearer if we identify these three stories not in Nahal's terms but rather as (1) that of the lovers, Jordan and Maria; (2) that of the Spanish people; and (3) that of the political and military machine. The second story, that of the Spanish people, is in some ways the most important single element in the novel because in that story Hemingway captures the spirit of the country trying to free itself through the conflict. Pilar and Pablo are important characters not because of what Nahal calls their "love-hate relationship," but because they each represent facets of the peasant mind--the gypsy set against the cunning, Pilar's endurance juxtaposed with Pablo's pathetic realism. But all the other peasant characters are important too--Anselmo, El Sordo, Augustin, Fernando, Rafael--each character comes through as an individual, and we receive a wide (and pleased) understanding of the real people involved in this--or any-- civil war.

It is because we have this deep compassion for the Spanish people, Loyalist and Fascist alike, that the other two "separate" stories have such impact. Robert Jordan's love for Maria is more believable because she represents the native element he so much admires; she has also been victimized by the war machine--yet even the threat of new danger does not frighten her. And had Jordan not admired both the peasants and Golz's acute military mind, his own dilemma would have been less tortured. Indeed, rather than finding these story lines separate, it is difficult to imagine the book without any one of them, especially since they all meet--and find resolution--in the bridge.

Just as this interwoven story line is new for a Hemingway novel, so too is the shifting point of view. The fruit of his experiments with point of view in To Have and Have Not and several stories, his versatile perspective in For Whom the Bell Tolls moves from omniscience to Jordan's first person (or the dialogue of his divided first), to Pilar's, returning easily in each case to omniscient. (The stringent limitation of Jake Barnes' first person was never again to stalemate Hemingway. His concern in 1925 with the "rules" was evident when he tried to revise The Sun Also Rises by writing it in third person, never realizing that a combination of several perspectives might be possible.)

Another effect reminiscent of To Have and Have Not is Hemingway's ability to build tension by juxtaposing scenes in the last third of the novel, alternating Jordan and Maria's love scenes with segments of Andrés' journey to headquarters. As the lone gypsy tries to stay alive through his own lines, his struggle becomes such a vivid image for the absurdity of all war that Hemingway has no need to make any didactic statements. Therefore Pilar--who serves as vehicle for many of Hemingway's attitudes throughout the book--almost disappears from this latter section.

A further modification of Hemingway's earlier novel format is the inclusion of longer passages of description. No longer does dialogue have to carry the action. When it does, however, as in the scenes between Andrés and the guards, or between Pablo and Jordan, it is excellent and well-paced. But there are in this novel a great many scenes when dialogue is used very sparingly, and a few when there is no dialogue at all. Part of Hemingway's emphasis on description in the work comes, one might assume, from his interest in the country and his love of its people (his working title for it was The Undiscovered Country). Part of it is also a proof of his late writing skill, for, in his early Paris days, he had much admired Cézanne's landscapes:

> He, Nick, wanted to write about country so it
> would be there like Cézanne had done it in painting
> .... Cézanne could do people, too. But that was
> easier, he used what he got from the country to do
> people with.... People were easy. Nobody knew
> anything about them. If it sounded good they took
> your word for it.[18]

When one considers that Hemingway was also writing about

the Spain that he loved in <u>The Sun Also Rises</u>, the differences in his descriptive method are apparent.

Descriptive as it is, <u>For Whom the Bell Tolls</u> is never static. Part of Hemingway's success in creating the feeling of urgency that permeates the book comes from his techniques of opening each chapter with action. Characters are often in a new place, or about to make some kind of change: "They came down the last 200 yards." "They came down to the mouth of the cave." "Robert Jordan pushed aside the saddle blanket ... and, stepping out, took a deep breath of the cold night air." "Pablo stopped and dismounted in the dark." Place, person, movement is precise. We are immediately oriented and in motion. And the slower passages, those of soliloquy, are nearly always placed <u>within</u> the chapters so that the reader is adequately prepared for them.

Hemingway seems here to have developed even further the ability that was already evident in <u>The Sun Also Rises</u> and many short stories--the ability to write rhythmically balanced paragraphs so that he was writing balanced chapters. In <u>For Whom the Bell Tolls</u> chapter length varies tremendously (Chapter 33 has only three pages; Chapter 43 has 41) but each unit has its own justifiable rationale. We leave each chapter feeling satisfied; the action has truly been completed.

Closure for each chapter plays an essential part in this feeling of completion. In Chapter 6 Jordan says simply, "Good. I will get my things." Chapter 24 ends with his deciding against helping El Sordo; Chapter 31 ends with his blessing on Maria. But more than a physical stop to action, each chapter ends with either a short statement or a short paragraph, and usually a short sentence. This brevity is in definite contrast to the openings of these chapters which are often long paragraphs containing many long sentences. Chapter 13 for example opens

> They were walking through the heather of the
> mountain meadow and Robert Jordan felt the brush-
> ing of the heather against his legs, felt the weight
> of the pistol in its holster against his thigh, felt
> the sun on his head, felt the breeze from the snow
> of the mountain peaks cool on his back and, in his
> hand, he felt the girl's hand firm and strong, the
> fingers locked in his.

In contrast, this chapter ends with Jordan agreeing with Pilar, simply, " 'Yes,' " he said, 'I guess you are right.' " There is this almost musical ritard at the end of nearly every chapter.

Perhaps more impressive than the balanced structuring of each chapter is the way Hemingway so tightly fuses the various themes of the novel within each single chapter. For example, most writers would probably be tempted to let Pilar's long account of the village executions stand alone because its impact is unquestionable. It is important to the theme of the endurance of women, however, that Pilar tell the story so that we are privy to her own reactions to the killings, and so Hemingway sets the story within a chapter filled with feminine characterization. Pilar's wanting to rest, her perverse discussion of her ugliness--the opening of the chapter lets us know we are in Pilar's power. And the ending too reminds us that we must think again about the women whose lives are also destroyed in such wars, as Maria is shaken by Pilar's story and wants only to escape: "Are there no pleasant things to speak of? Do we have to talk always of horrors?" By giving the story this full and convincing setting, Hemingway has deepened its impact, and its implications.

There is as well an interesting rhythm to the novel as a whole. Many of the opening chapters, in which Hemingway describes both country and characters, run from 12 to 15 pages in length; the average length of chapters midway in the book, as the tempo of action increases, is more generally six or seven pages (indeed, the shorter chapter length is partly responsible for the faster tempo). Within this procession, there are well-placed peaks of interest, which usually combine at least one long chapter with several shorter ones.

The first such peak occurs in Chapters 10 through 13. Chapter 10 is Pilar's story of the village, containing 30 pages. It is followed by a 22-page account of El Sordo and his camp, and then a five-page Chapter 12 which in its abruptness intensifies the mood of anger for the waste of war which has been building in the previous two chapters. Chapter 13 is the last long chapter of this section. With 20 pages, it begins with Jordan's making love to Maria and then moves to Jordan's thoughts about love and war and the new perspective he must now have on the latter. So Hemingway has created a montage of past events, new information about the present, and the personal present, all used to present the basic theme of war's travesty.

The next peak of compression occurs in Chapters 17 and 18, 17 being the short (seven-page) unit describing the unbearable tension among Pablo's band in the cave, paired with the long Chapter 18, 24 pages focusing on the Gaylord clientele, particularly Karkov. In Jordan's conversation with the Russian journalist, we are told much about Jordan's philosophy, and we also see in forceful juxtaposition the ways war maims the people while only brushing the commanders.

In one sense, this beginning portion of the novel has been exposition. The remaining 24 chapters are largely action chapters, broken only by two sections of more intense presentation.

Chapters 26 and 27 comprise the third such break in the more straightforward narrative. The short Chapter 26 finds Jordan reading the letters he has found in the Fascist cavalryman's pockets. Like the scenes when the Loyalists hear their enemies talking and like the scenes with Lt. Berrando toward the end of the book, this is graphic illustration of Hemingway's point that the sides in civil war are nearly indistinguishable. And then he moves quickly to the El Sordo massacre, a story that takes 16 pages to tell. By so coupling the chapters, his effect is much stronger because the reader is moved through both tragic emotions, pity in Chapter 26, and horror in 27.

The next peak of compression is also a long-short pairing. In Chapter 31 Maria first tells her story, in the four-page Chapter 32 Hemingway moves once again to Gaylord's. One effect is similar to that of Chapters 17 and 18 --first we feel the effects of war on the people who must endure it; then we see the men who run it, lavishly protected from its damage. Maria has been nearly destroyed by the war, yet at Gaylord's, the Spanish whore Delores is treated as another Joan of Arc. Karkov's bitterness about the "flower of Spanish womanhood" echoes Hemingway's attitude, particularly since Maria--the true saint in the novel--has been deflowered not only in losing her virginity but also her womanly hair. When Karkov's mistress begs to go along to see the surprise attack as though it were a circus, we hear again Jordan's thoughts from the previous chapter, "There is no finer and no worse people in the world. No kinder people and no crueler" (355).

As though the contrast between Chapters 31 and 32 were not strong enough, Hemingway follows the scathing

picture of Gaylord's with further illustration of the duplicity
of the Spanish, the three-page Chapter 33 in which Pablo
sabotages the mission. The three-chapter section thus com-
prises another "Night Before Battle" very similar in mood
to the 1938 short story.

From then on the novel moves in short chapters until the last two, which again benefit from the same kind of
pairing. Chapter 42 is the long study of Comrade Marty and
his inept brutality; Chapter 43 is the bridge blowing, the escape, and Jordan's end. Again, we see vividly the results
on "the people" coupled with the glimpse of war as the game
that it is at headquarters. Whatever Hemingway had left un-
said in this novel, his structure surely clarifies. The reader is seeing each major action, each devastation of the
people, each casualty--whether of body or spirit--in conjunction with a view of blithe, cynical Gaylord's Hotel. As Jordan had correctly surmised half way through the novel,

It is like a merry-go-round, Robert Jordan
thought. Not a merry-go-round that travels fast,
and with a calliope for music, and the children
ride on cows with gilded horns, and there are rings
to catch with sticks, ... and a wheel of fortune
turning with the leather flaps slapping against the
posts of the numbered compartments, and the pack-
ages of lump sugar piled in pyramids for prizes.
No, it is not that kind of a merry-go-round; although the people are waiting, like the men in caps
and the women in knitted sweaters, their heads
bare in the gaslight and their hair shining, who
stand in front of the wheel of fortune as it spins.
Yes, those are the people. But there is another
wheel. This is like a wheel that goes up and
around.
It has been around twice now. It is a vast
wheel, set at an angle, and each time it goes
around and then is back to where it starts. One
side is higher than the other and the sweep it makes
lifts you back and down to where you started.
There are no prizes either, he thought, and no one
would choose to ride this wheel.... There is only
one turn; one large, elliptical, rising and falling
turn and you are back where you have started
[225].

This image of the wheel of chance--war run by the whim and

petty jealousy of madmen--is more than a thematic insight.
It also suggests the pattern of the novel, as Jordan prepares
to die in the same meadow where he began his odyssey, with
Hemingway's careful description being almost an exact copy.
But, with Hemingway's also characteristic irony, many things
have changed and the ending is in no way like the beginning;
for Jordan has learned love, and gratitude, and compassion,
and tolerance. It has been a true odyssey, but an odyssey
of the spirit. As Jake Barnes had told Cohn, "going to another country doesn't make any difference. I've tried all
that. You can't get away from yourself by moving from one
place to another."[19]

The unified structure of For Whom the Bell Tolls is
a splendid achievement, giving much proportion, and consequently much meaning, to the many events within the book.
The arrangement of it is especially impressive when one considers that the flashbacks of Pilar's story and Maria's, and
Jordan's own flashbacks to Gaylord's, could have occurred
anywhere in the novel. The only major scenes really bound
to the plot chronologically are El Sordo's battle and the Gaylord scene the night before the attack, but even these could
have been placed differently. That Hemingway was well
aware of his accomplishment in this work is evident in his
comment to Baker that the novel contained "no loose writing
and was all of a piece, with every word depending on every
other word" (351) straight through.

The novel also gives evidence of other Hemingway
writing experimentation during the thirties. Having recently
written a play may also have caused some changes in Hemingway's narrative method. Unlike The Sun Also Rises and
A Farewell to Arms, For Whom the Bell Tolls can in no
sense be considered a travel book. It begins, and ends, on
the same hillside, and only Andrés sees another area of the
country. It is the first novel that covers a severely limited
time span; like "Snows" and Across the River and Into the
Trees and The Old Man and the Sea to come, Hemingway
presents only Jordan's last three days alive. So we have the
dramatic unity of place and time, enriched by not only Pilar's
and Maria's stories but also by Jordan's own shorter flashbacks. And, like Harry in "Snows" and Cantwell in Across the
River, Jordan too knows that his death is imminent. Hemingway seems to be using the psychology that Flannery O'Connor
was to speak of: "It is the extreme situation that best reveals what we are essentially."[20] The knowledge of his at
least probable death appears to make Jordan more preceptive

and yet more compassionate; it also makes him, we surmise, more introspective, for his long passages of musing
seem strangely out of character for the man of action he
early identifies himself as being.

The closing stream-of-consciousness passage is a fit-
ting denouement to Jordan's life as a character. "Night Before Battle" had given Hemingway an earlier chance to draw
a man's last few hours, and in "Snows" and To Have and
Have Not he extended those preliminaries to the death itself,
obliquely in both cases. The effect of these deaths, however, in comparison to the earlier passages in the respective
narratives, was disappointing. Perhaps Hemingway's prior
experience was one reason for his ending the work befor Jordan's actual death. But the dialogue between Jordan's two
views of suicide is effective in that it gives the ending that
same saving ambivalence which operates throughout the novel.
Jordan is not a super-hero; Jordan is an all-too-human man.

Considering the many forerunners of at least parts of
For Whom the Bell Tolls, one is amazed at the unity--both
structural and motivational--of the actual book. Being so
filled with his knowledge about the war, Hemingway was in a
difficult position to write; there was really too much material at hand. What seems to have happened, in Hemingway's
writing the many columns, the short stories, the play and
even To Have and Have Not, was that he practiced creating
mood, tone, and setting. He also practiced being selective:
he did not include in this novel many of the characters or
situations of the earlier writing.

What he more importantly did was to create a fiction
that expressed the truth of the situation, the lives of the
people in Spain--or perhaps in any country--better than any
factual story could have. In "The Butterfly and the Tank"
he had questioned the discrepancy between appearance and
reality; in fact, a man was killed because of that discrepancy.
And so in For Whom the Bell Tolls Hemingway was much less
tied to the realities of his own experience than he had been
in much of his other writing (The Sun Also Rises, A Farewell to Arms, Green Hills of Africa, and Death in the Afternoon). No wonder he was excited about this novel--" 'a real
one,' " he declared to Baker.[21]

Hemingway also seems much less self conscious here
about his writing than in To Have and Have Not. The only
place in For Whom the Bell Tolls that he gets off the track

to talk about writing per se comes at the close of the long flashback to Gaylord's, Chapter 18, when Karkov tells Jordan he wants him to know the whole story of the war--the good and the bad things--so that he can write about them "truly," and Jordan thinks to himself,

> But I will have to be a much better writer than I am now to handle them.... The things he had come to know in this war were not so simple [248].

The writing of the novel proved--to Hemingway as well as to his readers--that he did know how to handle a great many things. One is reminded of his 1935 comment that

> most of us have written very little of what we know because ... we have to learn how to handle what we are going to write. So we write the part of what we know that we can handle with our equipment as we go along. 22

Hemingway was working, too, out of those long years of his own personal quest--for purpose, for love, for truth. And perhaps he was well aware that his characters in For Whom the Bell Tolls were weighted on the side of the great ones, that Maria and Pilar were almost too noble to be true, and Robert Jordan too. But then, hadn't he planned to call the book The Undiscovered Country?

Chapter Six

THE SEARCH FOR LOVE AND THE LAST YEARS

ACROSS THE RIVER AND INTO THE TREES

By 1950, when Across the River was published, Hemingway's phrase "undiscovered country" had changed to "unknown country"--and it represented not the generic people of Spain but the specific Italian girl, Renata. The image appears during the lovemaking scene in the gondola, and helps to emphasize the change in theme during the ten years since Hemingway had written For Whom the Bell Tolls. From a concern with a country's fight for life, he moved to a preoccupation with a single man's fight for a meaningful life, and death.

Colonel Richard Cantwell owes no loyalty to his occupation, though Renata believes he must have loved some of it; but any loyalty has been defiled because of the negligent and cruel commands he has survived, and the unmanning things he has been ordered to do. The same bitterness that colors the closing of For Whom the Bell Tolls is apparent throughout Across the River and Into the Trees, but Hemingway handles his narrative line somewhat differently. We see the cynic Cantwell, the strange mixture of violence and gentleness, but it is only in the last fifty pages of the novel--as he tells Renata about war, and finally thinks the worst of himself--that we are given the means to understand why he is such a dichotomy of hatred and kindness. As he explains to Renata, most military decisions are unrealistic, calculated for public relations value rather than military acumen:

> The phone rings and somebody calls from Corps who has his orders from Army or maybe Army Group or maybe even SHAEF, because they read the name of the town in a newspaper, possibly sent in from Spa, by a correspondent, and the order is to take it by assault. It's important because it got into the newspapers. You have to take it.

> So you leave one company dead along a draw.
> You lose one company complete and you destroy
> three others. The tanks get smacked even as fast
> as they could move and they could move fast both
> ways. [1]

Yet if the decision is wrong, for whatever reasons, men die
just as quickly no matter what the rationale.

Later, playing Dante for himself, Hemingway gives us
Cantwell's everpresent memory, his personal burden of
death,

> He looked up at the light on the ceiling and he
> was completely desperate at the remembrance of
> his loss of his battalions, and of individual people.
> He could never hope to have such a regiment,
> ever. He had not built it. He had inherited it.
> But, for a time, it had been his great joy. Now
> every second man in it was dead and the others
> nearly all were wounded. In the belly, the head,
> the feet or the hands, the neck, the back, the lucky
> buttocks, the unfortunate chest and the other
> places. Tree burst wounds hit men where they
> would never be wounded in open country. And all
> the wounded were wounded for life.
> 'It was a good regiment,' he said, 'You might
> even say it was a beautiful regiment until I de-
> stroyed it under other people's orders.'
> 'But why do you have to obey them when you
> know better?'
> 'In our army you obey like a dog,' the Colonel
> explained. 'You always hope you have a good mas-
> ter' [242].

Cantwell seems to be modeled after an older Robert
Jordan, but Jordan--had he kept Maria and his love intact--
would not have come to this withered end. Until Renata,
Cantwell had lived a loveless life. His description of his
former wife, the power-hungry journalist, suggests that he
had had as much competition there as in his military career.
Even his heart condition reflects years of frustration serving
under the--to him--inept commanders, torn between consci-
ence and orders. [2] Hemingway reinforces this picture of
Cantwell by using as a refrain throughout the novel his description of Renata--"my last and true and only love." [3]

So the story becomes another love story--apparently, love for Renata, but more generally of love for all the other victims of life (the analogy between life and war is as clear here as it was in A Farewell to Arms and For Whom the Bell Tolls). Hemingway begins early to establish Cantwell's basic compassion. On page 33 he says simply that he "never hated" the enemy; on page 71 he muses that he loved only people "who had fought or been mutilated." In the dialogue that follows--between the good and the tough sides of the colonel--Hemingway makes the progression to what is for the laconic Cantwell, a declaration of love:

> Other people were fine and you liked them and were good friends; but you only felt true tenderness and love for those who had been there and had received the castigation that everyone receives who goes there long enough.
> So I'm a sucker for crips, he thought, drinking the unwanted drink. And any son of a bitch who has been hit solidly, as every man will be if he stays, then I love him.
> Yes, his other, good, side said. You love them. I'd rather have fun.
> And fun, his good side said to him, you have no fun when you do not love.
> All right. I love more than any son of the great bitch alive, the Colonel said, but not aloud [71].

Cantwell's relationships with the Gran Maesere, Arnoldo, and even Jackson testify to the same basically compassionate nature, so that his love for Renata does not seem odd. His love does, however, give some rationale for his obsession with his appearance--his ugliness set against Renata's young beauty. Because Hemingway never before emphasized physical description, the reader must see this somewhat boring concern of Cantwell's as primarily a means of characterizing his state of mind--every glance in the mirror reminds him of his great luck in having Renata, just as every twinge of his heart reminds him of his impending death. Hemingway uses the descriptions of Cantwell's face almost as an objective correlative; his ugliness suggests age, and age suggests loss and death.

Cantwell's situation, like Jordan's, is in itself ironic. Maria and Renata--one suggesting the Virgin, the other, rebirth[4]--both bring meaning into lives that are otherwise sterile and cold, yet each man's time with his woman is short because of his life as soldier. And the girls' responsiveness, their generosity, their youth are the only possible ideal characteristics for them. (Hemingway has shown us, in "Snows," "Short Happy Life," and the flashbacks in Across the River what happens when woman is also competitor.) Yet Renata too has her code--she cannot marry Cantwell because he is a divorced man; she has her own family duties and conventions. Like Maria, she has pride and dignity to equal Cantwell's. The love relationship, Hemingway suggests, does not debase; one person does not live from the other.

The correspondences between Across the River and Hemingway's other novels are numerous, yet despite them, the novel is far from successful. Its weaknesses include its slow pace; repetitious dialogue; an obvious ending (not true of For Whom the Bell Tolls); and a boorish hero (some of the manly jokes are nothing but crude, and belie Cantwell's apparent sophistication in other areas), if not a sentimental one. But had Hemingway created a believable old colonel, the entire novel might have worked. It gives the reader an impression similar to that of To Have and Have Not: that this is an incomplete story, if not in plot, in composition. If Hemingway had given this book the time, the settling, or--perhaps more important in his own process of creation--the pre-writing, all elements of the story would probably have been more fully presented, and perhaps in less space. The numerous short scenes of Cantwell in conversation with waiters, drivers, and hunters could have been consolidated, or made more integral to the pervasive themes (or cut, as the vituperation of Truman and the system of Presidential selection would surely have been).

As Baker recounts, Hemingway had recovered from World War II with all of his knowledge from World War I and the Spanish Civil War only more firmly established, and had again begun work on the long sea novel--of which The Old Man and the Sea was to be a part. It was in the midst of this writing that he visited Italy and met illustrious Italian families, among them the Ianvich, with the lovely eighteen-year-old Adriata. So the work on Across the River and Into the Trees grew largely from what Baker terms "only a story about shooting ducks" into the broader novel of love and war. Its intent was admirable, and certainly in keeping with Hemingway's recent activities--another war, another marriage-- but as artistic work, as novel, it seems to have been premature. (Hemingway appears to recognize this himself. He is surprised at how fast the writing goes, he is delighted to be able to "use" all that war material. [5]) In brief, Across the River is more of an accidental novel; Hemingway had not prepared himself to write it through the long-term thinking and actual production of shorter related materials. The whole process is much different from that involved in writing For Whom the Bell Tolls and The Old Man and the Sea, and the final effect of the book more nearly resembles that of To Have and Have Not or the more recent Islands in the Stream. It is characteristic Hemingway, but it is not the best Hemingway.

THE POEM OF SANTIAGO AND MANOLIN

The process of writing The Old Man and the Sea was the longest of any Hemingway experienced. It began in 1935 when Carlos Gutiérrez had told him about the old Cuban fisherman and the giant marlin, and Hemingway had toyed with writing it several times in the interval. Since about 1944 he had been working intermittently on parts of his trilogy--The Earth, The Sea, and The Air, particularly the Sea sections. Just as in 1933 to 1937 Harry Morgan's love for the sea had given rise to some excellent descriptions of it, so Hemingway had included many such passages in his 1946-47 Garden of Eden. Indeed, since acquiring the Pilar in 1934, Hemingway had become a water man rather than an earth man:

> You take Yoknapatawpha County, and I'll take the ocean.... It's one of the last unspoiled places ... the place I love best and that moves me the most. [6]

So, working from a plot that was already his--and had been for seventeen years--with a setting he had previously described often, Hemingway began The Old Man and the Sea in a flush of victory. In less than two years he had written the entire Across the River and Into the Trees, and had finished The Sea When Absent (evidently the "Cuba" section of Islands in the Stream). Over the Christmas holidays, Adriata was their guest, and Hemingway was living the part of being the great writer: in two months The Old Man was finished--and then he went on to write the "Sea Chase" section of Islands. [7]

Such production for Hemingway was nearly unbelievable. By this stage in his life, his standards for good writing were so high he could seldom meet them. The problem as he grew older--and recalled the great fiction he had already written--is evident in his comment to William Seward,

" 'But every time it is harder to beat the last one when you write each time to complete fulfilling of how well you can write.' "[8] This was the man who, when he began The Sun Also Rises, was "still having a difficult time writing a paragraph"[9]--precisely because he was, from the beginning, so self-conscious of "getting the words right."[10] And although his first novel was a masterpiece, as were A Farewell to Arms and For Whom the Bell Tolls, Hemingway could never rest on laurels. Yet, after The Old Man and the Sea, he tended to be more at peace; in fact, he wrote in August of 1952 about the Santiago story, "It's as though I had gotten finally what I had been working for all my life."[11] The focus here, then, is on Hemingway's last great satisfaction, the lyric novel that may be his greatest book because in it all segments--structure, imagery, word choice, characters, plot--create a single organic whole. Hemingway began as a poet and so he ended--and, well aware of Dylan Thomas' remark that the greatest poems have in them both love and death, he captured in this work several great loves, and a truly noble death.

Once again poet-like, Hemingway never relinquished his insistence on both the rightness of each word or on the author's duty to "stimulate expectation."[12] Readers had to be kept interested; literature could never exist as a static picture. Verbs were prized; adjectives made useful. For Hemingway, the principle of active writing operated at a double level in The Old Man and the Sea. There are many verbs and surprisingly few adjectives in the book, considering that much of it is description; but in a broader sense, Santiago's struggle is always dynamic. There is movement, verve--even when only the stars are moving. The book's original title (The Sea in Being) suggested this dynamism, reflecting the source of Hemingway's later pride as he said, "The emotion was made with the action."[13] Had Santiago not cared so much, he would not have gone out so far; had he not revered the fish, he would have cut the line and come home; had he not come to love it, he would not have struggled so valiantly to save little more than its carcass. Just as every word in the book is there for a purpose, so is Santiago's every act. His dialogue with his left hand is a vivid reminder of the importance of each gesture, each movement.

By focusing on the immediate action, Hemingway follows Imagist doctrine and also avoids the sentiment inherent in his choice of hero. Santiago is pure pathos--alone except for an unrelated boy, poor, comfortless, unlucky, and old;

yet because Hemingway presents him as proud and courageous, aligned with the arch young lions, that is the way we see him. As Pound commented, the poet can control his readers' reaction, as the journalist cannot: "in journalism the reader finds what he is looking for, whereas in literature he must find at least a part of what the author intended."[14]

Perhaps this is one of the most difficult of the Imagist tenets to employ, the fact that the author controls without interfering. He presents; he renders the story; but his control is limited to the selection of details. Hemingway's choice of the singular noun shirt in this brief opening description of Santiago is one such telling detail.

> Once there had been a tinted photograph of his wife on the wall but he had taken it down because it made him too lonely to see it and it was on the shelf in the corner under his clean shirt.[15]

The reader is led through the quick impressions--a photo, and colored at that, must have been a great tribute to his love; then removing the photo, the primary reaction of his sadness; then two more lines reinforcing his poverty: the shelf may well be the only shelf, just as the single shirt may be his only change. In one sentence Hemingway has conveyed both Santiago's passion, and his poverty.

The same care with detail is even more evident once Santiago is in action, fishing. Many of Hemingway's paragraphs follow the pattern of (A) large narrative statement, then (B) an accumulation of reinforcing details, and finally (C) the summary statement that gives the otherwise objective paragraph its determination. When Santiago baits his hooks, Hemingway leaves no question that the old man is an expert.

> [A] Before it was really light he had his baits out and was drifting with the current. [B] One bait was down forty fathoms. The second was at seventy-five and the third and fourth were down in the blue water at one hundred and one hundred and twenty-five fathoms. Each bait hung head down with the shank of the hook inside the bait fish, tied and sewed solid and all the projecting part of the hook, the curve and the point, was covered with fresh sardines. Each sardine was hooked through both eyes so that they made a half-garland on the projecting steel. [C] There was no part of the

> hook that a great fish could feel which was not
> sweet smelling and good tasting [30].

The final tone, established through the adjectives "sweet
smelling and good tasting," comes as no surprise to the
reader, even though he has been reading about baits, because
earlier in the description, Hemingway had used the words
solid, fresh, and particularly half-garland. The reader is
thus viewing the entire process as Santiago would--the fish
are beautifully fresh, the act of fishing is a ritual.

Working in a nearly poetic condensation, Hemingway
turns frequently to figures of speech--patterned in a series
--as a way of giving extra meaning to his seemingly simple
descriptions. Our initial picture of Santiago depends largely
on this use of connected images. We first see his patched
sail, looking when furled "like the flag of permanent defeat" (9). Then Hemingway gives us Santiago's scars, "as
old as erosions in a fishless desert" (10). Defeated, fish-
less--the images are rapidly taking us one direction until the
author moves, quickly, to Santiago's eyes: "Everything about
him was old except his eyes and they were the same color
as the sea and were cheerful and undefeated." The identification with the sea, coupled with the direct contradiction of
"undefeated," establishes the tone Hemingway wants. But we
also have the facts--and it is not because of the existing
facts that Santiago is whole, but rather because of his spirit.

Operating through the writing is a kind of rhythmic
identity, evident in the excerpt above, which William Gass
has recently described in his discussion of Gertrude Stein:

> Her success in uniting thought and feeling in the
> meaning and movement of speech showed that
> rhythm is half of prose, and gave it the power of
> poetry without the indecency of imitation. . . .
> [S]ometimes she brings prose by its own good meth-
> ods to the condition of the lyric. [16]

As his experiments with language in his earlier novels had
shown, Hemingway was also concerned with this rhythmic
identity as an integral part of the whole effect. The rhythm
of The Sun Also Rises is laconic, abrupt; of For Whom the
Bell Tolls, moderately smooth, with much longer sentences.
Hemingway's attempts to use the Spanish language, and the
more personal pronoun forms, were ways of attaining the
flavor--at least partially a rhythmic concern--of the Spanish

people (the duration of the word <u>thee</u> is longer than <u>you</u> no matter how slowly the latter is said). Even Richard Cantwell's crudities help create the disjointed, even stacatto measures of <u>Across the River and Into the Trees.</u> But nowhere else does Hemingway match so well the language of his persona with the narrative voice of the novel. Santiago's tranquility sets the pace for <u>The Old Man and the Sea,</u> in keeping with his slow, chary, and deceptively uncomplicated speech.

The passage describing Santiago's baits also illustrates the somewhat idiosyncratic use Hemingway makes here of the compound structure, particularly the connective <u>and</u>. In its simplest position, the <u>and</u> coupling suggests that there is no judgmental relationship between the clauses connected: "He was an old man who fished alone in a skiff in the Gulf Stream and he had gone eighty-four days now without taking a fish." It is not <u>because</u> he fishes alone that Santiago has caught nothing. The simple statement of apparent fact does what it purports to do, puts down the facts, with no causation or blame.

Hemingway achieves the same kind of objective tone when he uses the structure in more emotional situations, "The old man had taught the boy to fish and the boy loved him." Perhaps Manolin did love Santiago partly because of his having taught him, but rather than oversimplify the relationship, Hemingway again uses the simple coupling which leaves more to the reader's own insight. The structure-- for all its apparent simplicity--is thus suggestive.

At times several of these compound sentences must work together as a unit, to help reinforce the impression the reader will probably draw from the first sentence. In his description of Manolin and Santiago stopping for a beer, Hemingway sketches the milieu of the fishing village in two such connected sentences:

> They sat on the Terrace and many of the fishermen made fun of the old man and he was not angry. Others, of the older fishermen, looked at him and were sad.

That Santiago was not angry is a bit ambivalent--is he beaten or indifferent? or has he "the peace that passeth understanding," the wider tolerance? The follow-up sentence shows that the latter interpretation is the one Hemingway intends to reinforce; the older fishermen share his knowledge.

It is one matter to look at single words and sentences and nod sagely, thinking, "Yes, that's Hemingway's 'one clear sentence,' and there is the 'no ornament except good ornament'"; it is more impressive to see all these single elements joined into a longer passage which works, and conveys surprising richness. The page of dialogue between Santiago and Manolin essentially presents their past relationship, their present love for each other--and the effect that love has on Santiago--all amid more commonplace detail about the village and the fishing process.

> 'How old was I when you first took me in a boat?'
> 'Five and you nearly were killed when I brought the fish in too green and he nearly tore the boat to pieces. Can you remember?'
> 'I can remember the tail slapping and banging and the thwart breaking and the noise of the clubbing. I can remember you throwing me into the bow where the wet coiled lines were and feeling the whole boat shiver and the noise of you clubbing him like chopping a tree down and the sweet blood smell all over me.'
> 'Can you really remember that or did I just tell it to you?'
> 'I remember everything from when we first went together.'
> . . .
> 'If you were my boy I'd take you out and gamble,' he said. 'But you are your father's and your mother's and you are in a lucky boat.'
> 'May I get the sardines? I know where I can get four baits too.'
> 'I have mine left from today. I put them in salt in the box.'
> 'Let me get four fresh ones.'
> 'One,' the old man said. His hope and his confidence had never gone. But now they were freshening as when the breeze rises [12-13].

In Manolin's comparatively long memory of the fish, Hemingway writes his usual active prose, relying on the many -ing words, but he more importantly resolves the boy's memories happily. Even though Santiago is "clubbing" the fish, his action seems as natural to the boy as "chopping a tree down," and the heavy blood smell he recalls as "sweet." That a five-year-old child had such a reaction to what must

have been a gory and frightening scene shows clearly the
trust he had in Santiago. Hemingway then goes on to show
in turn the power of Manolin's love on him, with the closing
image. By placing the descriptions of Santiago throughout
the section, Hemingway keeps the old man before us, even
when Manolin carries most of the dialogue. And by estab-
lishing tone through nature images, he reinforces the impression of Santiago as sea-like, old, strange, proud, and unbeaten.

The relationship between Manolin and Santiago is poignantly done, particularly when one considers that the boy appears in only one-fifth of the novel--in the first eighteen
pages and the last six. The structure of the book is thus
like that of The Sun Also Rises, with Jake and Brett together
in Parts I and III, as are Manolin and Santiago. Yet when
Santiago is alone, he thinks often of the boy, and his
thoughts of him become a kind of refrain.

It begins, "I wish I had the boy" (51), and then modu-
lates into "If the boy were here" (56, 62, 83); finally reaching its climax in a threefold repetition, as the coils of line
tear Santiago's hands,

> If the boy was here he would wet the coils of
> line, he thought. If the boy were here. If the
> boy were here [83].

Santiago has no time to pray, he tells God in his numerous
attempts to bargain, but his thoughts of Manolin come at
points of crisis, and--structurally--seem to substitute for the
prayers another man might be saying. That this effect is in-
tentional--Manolin as Santiago's only hope, only love--is re-
stated later when Santiago justifies killing the marlin,

> Besides, he thought, everything kills everything
> else in some way. Fishing kills me exactly as it
> keeps me alive. The boy keeps me alive, he
> thought. I must not deceive myself too much [106].

Using structure as well as immediate presentation,
Hemingway drew this all-encompassing love relationship, perhaps the most convincing of those in any of his novels. When
Manolin says, "I remember everything from when we first
went together," we accept his exaggeration, as Santiago does,
as evidence of his selfless love for the old man. His willingness to bargain, to beg, to steal food and supplies for him

--and to go against his parents' wishes--is further evidence
of that generous relationship. With Hemingway's definition
of love as generous giving, the similarities between Manolin's devotion to Santiago and Maria's to Jordan and, to an
even greater degree, Renata's to Cantwell, are evident. Sex
aside, much of each of these relationships exists in the near-
reverence of youth for the enduring wisdom of age. In
<u>Across the River and Into the Trees</u>, Renata wants to learn
from Cantwell; true, she thinks his talking about war will in
some way exorcise his bitterness, but her thirst for information must have some basis in interest as well. The closest parallel to the love between Manolin and Santiago, of
course, is that between Jake and Brett. Also sexless, that
love was proven chiefly in Jake's desire to give whatever he
could toward Brett's happiness--and only because society
finds bullfighters more objectionable than cups of coffee did
Hemingway's first novel fail to have its appropriate effect.

Manolin wants everything good for Santiago; there is
no jealousy between competing fishing boats here. He is confident in his position with the old man; there is no timidity
or artifice. One of the best evidences of this is the fantasy
Santiago and the boy create about the yellow rice and fish.
Only very confident lovers joke (as Santiago does with
God).[17] Such scenes create the aura of tranquility, of surety, that this novel maintains throughout. Like Shakespeare
in <u>The Tempest</u>, Hemingway has realized the value of humor
in the midst of the life-and-death struggle that the book really is, and he uses it well: the old man's thoughts about Joe
DiMaggio's bone spur, and his childlike wondering about it,
occur at some of the highest peaks of action. And the comic dialogue between Santiago and Manolin about fear is a skillful touch of the raspberries to any former Hemingway reader.
To come from Robert Jordan's near-obsession with fear,
fear as an index of manliness, to Santiago's mocking comments on the baseball teams is progression indeed:

> 'The Yankees cannot lose.'
> 'But I fear the Indians of Cleveland.'
> 'Have faith in the Yankees my son. Think of
> the great DiMaggio.'
> 'I fear both the Tigers of Detroit and the Indi-
> ans of Cleveland.'
> 'Be careful or you will fear even the Reds of
> Cincinnati and the White Sox of Chicago' [17].

Santiago--and Manolin in his tutelage--seems to be almost

beyond man's usual concerns with mortality--hence, his "strangeness"[18] and perhaps his complete resolution (Cantwell's ability to spit might be an intermediate stage in this progression). Yet Hemingway includes enough detail to show that Santiago is a realist, not a romantic; he knows he will have to use "tricks" on the fish because his strength is not what it was when he was young. And he accepts his fate realistically, too, knowing that he "went out too far."[19] The fish--though an impossibility--was not impossible to catch; it was only bringing it back such a long distance, unscathed, that was impossible.

Admittedly, Santiago shares many traits with the best of Hemingway's heroes, Jake Barnes and Robert Jordan. He does not admit to a limited set of hopes for man; there are no impossibilities. The central image occurs near the center of the story when Santiago, bemused at the size of the marlin, considers man's "luck":

> I have never seen or heard of such a fish. But I must kill him. I am glad we do not have to try to kill the stars.
> Imagine if each day a man must try to kill the moon, he thought. The moon runs away. But imagine if a man each day should have to try to kill the sun? We were born lucky, he thought [75].

This is the same kind of reversal in our normal perception of events that Hemingway uses as Santiago sits cramped all night in the cold boat, "The sack cushioned the line and he had found a way of leaning forward against the bow so that he was almost comfortable. The position actually was only somewhat less intolerable; but he thought of it as almost comfortable" (47).

Calling it optimism is too pale. Santiago's outlook is stoicism at its best, somehow infused with a living, growing hope. And the presentation of it is amazingly effective, partly because of the author's shifting point of view.

Trying to categorize Santiago's philosophy makes one eager for generalities, and we tend to summarize all the Hemingway heroes, noticing how few suicides there are in any of the fiction, although nearly every character at some moment has a right to at least contemplate the act. One of the difficulties with identifying with Jake Barnes was our sparse knowledge about his real feelings, the restrictions of using the first person point of view with a laconic and rather tough-sounding narrator. By the time of The Old Man and the Sea, Hemingway had learned not only to move easily between first person and omniscience (and here to include dialogue for more necessary insights), he had also learned to give the reader didactic help at crucial moments. Rather than have us believe what Santiago says--that the pain is nearly comfortable--Hemingway tells us how it really was. And rather than have us slide over the moon-sun passage, he adds a summary image a few pages earlier, so that Santiago's position is crystallized in our minds. It is all hopeless.

> The old man had seen many great fish. He had seen many that weighed more than a thousand pounds and he had caught two of that size in his life, but never alone. Now alone, and out of sight of land, he was fast to the biggest fish that he had ever seen and bigger than he had ever heard of, and his left hand was still as tight as the gripped claws of an eagle [63].

Soon after this, we have one of the few flashbacks in the book, as Santiago thinks of his Indian wrestling with the strongest man on the docks. They had gone one night and one day and, for no rational reason, Santiago had won. So Hemingway tells us, in effect, that spirit can go a long way. It cannot, however, overcome everything.

> Santiago is never broken, but then Hemingway has also told us that "man is not made for defeat.... A man can be destroyed but not defeated" (103). What is new in this novel is the explicit injunction to think. Contrary to the earlier admonitions of Barnes, Henry, Morgan, Jordan, Thomas Hudson, and Cantwell that they not think--because, we suppose, Hamlet-like, they would be too fearful to act-- Santiago in all his wisdom admits, "But I must think.... Because it is all I have left." Then he improvises the weapons he has lost, and later repeats, "Think of what you can do with what there is." In this synthesis of thought and action, Santiago works just as Jordan surely has, to the best of his ability, using what he has but never mourning, as Cohn might have, for what he did not have and could not hope to obtain. Hemingway's theme has changed little throughout his writing, but his method of expressing that theme has been modified toward greater directness and greater

emphasis on the final effect. The latter part of the novel is the most didactic of any of Hemingway's writing.

The "Cuba" and "Sea" sections of the posthumously published Islands in the Stream run a close second, however; and in the Thomas Hudson story is found the same emphasis on endurance. By depriving Hudson of his three sons, two at the close of the "Bimini" section and the third during the "Cuba," Hemingway has set up a different kind of endurance test, a torture of the heart rather than the body. Hudson, describing life as a series of tests, thinks to himself that all will be well "if we can get by this one and the next one and the next one."[20] As he summarizes his own position, "Get it straight. Your boy you lose. Love you lose. Honor has been gone for a long time. Duty you do." Again Hemingway gives us a man who has known love--like Santiago--but is now bereft of it all. (The first part of Islands works largely to establish how great his devotion to his sons is, and how lost he is in their absence.) Unwieldy as some parts of the novel are, and unfinished, the book is still a moving study of man's bereavement. Just as Santiago loses parts of the fish to the sharks, so Hudson loses parts of his own life until finally, as his behavior in the "chase" section suggests, that life means little. His actions show that all he does have left is duty. (Once injured, in another reasonless aberration of fate, Hudson does think of his painting--"life is a cheap thing beside a man's work"--but it seems to be a definite afterthought.)

The transfer of emotion from this mass of writing, loosely connected as the "sea novel," to The Old Man and the Sea is evident. Whereas Hudson is concerned with his love for his sons and his first wife, Santiago has Manolin. The somewhat inarticulate conversations between Hudson and his boys seem stilted (one exception is young Tom's reminiscence of his early days in Paris) compared with the direct expressions of Manolin and Santiago. But then these characters are simpler, and their laconic language is borne out by substantiating actions. In Islands in the Stream, so many people are involved that giving any one of them sufficient emphasis is difficult. The situation may have been closer to the author's own, but it was much harder to achieve artistically than the single man - single boy of The Old Man. Only once in Islands does Hemingway achieve a similar concentration, when David tries to land the fish. There also the action is meaningful; it is focused on only several characters (with Hudson's position as separate yet horribly involved clearly drawn), and the scene moves quickly. Like Santiago's feeling for the marlin, David's reaction to his fish is compelling--his injured hands and feet, his feeling of union with the fish, his reticence, and his love for it. The boy's experience is, however, finally less effective than Santiago's because of the constant interruptions from the other six people on the boat, and also because Hemingway uses the third-person point of view to convey the boy's reactions.

In Islands, too, the fishing experience is primarily an initiation process, giving us greater insight into Hudson's fears for his sons--fears that the novel shows, perhaps too quickly, were well founded. The scene ends when the fish breaks away. In The Old Man and the Sea, by extending the story so much further, by taking us past the excitement of the catch, the fight, and the possession, Hemingway emphasizes what a man can endure (just as in Islands the successive two parts of the novel do this for Hudson). By shifting emphasis from catching the fish to staying with it, Hemingway changes the nature of the story. In the course of the earlier work he shows repeatedly Santiago's doing what he as man "had to do," and much more, until he finally waits, unarmed, for the last sharks, wondering "what can a man do against them in the dark without a weapon?" (117).

It has been called existential, the fact that Hemingway gives his hero this dilemma, and makes him face it. But how similar the whole situation is to that of the scene in Faulkner's The Unvanquished, when Bayard Sartoris asks, "How can you fight in the mountains, Father?" and the answer comes, "You can't. You just have to."[21] The Old Man and the Sea is the novel Faulkner admired. For it is the first one Hemingway had written in thirty years in which the hero stood it all. And lived.

The catharsis here, in this spent resolution of Santiago's struggle, must remind any reader of the effects of Greek tragedy. The classic intensity of focus is evident in the limitation to three characters, the nearly single setting (village, ocean, village), the three-day time span (unified by the single action), and the resolution of that single action. So tightly unified is the story, in fact, that some of the telescoping of time is so heightened that it creates irony. As Santiago pulls on the line, for example, Hemingway writes,

> This will kill him, the old man thought. He can't do this forever. But four hours later the fish was still swimming steadily out to sea [45].

The juxtaposition of time information with Santiago's incorrect "knowledge" does more than convey fact; it also foreshadows the falsity of many of Santiago's expectations. And we are reminded again of the Hemingway thesis: even the greatest of men can seldom be in complete control of all circumstances.

Structurally, too, Hemingway emphasizes this axiom. It takes Santiago 94 pages to get the fish, and only 18 to lose it to the various sharks. The concentration, even in terms of space and detail, falls on Santiago's purely voluntary exposure to danger. For the first time in twenty years, the hero of a Hemingway novel was not chafing under "orders." (As Hudson said, in the passages written immediately after The Old Man and the Sea, "There are worse places to be than on your own" [343].) Santiago could not complain about the higher powers--except the highest fates of all, those that willed him toward his destiny. Like Jake Barnes, Santiago's duty is only to himself and his ideals; similarly, only those who know him well, who understand him, can judge him. Therefore Hemingway concludes the novel by letting Manolin give his reaction to Santiago's experience, fittingly, in actions as well as in words: crying, warming and rewarming Santiago's coffee, and keeping guard as the old man sleeps. Here, love is a secure and confident relationship.

The actual ending works perfectly to complement the rest of the book. It is no deliberate Christian ploy to have Santiago carry the mast up the hill (on page 26 he carried it down), and then lay face down on his bed (this is the falling action of an exhausted man, not a person going to bed). For those who read these last ten pages as evidence of Hemingway's Christ symbolism, one must suggest that Santiago's not saying the promised prayers provides an antidote to that interpretation. Instead, we must view the last few passages as (1) a summation of the theme that runs, obviously and yet skillfully, throughout the book--man's incredible ability to survive, and more, to dare; to make it, whole in spirit and body; (2) a return to the enduring love that Manolin gave, and Santiago lived for; (3) a necessary ending to the apparent "plot"--Santiago alive, his reputation vindicated, and the marlin skeleton disposed of; and (4) one of the most masterful of Hemingway's exercises in juxtaposition.

Once Santiago is asleep, focus shifts again to Manolin whose tears of joy and sorrow, occurring three distinct times, are the best single testimony to Santiago's courage.

Then the last few pages of the novel shift setting kaleido-
scopically: Manolin watching Santiago, going for coffee, talking with the crowd gathered near the skeleton, talking with
Santiago, and then again returning to the village. As the boy
hurries back and forth, we sense the reactions of the entire
village, and even of the outsiders, those uninitiated observers
who usually appear in a Hemingway novel, but often to the
detriment of any total effect. Here, however, after the laconic dialogue of Manolin and Santiago, with even his evident
suffering described only as "Plenty," the ending image of the
tourists' ignorance has a triple-edged effect. The evidence
of Santiago's greatest catch is now garbage and, as such, has
no meaning for any but the initiated. Even when the waiter
tries to explain what has happened ("Tiburon." "Eshark"),
the tourists hear him incorrectly. In the vapid, "I didn't
know sharks had such handsome, beautifully formed tails,"
Hemingway has caught the tone of facile indifference he de-
spised. Yet in this novel--rather than belabor the ignorance,
or admonish, or let Manolin comment--he instead moves
quickly back to the sleeping Santiago, strangely at peace with
his pain, the pain which signifies life, dreaming once again
of the lions, as Manolin stands watch. We are given Santiago's peace in the envelope of Manolin's concern.

The relationship between Santiago and the marlin has
been made much of, and rightly so, for the sense of wonder,
the immensity, the brotherhood is beautifully conveyed. But,
as the structure and imagery of The Old Man and the Sea
prove, it is the love between imperfect human beings that lies
at the core of Santiago's experience. It is that love which
redeems Santiago; and it is that love to which he returns.

Chapter Seven

FAULKNER: ON FACTS AND TRUTH

Just as Hemingway ended with The Old Man and the Sea, his poem to love and awareness of life beyond self, so Faulkner's last novel was in many ways the same kind of distillation. The Reivers, too, is a chronicle of love. Like Manolin, Lucius Priest learns from older men, but the story employs reversals, and its treatment is more obviously comic. Lucius, like Lucius Apulius in his own earlier "golden book" (see Appendix III), has learned about choice, free will, responsibility, and virtue--Faulkner's pervasive themes throughout his writing. That the emphasis on virtue, on love, became so apparent in the late writing of both Faulkner and Hemingway can be attributed partly to their use of simpler styles, and partly to their choices of situation and character. The themes had, however, existed throughout their writing.

The heart of each of Faulkner's nineteen novels, and each of Hemingway's six, had from the beginning been love:

> love really is the central subject of all his [Faulkner's] greatest work. We may go even further and say that all of Faulkner's significant writings constitute merely a series of variations on a single idea: the importance of love. [1]

With Lawrence Bowling's view, Cleanth Brooks concurs, in both his 1963 The Hidden God and the later William Faulkner, and even more recently has presented Soldiers' Pay as not a war novel so much as a study of "various kinds of love: Don Juanism (Jones); romantic love (Joe Gilligan); puppy love (Julian Lowe); self-love (Cecily)...." [2]

Perhaps here the similarity in backgrounds has once again been formative. As we have seen, both Hemingway and Faulkner were from small enough towns that they, their families--indeed, every family--had identity, and resultingly, responsibility. When a child is known, he acts with some cognizance of that recognition.[3] Another facet of the small-town environment is that a boy can still learn to know the land. As Hemingway and Faulkner both show so vividly in their writing, such knowledge was for them crucial. In 1952 Faulkner was to praise the South precisely because "It's the only really authentic region in the U.S., because a deep indestructible bond still exists between man and his environment."[4] (The same might well be said of Upper Michigan, especially in the twenty years Hemingway knew it best.)

Because their families were close to both men, they had studied that tangent of life. They were aware of the importance, both positive and negative, of the most commonplace responses; and much of their early fiction deals with simple, familial situations. While the study of the family dominated much of Faulkner's work, Hemingway approached it more obliquely; but its importance in the short stories, in A Farewell to Arms, in To Have and Have Not, and in Islands in the Stream is also clear.

The concept of a just and nourishing family life is so important to their fiction, indeed, that its presence underlies many of their dramatic situations. We know what is wrong with the doctor's marriage even before we see his wife burning his collection of artifacts; we sense the kind of mother Caroline Compson is as soon as she moans about Christmas (it does not take Faulkner to tell us that she "wasn't much good"[5]). Interestingly enough, both Faulkner and Hemingway chose to point their ideals negatively; we seldom see the harmonious family or the smoothly working marriage. As Bowling describes the method,

> Another reason why readers overlook the significance of love in Faulkner's writing is that its importance is often emphasized indirectly through its absence or perversion. The need for love is the central issue in the most un-lovely of Faulkner's books--such as The Sound and the Fury, Absalom, Absalom! and Sanctuary--in which we behold the depravity and desperation and horror of human actions divorced from pity and compassion and sacrifice.[6]

To this list, one could easily add not only most of Faulkner's other fiction, but also To Have and Have Not, Across the River and Into the Trees, and The Sun Also Rises.

The sensitivity of Faulkner and Hemingway to innovation in the arts gave them apparently new modes for expressing the ageless truths, but under the new technical trappings, their stance toward life differed very little from that of Shakespeare, Tolstoi, Conrad, or Melville. As Faulkner stated in his West Point seminar,

> basically the drives of the heart are the same.
> It's the verities, for the verities have been the same
> ever since Socrates, which are courage and pride
> and honor--compassion. It's a man's knowledge
> that at bottom he is not very brave, that he is not
> very compassionate, but he wants to be ... yet
> still he tries.... [T]hey are the verities which all
> the writing is about.[7]

In this preoccupation with relationships among people, both Faulkner and Hemingway may be the best students Sherwood Anderson ever had. For Anderson was never the aesthetician that the Imagists were (indeed, he was a near romantic in his mystical approach to writing); he believed rather that the artists' first commitment was to drawing character sympathetically:

> The material age has had its say and has said nothing.... [T]hat terribly abused word "love" is at
> the bottom of all the decay. When men do not dare
> love, they cannot live, and the men of our day did
> not dare love either God or their fellow men.[8]

His "Testament" prose poems, his Mid-American chants, and nearly all of his fiction repeat this concern, with varying degrees of artistic success. It is interesting that in 1925 Faulkner recognized Anderson's strengths (and concurrent weaknesses) when he praised Winesburg for showing Anderson's sympathy with his characters, "a sympathy which, had the book been done as a full-length novel, would have become mawkish."[9] Somewhat later, Faulkner himself declared, "I was just trying to write about people, which to me are the important thing. Just the human heart, it's not ideas."[10] And, correspondingly, Anderson later reacted to the same sympathy in Faulkner's delineation of his people, as he acknowledged that Faulkner did sometimes write "of terrible happenings," but still felt that the younger writer had "an inner sympathy with the fact of life itself."[11]

Having such an inner sympathy was in no way parallel

with the practices of the Realists, however, for the word
fact--and the fictional technique of accumulating facts--were
anathema to Anderson. Only the writer's imagination can
give art the form it requires: " 'it did not come out of reality,' I said to myself, 'but out of that strange, more real
life into which I have so long been trying to penetrate and
that is the only real reality.' "[12] Hemingway's use of this
attitude has already been illustrated, but he is never so clear
in his statement of the position as is Faulkner, who frequently derides "facts": "facts and truth don't really have much
to do with each other."[13] "Fact is not too important and
can be altered by law, by circumstance, by too many qualities, economics, temperature, but truth is the constant thing,
it's what man knows is right and that when he violates it, it
troubles him." "Facts bear no relation to truth."[14]

Much like Pound's censure of the journalist's use of
fact, this attitude is in no way at odds with Anderson's emphasis on the local as a means to the universal. Everyone
in the twenties, it seems, was reading John Dewey. As early
as Mosquitoes, that quixotic novel that can best be justified
as Faulkner's Portrait of the Artist,[15] Faulkner too is repeating,

> Life everywhere is the same, you know. Manners
> of living it may be different ... but man's old
> compulsions, duty and inclination ... they do not
> change.[16]

In his 1953 essay on Anderson, Faulkner reminisced that
from the older writer he learned "that, to be a writer, one
has first got to be what he is, what he was born.... You
had only to remember that you were. 'You have to be somewhere to start from: then you begin to learn.... You're a
country boy; all you know is that little patch up there in Mississippi where you started from. But that's all right too.
It's America too.' "[17]

The modernist tendency to work through the concrete
particular is one corollary to this principle of finding the universal through the specific. Faulkner would have been aware
of this aesthetic from many different sources--his wide and
eclectic reading, his friendship with Phil Stone, his pride in
knowing avant-garde literature, as his essays in Ole Miss
show. Despite the fact that Faulkner never met Ezra Pound,
there is much evidence that he too was an admirer of the
champion of the concrete image in writing. By 1919 Joseph

Blotner recounts, "William Faulkner and Phil Stone were interested in Ezra Pound and the imagists as well as T. S. Eliot."[18] In November of that year, Faulkner wrote a poem titled "Cathay" (Pound's collection by that name had appeared in 1915), and later Faulkner himself recalled having read Japanese poems in translations by Pound. Blotner suggests too that Faulkner's 1920 Marionettes contains imagery similar to that in Pound's Chinese poems.[19]

By 1925, when Faulkner made his trip to Europe, he had already " 'got past Verlaine, Eliot, Pound and Joyce.'"[20] He carried with him letters of introduction to the latter three, letters which he never used. Inherently timid, Faulkner was content to watch the established writers from a distance; however, Blotner writes that

> Once they saw Ezra Pound, Spratling thought. Faulkner talked a great deal about him, he remembered, and admired him tremendously [452].

In 1931, Faulkner no doubt took great satisfaction from the fact that he and Pound were both listed as contributing editors to the magazine Contempo.

Many structural devices in his poems and prose suggest that Faulkner was well aware of both Imagist and Vorticist aesthetics. Important as Pound was in the formation of these principles, for Faulkner a more immediate influence was his friendship with Sherwood Anderson. Like Pound, Anderson too insisted on presentation, not "preaching." His admiration for Turgenev, Tolstoi, and Dostoevski stems not only from their "love of human life" and "tenderness," but also their "lack of the eternal preaching and smart-aleckness so characteristic of much Western writing."[21] Faulkner too resented any writer's taking 1000 pages to tell a story, and was consistently re-writing his own fiction to avoid discursive story telling.[22] He clearly distinguished between stories of "message" and stories of "character," as he here describes the problem:

> I think that the writer is too busy trying to create flesh-and-blood people that will stand up and cast a shadow to have time to be conscious of all the symbolism that he may put into what he does or what people may read into it. That if he had the time to--that is, if one individual could write the authentic, credible, flesh-and-blood character and

at the same time deliver the message, maybe he
would, but I don't believe any writer is capable of
doing both...: either he is delivering a message
or he's trying to create flesh-and-blood, living,
suffering, anguishing human beings.[23]

In terms of fictional technique, Faulkner's tendency
to emphasize character instead of message led him to prefer first person or stream of consciousness methods. As
early as 1931 he had expressed the theory that novelists
should "let the characters tell their own stories instead of
filling page after page with exposition."

In the future novel, or fiction--Mr. Faulkner con-
tends--there will be no straight exposition, but instead, objective presentation, by means of solilo-
quies or speeches of the characters, those of each
character printed in a different colored ink. Something of the play technique will thus eliminate much
of the author from the story. And the consequent
loss of personality? Is not all writing interesting
and important only insofar as it expresses the personality of the author? All exclusive of the story,
Mr. Faulkner says, is dead weight. What is interesting in Dickens is not the way he takes things,
but 'those people he wrote about and what they
did.'[24]

Faulkner's own most striking attempts to employ this meth-
od--The Sound and the Fury and As I Lay Dying--proved to
the critical world how effective and yet how difficult such
stark presentation could be. Hemingway's writing also illustrates this belief in the efficacy of the supposed absent author; and, just as they had Hemingway's, critics also misread Faulkner's characters.[25]

Precisely because neither Hemingway or Faulkner
would expound on characters' motivation, a wide range of
"interpretations" about their characters now exists; but such
a range is evidence only of imperceptive reading, and of the
critics' failure to attend to the author's purpose in his total
work. A novel exists not to present a single character or a
single theme; a sketch or an essay, respectively, could do
either of those things, singly, better than a novel. The novel by definition is a wide canvas; it presents its truths
through the interrelation of characters. "Saneness, that is
the word,"[26] pleads Faulkner in one of the few comments

he ever made about the role of the critic. Often, in reading both these authors, readers seem to be testing their personal moral code instead of enjoying the experience of the story as story, a written, structured whole. As Pound said early in "The Serious Artist,"

> the good artist is not a theorist, who urges the reader to behave as he would like to behave. Art never asks anybody to do anything, or to think anything, or to be anything. It exists as trees exist.[27]

Modern art need not be the result of a philosophical formulation or a spiritual conviction, although, of course, it also may be. Traditionally, art, the act of creation, is by its very nature affirmative, joyous. As Faulkner describes his reasons for writing,

> ... primarily the writer, the artist, works because it's fun. He hadn't found anything that is that much pleasure. He is simply telling a story in the most moving and dramatic way that he can think to do it. He's not following any right nor any duty to improve you; he simply has seen something in the magic and passion of breathing which seems so funny or so tragic that he wants to tell you. And he is trying to tell you in the most moving and economical way he can, so that you will be moved, will laugh or cry, as he did.... He'd rather do that than anything else he knows.[28]

It is interesting to consider Hemingway's very similar statement written in 1924:

> It was really more fun than anything. That was really why you did it. He had never realized that before. It wasn't conscience. It was simply that it was the greatest pleasure. It had more bite to it than anything else. It was so damn hard to write well, too....

But Hemingway continues more somberly than Faulkner, "It was hell to do.... He felt almost holy about it. It was deadly serious. You could do it if you would fight it out.... It was a job. Maybe for all his life."[29] And in 1935,

> The only reward is in doing your work well and

> that is enough reward for any man.... If you be-
> lieve in one thing and work at it always, as I be-
> lieve in the importance of writing, you have no dis-
> illusion about that.... All you have is hatred for
> the shortness of the time we have to live and get
> our work done.[30]

The high personal seriousness in which Hemingway
held the writer's work differs somewhat from Faulkner's
emphasis on the writer's need to share his stories, on the
writer as story teller rather than spiritualist:

> As I see it, the writer has imagined a story of hu-
> man beings that was so moving, so important to
> him, that he wants to make a record of it for his
> own satisfaction or, perhaps, for others to read
> .... The novelist is talking about people.[31]

Not necessarily a lesser ambition, Faulkner's emphasis on
telling stories is also described by John Dos Passos:
"Storytelling is the creation of myths."[32]

Another difference between Hemingway and Faulkner
seems to be the way they regard their characters. Faulkner
often speaks fondly of his fictional creations, especially Lena
Grove, V. K. Ratliff, Eula Snopes. One feels as if to him
they were real people. Hemingway, conversely, has enthusiasm for the piece of writing in which a character appears,
but he seldom speaks so personally about the characters he
has created. With Hemingway, the effect of the whole was
important, whereas with Faulkner, "The story can come from
an anecdote, it can come from a character. With me it
never comes from an idea because I ... ain't really interested in ideas. I'm interested in people."[33]

"The first thing that a writer has is compassion for
all his characters.... He himself does not feel that he has
the power to judge."[34] The purpose of the writer is not
judgment but presentation: "It's not to choose sides at all--
just to compassionate the good splendid things."[35] Faulkner's
belief in this conviction is evident throughout his writing, and
his stance on this point is comparatively far from Hemingway's. In Hemingway's efforts to create heroes, he often
sacrificed characters like Robert Cohn, the doctor, Pablo because he was using them primarily as foils. For Hemingway,
some men's ways of living were simply objectionable. For
Faulkner, "the first thing he [the author] must do is to love

all mankind, even when he hates individual ones."

No critic has ever formulated a "Faulkner hero," partly because Faulkner's characters are drawn not from typed qualities but from the milieu and circumstances in which they live and struggle. Faulkner warned his readers against "assuming that a trait is good or evil in its own right. You must study the result. Anything that brings misery is bad."[36] But so far as fiction is concerned, even evil characters can serve artistic purposes. Faulkner once explained, "I just try to tell the truth of man. I use exaggeration when I have to, and cruelty as a last resort,"[37] and as he said regarding the Snopes clan, "They were simply an invention of mine to tell a story.... [O]ver-emphasized, burlesqued if you like, which is what Mr. Dickens spent a lot of his time doing, for a valid ... reason, which was to tell a story in an amusing, dramatic, tragic or comical way."[38] Some of Faulkner's own favorite characters are less than admirable (at least, from a moralist's perspective), but they are always remarkably drawn:

> My favorite characters are Sarah Gamp--a cruel, ruthless woman, a drunkard, opportunist, unreliable, most of her character was bad, but at least it was character; Mrs. Harris, Falstaff, Prince Hal, Don Quixote and Sancho, of course. Lady Macbeth I always admire. And Bottom, Ophelia, and Mercutio--both he and Mrs. Gamp coped with life, didn't ask any favors, never whined. Huck Finn, of course, and Jim. Tom Sawyer I never liked much--an awful prig. And then I like Sut Lovingood from a book written by George Harris about 1840 or '50 in the Tennessee mountains. He had no illusions about himself, did the best he could; at certain times he was a coward and knew it and wasn't ashamed; he never blamed his misfortunes on anyone and never cursed God for them.[39]

Impartial as he pretends to be, it is perhaps even more revealing that Faulkner's favorite characters from his own fiction are also among his most admirable: Dilsey ("brave, courageous, generous, gentle and honest") and Ratliff ("wonderful. He's done more things than any man I know. Why, I couldn't tell some of the things that man has done").[40]

According to Faulkner, the only way a writer could

really fail a character was to draw stereotypes instead of dynamic people. In an early review of Hergesheimer's novels, Faulkner criticized his characters because

> his people are never actuated from within; they do not create life about them; they are like puppets assuming graceful but meaningless postures in answer to the author's compulsions, and holding these attitudes until he arranges their limbs again.

He further condemns Hergesheimer for inflating the role of author, indulging in it for his own ego satisfaction. With the overstatement of youth, Faulkner calls him "an emasculate priest surrounded by the puppets he has carved and clothed and painted--a terrific world without motion or meaning."[41]

As early as 1922, Faulkner here equates life with motion. Man is capable of so much change because he is in constant movement: "change must alter, must happen.... [N]o matter how fine anything seems, it can't endure, because once it stops, abandons motion, it is dead."[42] This thematic concern has already been pointed out in numerous essays and at least two books, and rightly so: it is pervasive, and it is also central to much of Faulkner's characterization. The concept seems to have had its origin in Faulkner's March 1922 essay on American drama, where Faulkner determined that although the American language was a good resource for the American artist, it still might be less than adequate in what Faulkner saw as its essential, basic inarticulateness.

> Our wealth of language and its inarticulateness (inability to derive any benefit from the language) are due to the same cause: our racial chaos and our instinctive quickness to realize our simpler needs, and to supply them from any source. As a nation, we are a people of action; even our language is action rather than communication between minds.... [Our language] is employed only as a means of relief, when physical action is impossible or unpleasant, by all classes, ranging from the Harvard professor ... to the lowliest pop vendor at the ball park.[43]

Faulkner's chagrin over this condition may have been one impetus for his art because again and again his fiction becomes partly a rhetorical tour de force: rhetoric is used not only to reveal character but to obscure it. The reader must use a complex of signs, including the character's action, to read his words accurately. Anse Bundren, for one, sounds admirable, as does Mrs. Compson; and Jason and Jewel sound despicable. Faulkner's play with language as an extension/ fabrication of character is not perverse; it serves only to emphasize the wider scope of his approach to both character and fiction, the wholistic one.

Faulkner, like Anderson, James, Pound, Joyce, and many other modernist writers, believed in self-determination for his fiction. "The story will choose its own type of telling, own style." "The stories seem to shape themselves as they go along."[44]

I am convinced that the story you tell invents its own style, compels its style.[45]

As critics since Conrad Aiken, writing in 1939, never tire of pointing out--and rightly--Faulkner seldom did the same thing twice; and nearly every one of his fictional approaches seems justified. Michael Millgate puts it this way:

Nothing in Faulkner's career is more remarkable than the sheer bulk of his achievement and the extraordinary range of his experimentation, the variety of narrative techniques adopted in successive volumes. Even his earliest novels, Soldiers' Pay and Mosquitoes, incorporated distinctive experimental elements, and by the time he wrote his fourth novel, The Sound and the Fury, he was no longer tinkering with the problems of fictional form but undertaking radical new departures.... In other books of the 1930's and early 1940's the experiments were of many different kinds: chiefly stylistic in Pylon, chiefly structural in The Wild Palms, both stylistic and structural in Absalom, Absalom!, The Hamlet, and Go Down, Moses.[46]

Hemingway's own consistent experimentation shows that he too shares Faulkner's feeling that each novel is a specific problem, "one single urn or shape,"[47] a form to vary according to content. Parallel also was each writer's reliance on the dramatic scene as heart of his fiction. Whether the scene is the entire short story or whether a novel moves in clusters of scenes, the most powerful and vivid writing usually appears in the actual interchange among characters. Unlike

James or Conrad, whose characters often fascinate in complete solitude, Hemingway and Faulkner seem to work best with objectified, concrete scenes (even Hemingway's treatment of Santiago suggests something other than soliloquy). Present! Make it new! No ideas but in things.

Their awareness that the genius of fictional method--at least for them--lay in arrangement of material is also similar, and in this respect the influence of Impressionism seems clear. For Anderson, Hemingway, and Faulkner, Cézanne was highly significant; Faulkner too spent much of his 1925 sojourn in Paris frequenting the Luxembourg gardens. Richard Adams describes the transfer of method from Cézanne to fiction in this way, seeing the painter's real influence to lie in the way "the artists go about building the structures of the works."

> Cézanne proceeded by laying on patches of color here and there, filling more and more of his canvas, until the forms emerged--a complex and difficult way to make pictures which are complex and difficult to see. The viewer is forced to do a good share of the labor of composition, to enter into the process of constructing the picture along with the painter, to recapitulate and bring to life the painter's experience of the scene. For those who are not too lazy to do the necessary work, the result is a richly dynamic esthetic experience, which the artist does not present to the viewer so much as he allows and encourages the viewer to share it.[48]

The most essential quality of writing that Faulkner appears to have absorbed from Anderson, Shakespeare, and elsewhere which had little influence on Hemingway was that of an easy humor. As early as 1925 Faulkner judges Anderson's writing to be either good or bad largely on the basis of its effective humor. He feels that "Marching Men," "Windy McPherson's Son," and "Many Marriages" are bad writing because they lack humor; that Winesburg and most of the stories of Horses and Men are good, not only because they deal with humorous subjects but because the humor colors the writing even when Anderson is not "deliberately writing a story with a humorous intent."[49] This humor, a loving humor rooted not in spleen but in contentment with life, was to be Faulkner's own eventual accomplishment, once he had discovered V. K. Ratliff.

The difference between Faulkner's Introduction to
Sherwood Anderson & Other Famous Creoles and Hemingway's
The Torrents of Spring was precisely the tone of the humor.
Faulkner's gentle quips as he calls attention to the "soft
laughter" in the Vieux Carre, his parodies of Anderson's
mannerisms and lengthy details are deftly phrased; a reader
could almost read the parody as "straight" writing. And
Faulkner concludes with his apology to Anderson, the apology
that all American art takes itself too seriously, as does the
artist. "We have one priceless universal trait, we Americans. That trait is our humor."[50]

The pride with which Faulkner took his own use of
humor is evident not only in his comments about it, but most
impressively in his use of it in especially the later novels.
Humor, for Faulkner, was not an alleviation re the old comic relief theory so much as it was a valid point of view.
The anguished youth, like Quentin Compson, or the self-ali-
enated man, Joe Christmas, see little humor in any of life's
circumstances; Ratliff, Will Varner, Jennie Du Pre--Faulk-
ner's truly mature characters find comedy (and joy) in many
unexpected places. As Faulkner had said of humor in 1957,

> it's a part of man too, it's a part of life....
> [T]here's not too fine a distinction between humor
> and tragedy, that even tragedy is in a way walking
> a tightrope between the ridiculous--between the bi-
> zarre and the terrible.[51]

REARRANGEMENTS

It might be said that Hemingway's early friendship
with Anderson not only gave him the important introductions
to Paris figures, but also predisposed him to what he would
find there. Taken very generally, Anderson sounds a great
deal like Pound and Ford. He does speak much less often
about technical details, but the real difference between him
and the Paris group would become evident only in the execution of his own later writing (see Chapter One).

Hemingway knew Anderson during the Chicago winter
(1921) before he married Hadley Richardson and went to
Paris; Faulkner did not meet him until his New Orleans sojourn some four years later, in 1925. Despite the difference
in time, Anderson had changed very little; he was set on creating more novels with the same speed as he had short

stories, and the results were less than satisfactory (but so far he was not daunted by those results, or the critics' reaction to them). So that Faulkner received the same kind of advice and counsel that Hemingway had, with the additional now-famous remark that he should write about what he knew best.

That Anderson's general influence had such seemingly diverse results, at least stylistically, in the writing of Hemingway and Faulkner can best be explained in the wide differences between the pupils' other reading experiences and, perhaps more important, between their inherent approaches to writing. As we have seen, Hemingway gravitated naturally toward the lyric stance, the use of himself as persona, or as character with whom he might empathize, the use of and reuse of reasonably common experience. Hemingway was presenting emotional tones, not telling necessarily exciting stories; and his bent was only strengthened by his tutelage under Pound, Stein, Ford, and Joyce. Guided by the "Every word set on paper" maxim, Hemingway moved tortuously ahead in his writing, making every word work in several ways, and forcing each scene to carry at least double weight.

Faulkner, however, was a mixture of both the lyric poet and the chameleon story-teller, and in the coalescence of these identities may lie his primary narrative strength. Interestingly, much of Faulkner's writing is also marked by the single word charged with pointed ambivalence, scrupulous detail, the scene acting to implement both characterization and plot. For example, in Light in August, the brief scene of Mrs. Armstid, readying her egg money for Lena Grove: the implicit bitterness in her terse dialogue is achieved largely through her use of the seemingly vague pronoun them, here possibly referring to either children or chickens; and--probably--both.

> 'What are you fixing to do with your eggmoney this time of night?' he says.
> 'I reckon it's mine to do with what I like.' She stoops into the lamp, her face harsh, bitter. 'God knows it was me sweated over them and nursed them. You never lifted no hand" [19].

In addition to the impact of this dialogue, Faulkner has earlier used several images to depict Martha Armstid. She is described as handling the kitchen tools "with the abrupt savageness of a man," as being "manhard, workhard, in a serviceable gray garment worn savage and brusque, her hands on her hips, her face like those of generals who have been defeated in battle" (14). Like Hemingway, Faulkner uses imagery for more than description. The masculine traits signal Martha's loss of femininity (and humanity) through her long physical travail. Once Faulkner has so clearly established her condition, he then reverses her attitude--the one both Armstid and the reader have been led to expect--to show her as being still responsive, moved by Lena's plight, and willing to share the younger woman's difficulties. Even in this short sequence of details, a character appears in believable complexity. Martha Armstid is a vivid person in her own right; she also foreshadows the many other distraught and physically disabled women of the novel-- Mrs. Hines; the wife of the Rev. Hightower; even Joanna Burden--all of whom are the victims of the masculine right-eousness-puritan paranoia.

Repeatedly in all his writing, Faulkner employs the single detail for maximum thematic effect and the recurring image for both tonal and descriptive impact (Joe Christmas recurs throughout this novel as "carven, a large toy: small, still round headed and round eyed"--and, by implication, inherently blameless). Also like Hemingway's, Faulkner's narrative centers in scenes, which are frequently presented with little exposition. Joe crouches in the dietician's bedroom; Hightower sweats and becomes faint in the grocery; Byron is drawn to fight Lucas Burch. Each scene operates in numerous ways. And quite often, the reader's realization of theme--like the characters'--grows from observing an apparently slight happening. The situation is, once again, that we recognize truth through our apprehension of image or scene (scene serving many of the same purposes in fiction that image does in poetry, according to Handy, Beja, Alain Robbe-Grillet,[52] et al.).

These definite stylistic parallels between much of Faulkner's writing and much of Hemingway's may have gone partly unnoticed because Faulkner as raconteur frequently uses a wide base for his storyline, and the resulting rhythm of the total novel is inclusive, rambling, even ponderous. There is much to tell, in nearly every Faulkner novel, and the reader needs to know an incredible amount of detail. The impact of the single word or the separated detail is admittedly less noticeable in this matrix than in the somewhat spare context of much of Hemingway's work.

Despite his use of numerous story lines and many different characters, Faulkner frequently relies on a repeated image, a motif, to unify these seemingly disparate pieces. Different as Percy Grimm, Miss Atkins, and Hightower's grandfather are, Faulkner connects them by using the descriptive image, that each saw life as "a straight and simple corridor." When he later describes the philosophical stances of Hightower and Joe as circular, complex, his distinction between such attitudes becomes clear. The point is made, tellingly, almost entirely through imagery.

Working with the intricate and often convoluted plots that he seemed to glory in, Faulkner yet often depended on a pervasive tone (or organ base) to unify a novel thematically. Benjy's sounds in The Sound and the Fury conjoin with other expressions of man's agony. The haunting scent of the honeysuckle, which typifies for Quentin the sweet yet repulsing attraction of womenflesh, parallels and finally mingles with Caddy's smelling like trees, Jason's nausea at worldly smells, and Dilsey's acceptance of natural (and unnatural) odors. Light in August is toned to the somewhat mournful hesitancy of both Hightower and Joe, each fearing involvement in life, each searching for peace through conscious if erroneous choice, each bearing his life, as Joe thinks, "like it was a basket of eggs." The almost turgid movement of the novel itself parallels the slow turn of Hightower's wheel of realization, leaving the impact of the book, somber, heavy, completely solemn. The presence of the Juggernaut, the Player, and the chess game imagery also intensifies the basic tone.

The poet in Faulkner the novelist is also evident in his trust of organic form, in his inventiveness with each story, and in his real love for the effect words have--minted, combined, repeated. Cleanth Brooks writes perceptively in a 1968 essay about the effects Faulkner's somewhat rhetorical imagery has in his fiction, rather than in the formal poems; and concludes that the "poetry" gains by being juxtaposed with different textures of writing.[53] And, perhaps more importantly, the lyric emphasis for Faulkner is also clear as novel after novel, regardless of plot or character, returns to the same pervasive theme: man's endurance, his ability to survive, with honor, in a world he never made.[54]

It is helpful in this context to consider the supposed reservations that Hemingway and Faulkner had about each

other--given also, the great admiration that existed between
them. Despite the often-quoted Faulkner listing, which rates
Hemingway below four other American writers, including himself,[55] Faulkner consistently had great admiration for Hemingway. From the late twenties, when he and Phil Stone
placed Hemingway at the top, to his repeated defenses of the
novelist in the forties and fifties, Faulkner acknowledged
Hemingway's great skill and ability. Blotner quotes a particularly apt reprimand Faulkner delivered to Truman Capote,
as he was complaining about <u>Across the River and Into the
Trees</u>:

> 'Young man,' he said, 'I haven't read this new one.
> And though it may not be the best thing Hemingway
> ever wrote, I know it will be carefully done, and
> it will have quality.'[56]

He commented in 1957 that Hemingway "has done consistently probably the most solid work of all of us.... He is a
man who has never betrayed the--his integrity which one accepts to be a writer. He learned early in life a method by
which he could do his work, ... it suited him, he handled it
well. If his work continues, then it's going to get better."[57]

The reservations Faulkner appears to have had about
Hemingway's writing were still apparent even in these com-
ments--that he had, technically, played it safe ("it wasn't the
splendid magnificent bust that Wolfe made in trying to put the
whole history of the human heart on the head of a pin"[58]);
and that, until <u>The Old Man and the Sea</u>, Hemingway had
never found God, i.e., tradition, history, ritual ("Up to that
time his people functioned in a vacuum, they had no past"[59])
--but then Faulkner was never satisfied with his own writing
efforts either.

Hemingway made fewer public comments about Faulkner, but he several times listed one of Faulkner's books as
a favorite, and in private conversations admired his writing.[60]
Malcolm Cowley recounts Hemingway's high praise for Faulkner in 1945, saying that "Hemingway had written ... that
Faulkner had the most talent of all of them but was undepend-
able because he wasn't selective enough. 'I would have been
happy just to have managed him,' Hemingway had said."[61]
His occasional sarcasm about Faulkner fits the pattern Baker
has described: it occurred when Hemingway might have been
either jealous of Faulkner's success (after the Nobel Prize),
or disappointed in one of his books (as he was in <u>A Fable</u>).

Undoubtedly, their somewhat different approaches to the
method and purpose of writing kept them from complete
identification with each other; but the identification, nevertheless, was reasonably close. Both shared the stringent
view of writing as, first, art; and of writer as maker; and
Hemingway himself could have coined Faulkner's comment,
"Most writers are not literary men.... [T]hey're craftsmen."62

In addition to this central difference, in approach,
there are others. Hemingway had a much shorter apprenticeship period. When he was 22, he was already a part of the
Ford-Pound-Joyce-Stein group. When Faulkner was 22, he
had been away from any formal school for six years, had
attempted a variety of occupations, but was still far from
his career of novelist. Surrounded as he was, Hemingway
could hardly keep from writing; Philip Young cites among
Hemingway's large personal library four valuable books dating from these early Paris friendships:

> Joyce's Ulysses, 1922, unbound and stamped
> "Press Copy."
>
> Stein's Portrait of Mabel Dodge, signed "To the
> Hemingways with much affection. Gertrude
> Stein."
>
> Pound's XVI Cantos, 1924, No. 10 of 90,
> "Printed for Ernest Hemingway."
>
> Ford's No More Parades, dated Paris 31/10/24,
> Guermantes 25/4/25, a heavily-corrected type-
> script.63

Faulkner's career, contrastingly, was if not launched
at least nourished by his Oxford friend, Phil Stone, a perceptive reader with the inclination and means to buy the new-
est books.64 Evidence seems to indicate, however, that Phil
Stone was learning along with Faulkner, that he, Stone,
did not have an already formed canon. In no way was the
young lawyer another Ezra Pound.

Eventually, as we have seen, Faulkner did become intimate with Anderson, then at the peak of his reputation and
his own personal confidence. Their relationship was largely
an oral one; they exchanged stories, occasionally writing
them in letter form; but even this kind of exchange provided
no means of "correction." There seems to have been none
of the blue-penciling of a Pound.

Another important influence on Faulkner in 1925 was
the New Orleans literary circle--William Spratling, Roark
Bradford, Stark Young, Hamilton Basso, Lyle Saxon--and
The Double Dealer, [65] the little magazine which originated
in New Orleans, and existed largely to champion the "eternal verities," at no loss of craft. In many ways an admirable little journal, The Double Dealer differs somewhat from
The Little Review or Exile in that it preferred meat to method. While most of the modernist writers receive favorable
comment, Pound is censured in a 1922 review for his "bore-
dom, his effete sophistication." John McClure, an editor of
the magazine and here reviewer, went on ambiguously, saying that the book "contains much subtle and beautiful writing
and much that seems to be foolish, or, at any rate, merely
clever." [66] Because McClure became a good friend of Faulkner's, his less than wholehearted enthusiasm for Pound is
significant. McClure was more impressed at this time with
Sandburg, who customarily received high praise in the magazine. A 1922 editorial summarizes the journal's view clearly when it states that all innovation is acceptable so long as
it is profitable, but not if it exists only as an end in itself:

> Values are eternal. The old reminder. New
> gospels, new schools, new movements come and
> go ... but values--beauty, truth, humor, crafts-
> manship--remain. [67]

The Double Dealer was not unreasonable in its affections. There are excellent reviews of H. D., Aldington,
Fletcher, Cummings, Williams, and Joyce (the latter ac-
knowledging the tremendous importance of Ulysses). The
Double Dealer had in a 1921 editorial bemoaned the "neglect
of form," particularly in fiction, and throughout its official
prolegomena it emphasized craft. In fact, Sherwood Anderson is harshly criticized precisely because he has stated that
"technique is quite unnecessary to art"; [68] the reviewing critic is especially displeased with Anderson's Mid-American
Chants. (Because Anderson's writings--essays and the "testament" prose poems--were featured throughout the 1922 issues, some critics have considered the magazine an Anderson outlet, but these comments indicate no such relationship.
Even the reviews praising Anderson's prose point out that he
had difficulty sustaining long fiction.)

One of the most noticeable emphases in The Double
Dealer is that on humor. There are many pieces either by
or about Lafcadio Hearn; there is much emphasis on the

droll maxim as filler ("Journalism: Michelangelo painting a house"), the short aphoristic poem like Hemingway's "Ultimately," and the prose poem parable, like Hemingway's "A Divine Gesture."[69] In 1921 the magazine contained a series of essays titled "Tales of the Psychometric Reporter." And the opening editorial had in fact stressed that, with Twain, the greatest writers have realized that man's "only adequate weapon" is a "sense of humor."

Because Faulkner contributed to The Double Dealer from 1922 to 1926, we surmise that he read the journal; even this influence, however, like that of Anderson, came comparatively late in his maturity as writer. He had spent over a decade--he and Phil Stone--reading what was being done, and he had written of his own judgments with a confidence that bespoke experience. Perhaps because he was so independent of personal influences, Faulkner was able to sort through what was happening in modern art, and thereby to follow his own opinions. Particularly in his early writing, his reading, not his literary friendships, seems to have been the pervasive influence.

Chapter Eight

THE EARLY WRITING

The use Faulkner and Hemingway made of their reading seems to be as similar as their choices for that reading. They both felt that reading is a superb source for both materials and methods;[1] like being apprenticed to a carpenter, the writer learns his craft from watching other authors' stories in progress--particularly those of the great writers.[2] It is perhaps surprising that both Hemingway and Faulkner admired many of the same writers: Turgenev, Conrad, Melville, Joyce, Dostoevski, the authors of The Bible, Shakespeare, Mark Twain.*

For all their similarities, however, there are several important differences. The first is the comparatively normal amount of reading Hemingway did as a young man, compared with Faulkner's voracious consumption of books. Hemingway began writing at a younger age (he was only 24 when in our time was published, whereas Faulkner was 27 when his first poems came out, and 29 when his first novel appeared). There is little evidence, too, that Hemingway actually read some of the authors he supposedly admired (Conrad and James, for example).

The second, more significant, difference is Hemingway's nearly complete immersion in the Pound/Imagist

---

*The question here is more properly one of learning how to write than it is emulating any specific writer. One refrains from using the word influence with any discussion of Faulkner's writing, since his own comment on such studies is so devastating:

For some reason people seem to be interested not in what Mr. Anderson has written, but from what source he derives. The greater number who speculate upon his origin say he derives from the Russians. If so, he has returned home, 'The Triumph of the Egg' having been translated into Russian. A smaller number hold to the French theory. A cabinet-maker in New Orleans discovered that he resembles Zola, though how he arrived at this I can not see, unless it be that Zola also wrote books ['Sherwood Anderson,' The Dallas Morning News].

school of writing, contrasted with Faulkner's own distaste for
some of the writers involved in that group. During the very
early twenties, and perhaps before, Faulkner's taste ran
from Housman and Swinburne to Frost, H. D., and Conrad
Aiken; the former two for their vision and tone, the latter
particularly for his "musical forms."[3] As the line of the
Imagists and Vorticists grew spare and short, keeping "near
to the bone," Aiken and Faulkner delighted in the cumulative
effect of language in long strokes and passages. Faulkner
praises Aiken's polyphonic verse, his attempt to "synthesize
musical reactions," his rich variation. Like Aiken, Faulkner was never afraid to repeat himself, and often did, to
achieve rhythmic variety. He did, however, sometimes write
lines that Pound would have approved, as in "A Poplar":

> Why do you shiver there
> Between the white river and the road?
> You are not cold,
> With the sun light dreaming about you;
> And yet you lift your pliant supplicating arms as
> though
> To draw clouds from the sky to hide your slender-
> ness.
>
> You are a young girl
> Trembling in the throes of ecstatic modesty,
> A white objective girl
> Whose clothing has been forcibly taken away from
> her.[4]

The Oriental-like opening leads to the sequence of images
which builds the poem; since the poem has little meaning
aside from those images, Faulkner is using them in the best
contemporary manner, not merely as ornament.

Somewhat later than this 1920 poem, Faulkner still
uses the image as central, but builds on it also, forming
passages which could easily be shortened were it not for the
rhythmic effect he evidently desired. Only a suggestion of
the sensual power in Poem III of A Green Bough comes
through in this sixth stanza. (The identification of the beloved with the music in the cave has been made in a previous poem of the sequence):

> The cave is ribbed with music; threads of
> sound
> Gleam on the whirring wings of bats of gold
> Loop from the grassroots to the roots of trees

> Thrust into sunlight, where the song of birds
> Spins silver threads to gleam from bough to
>   bough.
> Grass in meadows cools his fancy's feet:
> Dew is on the grass, and birds in hedges
> Weave the sunlight with sharp streaks of flight.
> Bees break apple bloom, and peach and clover
> Sing in the southern air where aimless clouds
> Go up the sky-hill, cropping it like sheep,
> And startled pigeons, like a wind beginning,
> Fill the air with sucking silver sound. [5]

The assonance and compelling rhythm help create the effect of urgency which underlies the poem as a whole. Part of the impact of the poems in A Green Bough results from the arrangement of the separate poems into a unified collection; in his poems as in his short stories (and the later "blend" novels) Faulkner uses position to deepen or contrast effect. A Green Bough is a good collection, partly because of its ironic juxtapositions (and title) and partly because it includes masterful poems like XXII:

> I see your face through the twilight of my mind,
> A dusk of forgotten things, remembered things;
> It is a corridor dark and cool with music
> And too dim for sight,
> That leads me to a door which brings
> You, clothed in quiet sound for my delight
> [44].

The variation in line length and rhyme pattern here, as well as the apt choice of imagery, affirms George Garrett's view that Faulkner was a poet who knew "the value of words, rhythm, image, texture, and above all, structure ... a meticulous craftsman"[6] (see Appendix II, and Garrett's fine essay entire).

    Whatever Faulkner's later objection to Pound's influence, Blotner proves his earlier approbation. After 1925, Faulkner tended to echo the Double Dealer's complaint with the Imagists, that they were overconcerned with technique, to the exclusion of "spiritual beauty."[7] He chose to say little about Pound, Williams, and H. D. except that a "tide of aesthetic sterility" is engulfing modern letters, saving his cutting personal remarks for "the British nightingales, Mr. Vachel Lindsay with his tin pan and iron spoon, Mr. Kreymborg with his lithographic water coloring, and Mr. Carl

Sandburg with his sentimental Chicago propaganda."[8] Faulkner does conclude, in his biographical essay on poetry, that
he has become increasingly tired of modernist verse (this, in
1925), and has accordingly returned to the poems of Spenser,
Shakespeare, Shelley, and Keats; yet as late as 1957 in The
Town he is quoting lines from Djuna Barnes.[9] His own
cycles of formal poems in The Marble Faun (1924) and the
concluding sonnets of A Green Bough testify to that pervasive
interest, as does his statement in 1925 that poetry should
"revert to formal rhymes and conventional forms again."

     One is, however, hard put to overlook the admiration
Faulkner had for T. S. Eliot. From Mosquitoes through Pylon Faulkner used actual lines or phrases traceable to Eliot's
poems,[10] and one might conjecture that Faulkner's Requiem
for a Nun bears some slight relation to Eliot's Family Re-
union, when instead of living their lives blindly, Temple
Drake and Gowan Stevens awaken to the nightmare. Richard
Adams points out also that Eliot's early essays, published
during the years of Faulkner's development as writer, were
also important to Faulkner. Adams cites particularly "Tradition and the Individual Talent" (see Faulkner's use of impersonal as a term of high praise) and "Ulysses, Order, and
Myth," Eliot's essay which praises Joyce's mythical method
in terms that could now, in retrospect, also describe Faulkner's range of inclusion:

          In using the myth, in manipulating a continuous
          parallel between contemporaneity and antiquity, Mr.
          Joyce is pursuing a method which others must pur-
          sue after him ...; a way of controlling, of order-
          ing, of giving a shape and a significance to the im-
          mense panorama of futility and anarchy which is
          contemporary history.... Instead of narrative
          method, we may now use the mythical method.[11]

     Indeed, Eliot's influence on Faulkner may be seen to
be a great deal like that of Joyce, so important that Faulkner purposely, it seems, put readers off the scent by appear-
ing to deny his admiration. Both Joyce and Conrad were tremendously important writers to Faulkner,[12] with their significance ranging from method to theme to the emphasis on humor. Like Joyce, Faulkner is concerned with handling and
defining time; and often employs past and present juxtaposed.
Like Joyce, too, he relies even from his earliest fiction on
stream of consciousness technique in order to create his
world, more variously peopled than Joyce's, but as centrally

rooted. And a recurring theme in both is man's alienation, often presented with a cover of humor that sometimes only the initiated could understand as humor.

Although humor is less apparent in Conrad's writing, it also exists there, along with the characters of incomplete men repulsed by sex, the lush descriptions of mysterious nature, the themes that insist on probing to the center of man's relationship with man. Conrad's use of the image--extended to a controlling metaphor--has been recently compared to Faulkner's practice by James Guetti. And, among many other points of influence, Adams notes particularly that "the use of scrambled chronology, twice and three times removed narrators, and other devices of gradual revelation in Faulkner is easily traceable to Conrad, and there are occasional startling resemblances in style."[13] It is interesting that much of the Impressionistic method in fiction had its effect on Faulkner as well as Hemingway, but by different routes, with Hemingway learning through his personal friendships from Ford via Pound, and Faulkner learning directly from Conrad's writing itself. Again, with Conrad as with Joyce and Eliot, the actual lines and traceable borrowings occur more frequently in Faulkner's earliest fiction; the methods, however, remain throughout.

Many recent studies of Faulkner, Blotner's biography included, prove conclusively how well read he was; and how perceptive he was about his reading. Like most writers, Faulkner also stored away many suggestive possibilities for fiction, so that much of his late writing stems from things he had read many years before (as, his own Snopes trilogy bearing many similarities to T. S. Stribling's trilogy in the early thirties, or The Reivers having partial origin in a 1923 translation of Lucius Apulius' "golden book" (see Appendix III); or, more frequently, from things he had already written about once, but had for various reasons found necessary to resurrect (horserace stories, Civil War exploits, dauntless little old ladies). In these terms, Faulkner's earliest prose sketches, as well as his poems, are highly interesting. After his fifteen years as a poet, he turned to the prose sketches published in the New Orleans Times-Picayune from January to September of 1925. These pieces are of interest now not only for their themes, but also because they illustrate Faulkner's belief that action is necessary to fiction ("any story must have a conflict in it. You set it up, then solve it," Faulkner's brother John recounts being told[14]).

Several of these pieces show in embryo the way Faulkner seems to have worked from the core of "tales" that people in his area all knew, i.e., the Cullen accounts. "Sunset" opens with the newspaper paragraph describing the "facts" of a black gunman's death, after he had killed two whites and a Negro. "Black Desperado Slain" is the head-line, and the news item concludes that not only was the un-known black a terrorist, but that he was also insane. Faulk-ner then devotes eleven pages to re-creating the black man so that he becomes a sympathetic, childlike figure, trying desperately to reach his promised land of Africa, being duped and hurt repeatedly by blacks and whites alike. No one would help him; even the "cold, cold stars" were indif-ferent; and so in his uncomprehending ignorance, he had to die.

The two versions of the cobbler's story also illustrate what was to be an important fictional method for Faulkner throughout his writing, his tendency to pick up minor charac-ters--those only used at first to show facets of a major fig-ure--and give them a life, and story, of their own (Horace Benbow, Gowan Stevens, and Gavin Stevens, for example). One has only to read the several books now published which try to trace genealogy of Faulkner's characters to appreciate the fact that Faulkner did make numerous changes. His char-acters are nearly always subordinate to the story as a whole.

This early prose does much more than prefigure de-tails of Faulkner's later novels (Carvel Collins has identified many of these details in his perceptive introduction to the collected sketches. To his list might be added the violent speech of "The Longshoreman" that foreshadows Jason's idi-om, especially regarding Lorraine; the use of refrain in both sketches about the cobbler which anticipates the near-refrains in Absalom, Light in August, and The Sound and the Fury; the statement in "Out of Nazareth" that "Mankind is never as complex as we would like to believe ourselves to be" as a hint toward Faulkner's emphasis on simplicity to come; and the dying Negro's fantasy that he is a buzzard, which re-minds one of Vardaman's confusion about the fish). Interest-ing as these textual parallels are, the prose already shows Faulkner as a mature writer. It evinces clearly several bas-ic fictional methods which Faulkner was to use throughout his writing.

(1) The use of character's speech, in both rhythm and diction, as a primary means of delineation. The "New

Orleans" sequence places the monologues of a wealthy Jew, a priest, Frankie and Johnny, the sailor, and others in sequence. The Jew's refrain, "I love three things: gold; marble and purple; splendor, solidity, color" contrasts remarkably with the coarse idiom of the lover:

> Listen, baby, before I seen you it was like I was one of those ferry boats yonder crossing and crossing a dark river or something by myself.... [I]t was like a wind had blew a lot of trash and stuff out of the street. 15

(2) The use of poetic description, heavy with alliteration and assonance, sometimes for ironic effects, more often used seriously; and nearly always phrased in long, rhythmic sentences.

> He could feel sweat cold as copper pieces on his face and he ran toward the haystack and clawed madly at it, trying to climb it. His fear grew with his futile efforts, then cooled away [153].

Often the longer sentence is followed by a shorter one which acts as a summary image: "here was a wind coming up: the branches and bushes about him whipped suddenly to a gale fiercer than any yet; flattened and screamed, and melted away under it. And he, too, was a tree caught in the same wind" (157). Yet in some sketches, sentences are ineffectually short; in fact Faulkner in places sounds a great deal like the early Hemingway, relying on direct statement with some fairly easy word repetition to make his point:

> Things were beginning to look funny, and his shoulder hurt dreadfully. He dozed a moment and thought he was at home again; he waked to pain and dozed again. Dozing and waking, he passed the long day (156).

(3) The use of one character, often a completely sympathetic one like the idiot in "The Kingdom of God" or the old drunk in "Mirrors of Chartres Street," as a means of identifying other characters. Faulkner is to use this technique again and again, not only simply, as with Benjy or Darl and Vardaman, when our sympathy is easily given; but more ambivalently, with Quentin, Temple, Joe Christmas, Mrs. Armstid, and Mink Snopes.

(4) The use of inordinate coincidence like that of Light in August and The Wild Palms being expressly evident in "Chance" but used more perversely in "The Liar."

(5) The use of the naif or the physically impaired-- blind, crippled, displaced, or very old--as protagonist. Not one of Faulkner's main characters in his sketches is an intellectual; either they are young uneducated boys or tough ignorant men. Evidently taking his cue from Anderson's Winesburg subjects, Faulkner yet had varied his format by choosing many migrant figures--Italian, Greek, Oriental. In 1925 New Orleans was providing him more romantic subjects than he surmised Oxford could have presented. When he used Ek, in "The Liar," and the racing touts, he was closer to home-ground, although the racetrack stories here also remind one of Anderson. Faulkner's love for horses more than likely motivated most of his writing about them, but in these sketches, the attention falls not on the horse but on the men connected with it.

The few women that do appear also prefigure the Faulkner types to come: the very old woman in "Episode" who preens like a girl when the artist sketches her has the spirit of Aunt Jenny; but the women in "Jealousy," "The Liar," and "Chance" are mere Ophelias, necessary to the story's plot, unimportant in their own right. The collection is notable not for its treatment of women characters but rather for its absence of them. In the next five years, Faulkner was to learn a great deal about ways to use his feminine characters--notice the comparatively large number of important women characters in both Soldiers' Pay and Mosquitoes-- but his emphasis was to remain that of Shakespeare: in his fiction, like the country it usually mirrored, the role of women was largely passive. Women like Joanna Burden, Charlotte Rittenmeyer, Narcissa Benbow, and the early Temple Drake--for all their independence--are never heroines; and Mrs. Compson and Cora Tull are only hypocrites. Like Addie Bundren, Margaret Powers, Eula Varner Snopes, Lena Grove, Jenny Du Pre, Miss Habersham, and Nancy Mannigoe, few of Faulkner's successful heroines rebel. They remain feminine, and work within and through the established system.

The differences from Faulkner's later writing are largely technical. A rather traditional amount of authorial comment infiltrates each sketch, more often done through description than direct statement. Faulkner sets the reader's direction early in each piece so that the story unfolds

without many surprises (the element of mystery that several
of the sketches contain is necessary to keep the plot going at
all). The opening of "Yo Ho and Two Bottles of Rum" leaves
no question of allegiance for the reader; Faulkner describes
the Chinese sailors

> squatting quietly, meager and fleshless, small and
> naked as children; yellow wisps of men clothed
> modestly in shirts, still and unfathomable as mum-
> mies or idols

and then goes immediately to declare that the ship's officers
were "the scum of the riffraff of the United Kingdom, a scum
which even the catholic stomach of the dominions beyond the
seas refuses at intervals, vomiting it over the face of the
globe." After this, we are not surprised to hear the mate's
vindication of his murder of one of the Chinese (" 'Dammit,
sir,' Mr. Ayers said with justifiable exasperation, 'ain't I a
white man? Can't I kill a native if I want to?' " [215]).

Only a few years later, Faulkner is to use this apparent reliance on conventional description for his own ironic
ends, as in "A Rose for Emily," he includes much detail and
many illustrations, all the while omitting the details the reader really needs to know.

Another practice which differs from his later narrative method is that each sketch is told chronologically; every
one races to its climax. Partly because each is so short,
there is seldom any sustained interest in character. Only in
"Home," "The Cobbler," and "Sunset" does Faulkner use
any flashback; otherwise all are in present tense.

These differences occur in method, but thematically
the sketches prefigure the longer fiction. Already there are
many treatments of love, or lack of love. The romantic attachment of Frankie and Johnny, Antonio's jealous and consuming love for his young wife, the idealistic love of the cobbler are balanced with the complete lack of love in the relationship between Mr. Harris and Juan Venturia in "The Ros-
ary," and the noncommital weariness of Magdalen the prostitute. For some characters, idealistic love exists as a way
out of their sordid living: in "Home" Jean-Baptiste is saved
from becoming a criminal as he is forcibly reminded of his
home country and his family; in "The Kid Learns," Johnny
protects a young lady and dies as a result. His death is,
however, much more ennobling than his gangland life had

been, and Faulkner dignifies that end by calling it "Little
Sister Death."

Despite some use of romantic love situations, Faulkner is already working here with the broader kinds of love
he treats so fully in his mature work. Some stories illustrate social responsibility. The "black desperado" dies because not one person tries to understand or help him; the
country mice get just revenge because the bootleggers fail to
give them even minimal respect, as do the Orientals in "Yo
Ho." The idiot in "The Kingdom of God" wails when he
senses hostility. It remains for David to so trust his fellow
men that his life serves as exoneration for them. Faulkner's
title for David's story, "Out of Nazareth," suggests that David is misplaced on earth, but then as long as people exist
who can appreciate his worth, his presence is not wasted.
As the policeman reminded himself in his sketch, "life is
not like that.... Certainly man does not ever get exactly
what he wants in this world." Man's purpose is to survive
both the reality and the chance (the latter of which Faulkner
plays with in both "Chance" and "The Liar"), to live a little
beyond the epicurean level, and to bring joy to other people.
The pathos in Faulkner's characters--here, the cobbler, the
lonely priest, the childlike--usually results from their inability to fulfill themselves. They are, in short, lonely men,
frustrated by their isolation. That Faulkner sees the development of charity as running parallel with that of religion is
clear in his use of many religious titles and motifs.

No part of this attitude is at variance with Faulkner's
later philosophy, unless it be the simplicity of its presentation here, a simplicity that results partly from length limitations. Faulkner must treat these characters separately because he does not have space to interrelate them; he must
also present inadequate detail about some of them for the
same reasons (the racetrack men and the artists are especially weak because we know too little about them).

The full panorama of these sixteen sketches gives the
reader helpful insights into Soldiers' Pay, Faulkner's first
novel. It is a war novel in the same sense that The Sun Also Rises is, in that each book's hero bears irreparable
wounds as a result of World War I, and that he loses the
woman he loves because of those wounds. Comparing Soldiers' Pay with the Hemingway book, however, illustrates
clearly one difference in the authors' concept of character.
Hemingway consistently avoided caricature: that Jake

Barnes is a normal man despite his injury is a main point of Hemingway's novel. Donald Mahon, contrastingly, is one of Faulkner's grotesques--Mahon should have died months before; his speech is robot-like, and his appearance frightens everyone. There is no reason for Margaret Powers and Joe Gilligan to, in effect, lose their lives for Donald--and in that unreasonableness lies the strength of Faulkner's point. Margaret and Joe, not Donald, are the protagonists of the novel; they relinquish their own lives and their own chances for happiness together solely to make his last days bearable. Their sacrifice is his pay. Faulkner repeats his point again and again by emphasizing the element of chance, for the title is plural: Margaret's husband Dick Powers is shot by one of his own men, at close range, and also in the face; the mother of the man who killed Powers comes to mourn with the Mahon household, as does the commander who should more reasonably have been so killed. Some men, and women, do make sacrifices; others never have to. Each of the many characters in Soldiers' Pay in some ways helps Faulkner make his simple but convincing point.

Julian Lowe's mourning over not seeing action, or not being killed, is a marvelous bit of romantic adolescence, as are his "love" letters to Margaret. The Reverend Mahon's complete blindness to the situations surrounding him (Donald's health, Cecily's immaturity, Jones' falsity) makes him the most pathetic character in the novel. The Saunders' family has a valuable role not only because of Cecily, but also because the quiet running battle between Mr. Saunders and Mrs. (paralleled by that between Cecily and her younger brother) helps establish another primary theme: that there are great differences between men and women, and that Faulkner at this time finds the dice loaded in favor of women. Sometimes women use their strength positively (Margaret and even the stolid Emmy), but sometimes they use it to un-man their men (Mrs. Saunders, Cecily).

Margaret Powers is one protagonist of the novel because she is, as her name suggests, powerful in her own self-determination; loving, generous to the fault of marrying a dying man, and holy because of that very loving, which, for women, must often take the release of a sexual relationship. Faulkner uses the characters of Cecily and her mother as foils to Margaret. They are the proper ladies, who care nothing about their lovers except as acquisitions; yet they are the good women, and Margaret is, in society's view, the fallen female.

Faulkner begins emphasizing Margaret, once he has rather ambivalently involved her in the Mahon situation, by giving us an early stream of consciousness flashback, witness to her own bereavement (36-37). From the opening of the novel, then, we understand Margaret, and admire her. When she joins forces with Joe Gilligan (platonically, although Joes does literally sleep in her bed, as Faulkner plays a bit too hard against social convention) to care for Mahon, Lowe is the outsider and Joe is an equal partner. It is Joe who knows that Mahon will die. Faulkner's use of Mahon here, and throughout the novel, foreshadows his use of Benjy. Only the morally good characters have any real sympathy with either Benjy or Mahon. As Joe remarks after several weeks at Mahon's home:

> Do you know, while I was living and eating and sleeping with men all the time I never thought much of them, but since I got civilized again and seen all these women around here saying, Ain't his face terrible, poor boy, and Will she marry him? and Did you see her downtown yesterday almost nekkid? why, I think a little better of men after all. You'll notice them soldiers don't bother him, specially the ones that was over-seas. [16]

Just as Joe and Margaret are united in their compassion for Mahon, so they both abhor the fat stranger, Janarius Jones, whose satyr-like appearance is justified in (too) many episodes throughout the novel. Millgate and others have objected to Jones' presence, [17] but perhaps he is a less fantastic character than he might seem. Faulkner uses him initially to show the Rev. Mahon's poor judgment, his reliance on foggy bombast instead of heart. (That Jones is also an academic may have, at this time, doubly delighted Faulkner.) Once involved, Jones becomes the main mover of plot: it is fear of his blackmail that forces Cecily into planning marriage with Mahon, and that decision--and her later change of mind--leads to Margaret's eventual sacrifice. Faulkner also uses Jones in a most gratuitously evil scene, when Cecily mistakes him for Donald in the dark room, and he allows the conversation to run its course.

Jones' use is also a foil to Joe's honesty and inarticulateness--and Joe's eventual battle with him foreshadows Byron Bunch's fist fight with another of Faulkner's manipulators of people, Joe Brown. For Janarius is, as his name indicates, two-faced; and he will settle for any woman (or, perhaps, any man) as a sex partner. It is this opportunism with what Faulkner holds as the greatest of man's commitments that damns Jones. His use in Soldiers' Pay is not comic; it is evil.

Margaret has one scene with Jones in which she foreshadows Addie Bundren's bitter words about rhetoric, placing her also in the line of those protagonists who act rather than talk:

> Let me give you some advice ... the next time you try to seduce anyone, don't do it with talk, with words. Women know more about words than men ever will. And they know how little they can possibly ever mean [250].

In illustration of Margaret's view, the novel is filled with meaningless words, spoken particularly by all the visitors to the Mahon home (Faulkner's parenthetical asides are effective here), the Saunders (except for Mr. Saunders), and Jones. Mahon, Emmy, Joe and Margaret seldom speak. In an early scene, Margaret has reminded Joe of the pretentiousness--and inaccuracy--of words, especially in sexual connotations:

> 'They'll think you are one of them French what-do-you call-'ems the Loot brought back with him. Your good name won't be worth nothing after these folks get through with it.'
> 'My good name is your trouble, not mine, Joe.'
> 'My trouble? How you mean?'
> 'Men are the ones who worry about our good names, because they gave them to us. But we have other things to bother about, ourselves. What you mean by a good name is like a dress that's too flimsy to wear comfortably' [104-5].

Mr. Compson is to say it three years later, but it is more convincing coming from a woman. Indeed, much of Soldiers' Pay suggests that a woman has identity only as a sex object. The scenes at the dance and downtown are included primarily to make that point, as is much of the action surrounding Cecily. Cecily is living proof that women are to be used for gratification, and her every aim in being attractive, in dressing, and in talking, is to attract men. Faulkner reinforces her position by using a passage of introspection to show her seducer's pride after the act:

> I wonder if it shows in my face? ... It would be
> fine if (George Farr was a gentleman), if without
> talking men who had women could somehow know
> each other on sight ... an automatic masonry.
> When he remembered ... how she had run into
> the dark house in her nightgown, weeping, he felt
> quite masculine and superior and gentle [147].

Yet Faulkner has not used the obvious ploy of making Margaret, in contrast to Cecily, asexual. Margaret has to play
by the same rules as the younger woman, and Faulkner
shows her working cagily within those confines--sleeping with
Joe, kissing Lowe, even arming Mr. Saunders against his
wife with her own sensuality; and finally saving Mahon from
the despair of being unloved by marrying him. Conditioned
as each of these characters had been, a woman had nothing
of value to give except sex.

Eventually, Faulkner even softens his presentation of
Cecily by placing her in the sisterhood of used women. After her intercourse with George, she comes to realize how
meaningless the social labels were--man as protector; woman as protected.

> She wished for George. He should be here to
> help her. But what could he do? she reconsid-
> ered with that vast tolerance of their men which
> women must gain by giving their bodies (else how
> do they continue to live with them?) that the con-
> quering male is after all no better than a clumsy,
> tactless child [220].

It is this same kind of recognition that makes Emmy and
Margaret friends; their relationship in Soldiers' Pay suggests
that of Temple Drake and Nancy in Requiem for a Nun,
and Nancy's act of murder parallels in its selflessness Margaret's marriage to Mahon. For, as Margaret had reminded
Joe, when the very selflessness of her charity baffled him,

> So you are surprised to find a woman doing
> something without some obvious material end in
> view. Aren't you? ... I just happened to be the
> first woman you ever knew doing something you
> thought only a man would do [161].

Faulkner's second book might well be considered a
novel without a protagonist, although the ineffectual Mr.

Tallifero, in his Prufrock-like role, is on stage the most.
"Sex and death," the phrase that reoccurred in Soldiers' Pay,
is also used in Mosquitoes, but here the tone is one of
mockery. For all the 300-odd pages of talk about sex, there
is none in the novel. The gamesmanship of Janarius Jones
is here the rule, as is the constant talk about loving. But
the assembled characters care only for themselves, and any
love that is even pretended is to fill only the crudest needs.

The book begins and ends with the pathetic Tallifero
preening himself for a conquest; the story is repetitiously
that of his complete failure with women. In contrast, Faulkner attempts to use the withdrawn sculptor, Gordon, who
does feel passion of a kind--as his sculpting the headless
torso of the young girl suggests--but finds an outlet only with
a prostitute. He, at least, acts. Set against these two ex-
tremes are the unbelievably lethargic poet Mark Frost; Jul-
ius, the "Semitic man"; the British colonel, Ayers; Pete,
the young tough; and the most circumventive of all talkers,
Fielding Dawson, the prototype for Sherwood Anderson.
These are the "mosquitoes" of the novel; they exist seemingly only to sustain their own pleasures, as their gradual destruction of Mrs. Maurier's yachting party so clearly shows.

If they are attracted by anything besides their own
hedonistic pleasure, it is the young blonde Jenny. A forerunner of Eula Varner, Jenny oozes sensuality. She likes
men, she likes petting, though she seldom understands either.
Set against Jenny's rife sex is Patricia Robyn's lean hard
darkness, her innocence somewhat tempered by her quick understanding of people and her equally quick tongue. It would
seem that Faulkner's intention by using Jenny and Pat as
centers of masculine interest was to present the same kind
of dichotomy that he had in Soldiers' Pay with Margaret and
Cecily. This time, however, the dichotomy is much less
clear, partly because of Pat's relationship with her twin Gus
(we question her emotional freedom) and partly because
Faulkner has created so many characters that identifying
them each becomes as tedious as the conversations themselves.

Mosquitoes has been called Faulkner's Portrait of the
Artist because of the amount of talk about art it contains.
While there are a few points made in all the pseudo-sophisticated chatter about art and artists, Faulkner's intention was
surely more ironic than it was aesthetic. (Most of the artistic pronouncements come from Dawson, and he is presented

as contradictory at best.) What does result from all the conversation are truisms like artists need privacy; a work of art does not need to "mean" anything literal; artists experience epiphanies of insight; etc. The reader is happy to echo, with Faulkner:

> Talk, talk, talk: the utter and heartbreaking stupidity of words. It seemed endless, as though it might go on forever. Ideas, thoughts, became mere sounds to be bandied about until they were dead [186].

The novel changes slightly toward the end, when Gordon has sculpted the head of Mrs. Maurier, and has caught the tragedy of her wasted life. The viewers are taken out of themselves and forced to think about someone else, and the scene has its relatively forceful moments. The reader can find no real sympathy for her, however, because throughout the book she has been pictured as a domineering woman who uses art to augment her own social position. The change in perspective is too abrupt here, although Faulkner is beginning to realize the potential in his women characters. As the Semitic man said, "women can stand anything" (Faulkner's early emphasis on endurance begins here), even though Dawson undercuts that serious comment with, "And enjoy it" (and we are headed toward Temple Drake's inexplicable reactions to Popeye's use of her).

There is a popeyed man in Mosquitoes also, the materialistic Ayers, but he is foppish rather than terrifying. Perhaps another weakness of Mosquitoes is that none of the characters impresses us. Just as sex is frivolous, so too are the characters' passions about everything. In Mosquitoes, even death becomes a joke. The only circumstances which suggest mortality occur when Patricia and David, lost in the swamp the day of their romantic elopement, are chased by hordes of mosquitoes; and when the yachting party overloads a ship and it capsizes. Because the level of the readers' interest has been so slight, it comes as a surprise when Gordon makes his dramatic speech about this sense of tragedy, here described as grief:

> Forget grief.... Only an idiot has no grief; only a fool would forget it. What else is there in this world sharp enough to stick to your guts? [329].

If Faulkner does not here create any grief, any tragedy comparable to Donald Mahon's, he at least presents the
male artist's dilemma. Using the Freudian explanation of
creativity, Dawson mourns his inability to have children (and
of the women on board, only Jenny thinks she someday will
have children). But more significantly, Faulkner shows the
masculine idealization of women as identified with the ultimate creative process, positively, as with Dante and his
Beatrice,

> Dante invented Beatrice, creating himself a maid
> that life had not had time to create, and laid upon
> her frail and unbowed shoulders the whole burden
> of man's history and his impossible heart's desire
> [339].

and negatively, as Dawson describes women as not an "impossible heart's desire" but as "merely articulated genital
organs with a kind of aptitude for spending whatever money
you have" (241).

Several critics have pointed out that Faulkner's portrayal of Anderson is hardly complimentary here.[18] I con-
cur, but it seems that Dawson's attitudes about people, especially women, are the stances Faulkner disliked most, not
his ramblings about art. In fact, in Mosquitoes, Faulkner
seems to have disliked most of the characters he presented.
Such a relationship is hardly geared to produce sympathetic
characters, or moving fiction.

The kindest explanation for Faulkner's writing Mosquitoes, a novel which seems much less well-written and conceived than Soldiers' Pay, is that of Joyce Warren who sees
it as his Portrait of the Artist. Considering the characters
as types objectifying his prologomena, as she does with Mrs.
Maurier, Gordon, and others, is the best rationale for this
strangely uneven book. Also dating from these years, Faulkner's unfinished novel Elmer shares the same problems:
an artist as protagonist, tone shifting between comedy and
irony, a boring plot; there is also, however, experimentation
with time and free association, and some innovation in narrative structure.[19]

The tone of Sartoris, Faulkner's third novel, differs
greatly from that of Mosquitoes, with the beginning of his
emphasis on the "blind tragedy of human events" and the
"hopeless juggernaut of circumstance" (226) in which every

person attempts to live. The dichotomy within the cast of characters this time is much more sex oriented (in Mosquitoes, age differences were important; in Soldiers' Pay, experience levels), with Jenny Du Pre and Narcissa Benbow Sartoris having the capability to endure, and all the Sartorises from the Bayard before Old Bayard to the twin grandsons John and Bayard defying what life had to offer. That Faulkner admires Miss Jenny tremendously is evident; she is in complete charge of Old Bayard, the servants, and the household (the role that Dilsey plays later).[20] He speaks of Jenny's "indomitable spirit" and her "hopeless pact" (to care for Sartoris men) being made "with the fine and passive courage of women" (241); and of all the Sartoris women whose lives had been "modest and effacing as the song of thrushes beneath the eerie of an eagle" (299).

Yet Faulkner saves Jenny from his quasi-maudlin admiration by giving her a crisp, even tough, language pattern that sometimes successfully obscures her good heart. "Even niggers that eat here have got to work some," she mocks in a phrase very close to Jason Compson's. She warns Narcissa against marrying Bayard, and keeps up a running tirade about women ("We can stand anything," 212) and men:

> Men can't stand anything.... Can't even stand helling around with no worry and no responsibility and no limit to all the meanness they can think about wanting to do [58].

Set against this language pattern, however, is Jenny's very real love for the Sartoris men. And so we tend to value them as she does, for their daring, their stubbornness, and their dreams. The young Bayard is defeated because he fails in the last category--his dreams cannot match his grandfather's or his great-grandfather's, at least partly because the times have changed: there are no more railroads to build or wars to fight single-handedly. The best Bayard can do is race his car (and single-handedly kill his grandfather), hunt possum, or try to ride spirited horses. There are points in the narrative when Faulkner has sympathy for Bayard, but there are more in which he chastizes him for his foolhardiness. Much like Hightower, Bayard operates as though he is completely separate from all other human beings: he hurts his family and friends, and leaves Narcissa, pregnant with his son, without even a postcard (those he sends to Aunt Jenny). In a scene which lacks the tension of Hightower's realization in Light in August, but foreshadows that theme, Bayard finally does understand how wrong he has been, how every man must be responsible, at least to those he loves:

> He stared into the fire for a time, rubbing his hands slowly on his knees, and for an instant he saw the recent months of his life coldly in all their headlong and heedless wastefulness; saw its entirety like the swift unrolling of a film, culminating in that which he had been warned against and that any fool might have foreseen. Well, damn it, suppose it had: was he to blame? Had he insisted that his grandfather ride with him? Had he given the old fellow a bum heart? and then, coldly: You were afraid to go home. You made a nigger sneak your horse out to you. You, who deliberately do things your judgment tells you may not be successful, even possible, are afraid to face the consequences of your own acts [251].

Bayard's reaction, however, is not to repent but to run, until he finds a way of legitimately killing himself (he shies away from the onus of suicide during his visit to Mac-Callum's camp). That he dies in the air is more reinforcement for his passion for Johnny, his twin. Faulkner's use of Bayard's guilt for John's death, obsessive at times, is cumulatively effective for it places him in an isolation that no woman could ever share. Just as he had spent his last night with his first wife Caroline thinking that he would soon see John, so he came to his personal realization in the midst of the all-male hunting camp.

With Narcissa and Horace Benbow, Faulkner presents an equally close older brother-younger sister relationship (the forerunner of Quentin and Caddy's), as well as using Horace as an "artist of the beautiful" to foil Bayard's "savage" action. Although Faulkner never has Bayard come in contact with Horace's beautiful glass vases, we know without seeing what Bayard's reaction would have been. Horace as the impractical lawyer, a complete dupe in the hands of women, is the first of Faulkner's compassionate lawyer types, all of whom prefer rhetoric to passion. It is significant that Narcissa accepts her love for Bayard only on the rebound, only after she has been disillusioned upon hearing of Horace's affair with Belle.

Whatever version is read, Sartoris can easily be

seen as a continuation of the themes Faulkner was working with earlier, particularly those of Soldiers' Pay, but its emphasis creates a feeling closer to tragedy than did the earlier novel. Bayard Sartoris, like the other Sartorises before him, is never a victim of anything. Whatever happens to him is the result of his own choice; he is an active participant, whereas Donald Mahon had been almost completely passive. Because of the vigor of Bayard's character, the theme of responsibility is central. The definition of love also widens, as Faulkner moves from the love of man and woman to the less selfish familial love of Old Bayard, Aunt Jenny, and Narcissa. In Sartoris "sex and death" has been transformed into "love and death." As Faulkner presents Narcissa in his original book (now published as Flags in the Dust), she is a strong character whose somewhat Freudian ambivalences are more completely presented. Although she is intrigued by the Sartoris boys, she intuitively fears them. An image of power and serenity throughout the novel, she yet needs to be wanted--hence, she keeps the Snopes' letters; is confused with Horace's misjudgment; and is sexually attracted to Bayard. Narcissa is the one character damaged by the editing this original manuscript received before Sartoris was published. In the 1973 publication, pages 64-68, 134, 194, 287-99, and 341-47 are the major additions to her characterization, either as individual persona, or in conjunction with her brother Horace.

Part of the shift in emphasis occurs because Faulkner is able, by means of his legends and tales, to include a sense of historical perspective in the novel. The use of the short tale within the novel proper as substantiation for primary themes dates at least to The Odyssey, and Faulkner had used the Al Jackson stories in Mosquitoes in much the same structural manner. But in Sartoris this narrative material serves many purposes: it places the book firmly in the South; it crystallizes the family "traditions" which are innately important to any son whether those traditions make sense or not; it provides changes in texture and in narrative point of view; it inadvertently gives Faulkner many of his later novels, as he re-mines these experiences and develops them more fully.

This use of supplemental narrative is effective, as is the inclusion of Doc Peabody and other townspeople as chorus, to validate Miss Jenny's reactions. Other new techniques which Faulkner used more widely in Sartoris seems to be less viable. The short imagistic passages about the last rose, the misfit pups bred from the wild fox and the hunting

dog, and the mule--among others--seem too extraneous, too
contrived, coming as they do in the last third of the book,
to be fully defensible. The ostensible mystery of the
Snopes' letters to Narcissa is merely bothersome: that she
receives such notes is hardly the tribute to her womanhood
that Faulkner--in the longer manuscript--intended; and even
the ending episode drifts off inconclusively. (Enamored as
Faulkner was with the effect of these crude letters--having
used the device well in Soldiers' Pay--he came to realize
in Requiem for a Nun that the reader's imagination was a
more valuable asset: the letters used to blackmail Temple
Drake Stevens are never seen.) This epistolary strain in
Sartoris could well have been omitted, as could have many
of the stage-setting scenes throughout the book--endless pages
of Bayard drinking, or Horace ready to play tennis; long descriptions of the countryside; and how many times does Narcissa call at the Sartoris home before Bayard notices her?
While the structure of the novel seems reasonably well focused, beginning with Bayard's sneaking home from war, the
pace of the novel is often tedious. It does not approach the
ineptitude of Mosquitoes because we are interested in the
Sartoris characters, but it does not move with the expert
tempo of the major novels. Faulkner has yet to learn to select the crucial detail, not merely the interesting one.

Sartoris is, however, a major advance technically over
Soldiers' Pay and Mosquitoes because in it the writing seldom
calls attention to itself. Faulkner handles in third person
what he might earlier have done in self-conscious stream of
consciousness paragraphs, like the ending of Mosquitoes, as
well as Gordon's thoughts on form, David's on exhaustion,
Mr. Tallifero's on Jenny, and Margaret Power's on her first
marriage. Because Faulkner could not sustain these short
sections, the reader hardly adjusts to the new mode before
he is back in third person narration again. Undoubtedly
Faulkner's practice with the technique better prepared him
for writing The Sound and the Fury and As I Lay Dying, but
it hardly enhanced the early novels.

There is also less use of the repeated refrain to bring
the theme before the reader. George Farr's memories of
Cecily's outstretched legs ("two silver streams from a single
source") may be well described, but since George is a minor
character, this refrain seems to interfere with the progress
of the novel instead of enriching it. Faulkner has also
dropped his early practice of using one or two key adjectives
repeatedly to help the reader remember each character;

similarly he has stopped using single objects to identify characters, as Pete's hat, Theodore's pipe, Jenny's green dress. At times, especially in Mosquitoes, Faulkner seemed to be at the mercy of his rhetoric: entire passages would begin and end with the same sentence (see pages 168-169), and quite often the reader suspected that sentences themselves were lengthy and incremental only because Faulkner liked the sound of the rolling words.

In addition, in Sartoris Faulkner also relies less on coincidence, except for the fact that Bayard dies on the same day his child is born. Because the characters are better realized in Sartoris, Faulkner can trust their presumed actions to make things happen; he needs less help from deus ex machina.

Whereas Faulkner does still use juxtaposition as a primary mode of organizing his materials, Sartoris is told much more conventionally without the passages of short fragments of speech set against each other (see page 152 of Soldiers' Pay) or the chapters that include as many entirely different scenes as they have parts (Chapter V, Ibid.) Faulkner's tactic in Sartoris was to use minor characters to give the milieu and social color, instead of relying on the pastiche of random comment set into the novel at key points.

In at least three ways, however, Sartoris shows the logical extension of Faulkner's writing methods used in his earlier two novels. He still works from a concept of dramatic scene (Old Bayard and Mr. Falls in the bank; Jenny telling her great story--an image with which the original title of the book, Flags in the Dust, was connected; Horace with his newly-blown vase). He also withholds significant material until very late in the book, whether or not such withholding seems necessary. We don't know until midway in Soldiers' Pay that Dewey Burney shot Dick Powers, nor do we know until nearly the end the way Mahon came to be wounded. Similarly, Bayard does not think of the circumstances of John's death until fifty pages from the end, although his mad pursuit of destruction stems from the death of his twin. This gradual revelation of material is an important part of Faulkner's method of involving the reader--of, poetically, bringing the reader along with him into the experience; it stands in direct contrast to the mosaic-block approach of presenting all material, even events occurring simultaneously, in chronological order.

Faulkner's characteristic conclusion combines these two techniques masterfully. Usually a clearly defined scene, the ending of most Faulkner novels is often not the logical outgrowth of events immediately preceding it. Faulkner rather juxtaposes one image with, in effect, all that has already been conveyed, so that even the last few pages of a book are dynamic. No Faulkner novel ever just runs down. With Sartoris, Narcissa's rebellion in naming her child leads to Jenny's restatement of the Sartoris curse, but the mood is serene as Faulkner takes the reader "beyond the window" to Narcissa's "windless lilac dream" with its restful tone of "quietude and peace." Similarly in Soldiers' Pay Gilligan and the Rev. Mahon find themselves listening to the glorious Negro singing, and momentarily escaping their respective bereavements. The effect of the music on them is ambivalent, however, because as it dies they are brought back to "tomorrow and sweat, with sex and death and damnation; and they turned townward under the moon, feeling dust in their shoes" (319). Such reasonable open endings, in evidence throughout Faulkner's novels, are responsible in great part for the suggestive reach of the stories. He never has the last, limiting word; he adds only another further believable image to the long sequence already presented.[21]

In a final comparison, perhaps it is that sense of reach that gives Sartoris its relative power. The lives of the Sartoris family do go on, just as they do extend back, into the lives and the spirit of indomitable men. As Olga Vickery distinguished, in Sartoris Faulkner was engaged in "the making of a myth,"[22] and to Faulkner's own genius of vision the continuity of living was integral. Perhaps equally important was the fact that he made that myth well, writing economically instead of self-consciously, and writing with love instead of disdain.

Chapter Nine

FAULKNER: THE CRAFT OF FICTION

Even his earliest writing shows Faulkner's debt to
modernism and its absorption with largely poetic techniques.
His reliance on the single scene to convey character, tone,
and plot; his use of repeated motifs; his concluding images
--all echo practices of Joyce, Eliot, Conrad, and James.
In the same way his use of the repeated word or pun proves
his almost Joycean sense of humor.[1]

Percy Lubbock's The Craft of Fiction, first published
in 1921, was one of the few books in Faulkner's personal library devoted to the aesthetics of fiction. Since Lubbock's
study was one of the first to treat fiction as craft, and to
emphasize its need for design and symmetry, Faulkner undoubtedly read it with comfort. Knowing how a novel was
made was to be one of his enduring fascinations. Faulkner
would have agreed with what Lubbock saw as structural
method in the greatest novels ("the book is not a row of
facts, it is a single image");[2] with his concern that characters must be "true to themselves" at all times; and with his
concept of fictional method growing out of subject. To Lubbock, too, goes the credit for making valuable distinctions
about narrative point of view (in which area of method,
Faulkner's experimentation never stopped). As Lubbock had
written,

> The whole intricate question of method, in the
> craft of fiction, I take to be governed by the ques-
> tion of the point of view--the question of the rela-
> tion in which the narrator stands to the story
> [251].

Because the critical problem of reading Faulkner is
often primarily a technical one, it is not surprising that
some of the best critics on Faulkner's work are other
writers--Malcolm Cowley, Robert Penn Warren, Conrad Aiken. The heart of much of Faulkner's fiction lies in his

method of approach; this is as true of the successes like The Sound and the Fury and Absalom, Absalom! as it is of his comparative failures like Sanctuary and Pylon. It is also true that nearly all of Faulkner's "great" writing makes use of reasonably inventive narrative techniques: none of the major novels is written in the traditional chronology-oriented, omniscient narrator method of Soldiers' Pay or Mosquitoes. Whether the innovation of method somehow unleashes a different kind of creative force, or whether the striking combination of theme and method together forms the masterful effect, no critic can ever hope to say. The fact does remain, however inexplicable.

Most of Faulkner's writing--novel, short story (so far as the stories can be dated), and sketch--before The Sound and The Fury was done in a conventional third person or omniscient perspective (with the narrator at least assuming impersonality), and with events arranged in generally chronological order. Except in the story "Carcassone," the few stream of consciousness sections are obviously experimental and seldom integral to the writing. Flashbacks are usually handled within one character's memory, or as stories told by a character as narrator within the total narrative; the progression, as Faulkner's organization of Mosquitoes by days suggests, is in time sequence, even though the events may not actually "culminate" into a static resolution.

With Sartoris (and Flags in the Dust), however, Faulkner shifted to a structure dependent for its effect on a sequence of images. Although its five-part arrangement does follow a logical time scheme, Faulkner gains his mosaic effect by using strong dramatic scenes to conclude each of the five parts. These conclusions, because of their position and their culminating nature in each section, have more weight than most of the other passages of the novel. Part I ends with young Bayard's return home and Aunt Jenny's literal watch over him; Part II, with Bayard's tragic realization of how much time is really left to him:

> 'Hell,' he said, lying on his back, staring out the window where nothing was to be seen, waiting for sleep, not knowing if it would come or not, not caring a particular damn either way. Nothing to be seen, and the long, long span of a man's natural life. Three score and ten years to drag a stubborn body about the world and cozen its insistent demands. Three score and ten, the Bible said.

> Seventy years. And he was only twenty-six. Not
> much more than a third through it. Hell [138].

Parts III and IV attempt to break away from this tone of
doom, juxtaposing Horace against Bayard, and trying to involve the reader at least temporarily with Narcissa's own
tormented loyalties. But the novel ends precipitantly, continuing from the mood at the close of Part II, as Bayard
comes to his final understanding in Part IV, and spends the
concluding section searching for some reasonable end for his
burned-out life. The ending images for both Part III and IV
continue the tone of impending doom: the bloody tracks of
Narcissa's Snopes as he escapes his crime illustrate Bayard's own feeling of entrapment, and foreshadow the ending
of Part IV, Bayard's boarding the train on Christmas Eve,
leaving home and family forever.

In _Sartoris_, then, Faulkner used this sectional arrangement to stress thematic emphases which might otherwise have been lost in the movement of the apparent plot.

Faulkner's controlling device in both his long and
short fiction of this first decade of writing is his use of a
well-developed scene (_dramatic_, in Lubbock's terms), juxtaposed either with other equally dynamic scenes or, perhaps
more frequently, with passages of authorial comment. Faulkner's reliance on the latter differs from Hemingway's use of
as little storytelling as possible, and exists at least partly
because Faulkner seldom used the first-person point of view
while Hemingway nearly always did.

This fictional method is apparently justified in "All
the Dead Pilots," that haunting short story which echoes
many of the themes and situations of _Sartoris_ proper. As
the narrator of the story explains, the story is itself (like
so many of Faulkner's stories) "a composite" because its author had no philosophy to espouse; his purpose was chiefly
presentation--"a series of brief glares in which, instantane-
ous and without depth or perspective, there stood into sight
the portent and the threat of what the race could bear and
become, in an instant between dark and dark."[3] It is interesting that at the conclusion of the story Faulkner's image
for his collage-like method--those brief glares in the instant
between darks--is used to describe the brilliance of young
Bayard's life as pilot, and more, the attraction the Sartoris'
men had for women like Jenny and Narcissa: method and
character described through the same image:

> And that's all. That's it. The courage, the
> recklessness, call it what you will, is the flash,
> the instant of sublimation; then flick! the old dark-
> ness again. That's why. It's too strong for steady
> diet. And if it were a steady diet, it would not be
> a flash, a glare [109].

Cleanth Brooks makes the similarities between this particular story and Sartoris his bridge to read the novel as a story of another "dead pilot" rather than another Sartoris.[4] While many of Brooks' points are defensible, had this been Faulkner's main thrust, he would surely have spent less time in Part I of the novel recounting the family legends. That matrix of storytelling which Faulkner feels is essential enough to risk a slow and cluttered opening creates several narrative problems: who is to tell the stories? when are they to be told? what is to be done with them once they have been included? Old Man Falls and Aunt Jenny probably originated chiefly as narrators; Old Man Falls remains a vehicle (and with his idiom, thankfully, a limited one) while Jenny Du Pre comes to dominate the novel. Her importance lies partly in the fact that her dignity creates the prose style for the entire book. Notice that the recounting of the central Civil War-Sartoris legend is supposedly told by Jenny, yet there is no attempt to differentiate between the language of Faulkner's narrator and the idiom of the person, supposedly Jenny, telling this story. The diction and sentence rhythm are the same. Since the style in Sartoris differs considerably from that of Faulkner's earlier fiction, one might at least partly attribute his lengthier pace and more authoritative tone to his re-creation of Aunt Jenny's "richly solemn view" of both history and the Sartoris clan in relation to it--her voice "proud and still as banners in the dust." It seems unlikely that Faulkner would have felt necessary such emphasis on the very old characters--and their sense of propriety and right-- had he been interested mainly in Bayard as a Waste Land character. It may be that we critics tend to equate sociological time with artistic time; like the reception to The Sun Also Rises, viewing Sartoris as a book "about" World War I may be natural, but it may not be in all ways accurate.

In Sartoris as in most of the short stories and novels to follow, Faulkner's narrative voice is crucial to the effect of the story being told. We have seen his attempts to use letters, stream of consciousness, and large amounts of dialogue in even his earliest writing to let more characters than those narrating reveal themselves through their own language; for Faulkner, however, the narrating voice remains the powerful vehicle. Few authors have viewed the act of narration as so important, nor have presented it with such relish. In Sartoris, for example, Aunt Jenny's impassioned account of the avocado raid thrills the reader, whereas Old Man Falls' garrulous rambling invests John Sartoris' escape from the Yankees with a leisurely humor instead of drama; and Capsey's tales--told in short, bragging sentences--are only low comedy. Faulkner continually experiments with the variety of effects gained by having certain narrators tell certain stories--Byron Bunch serving as narrator for Hightower, or the reporter for Pylon. From these relatively simple narrative effects, he builds to the complexity of the four contrapuntal voices of Absalom, Absalom! or the three complementary voices of The Town.

But before he can reach the control of orchestrated narration--or the equally masterful achievement of using an almost unobtrusive narrator to perfectly color stories (imagine the Flem Snopes story through the eyes of someone other than Ratliff)--Faulkner serves his apprenticeship to conventional omniscient narration and also, pupil of modernism that he was, to stream of consciousness.

Most of Faulkner's early fiction is written either in omniscient third or in first person, the latter occurring more frequently in short stories than in novels. Quite a few of Faulkner's earliest published stories were written in first person, and it is possible that he grew more comfortable with that method because of its marketability as well as because he enjoyed those protagonists (Quentin in "A Justice" and "That Evening Sun"; the townsperson in "A Rose for Emily," "Hair," and "Death Drag"; and the fliers in "Honor" and "Ad Astra"--all characters or character types he was to use subsequently in longer fiction).

As was evident in Soldiers' Pay and Mosquitoes, Faulkner was intrigued with stream of consciousness, but his only short story which relies on that narrative method is "Carcassonne," the idyllic account of a Sanctuary-like theme. Probably because of his success with method, the story was one of his favorites.

Biographical evidence suggests that Faulkner's narrative method might well have been determined at this point in his career by economic concerns. The late months of 1929 were difficult ones for Faulkner. He was writing well, and he knew it, but he still could never expect to live from his earnings as a writer. His precarious economic situation was especially frustrating since he had married Estelle Oldham, and had a family of four to support. Consequently, in the early thirties, his writing appears to be moving in two directions--one, that of marketable fiction: most of the short stories and Sanctuary (long famous for his admission that he wrote it to make money). With three novels behind him, and no short story as yet published, Faulkner turned his attention to the writing and distribution of short fiction because, as James Meriwether points out, one story sold to a magazine like Saturday Evening Post would profit Faulkner as much as any of his early novels had. Meriwether documents Faulkner's record of sending out stories 129 times from (approximately) January of 1930 to January of 1932, with 20 accepted for publication in various magazines. With the money from these stories and Sanctuary, Faulkner could buy a house of his own, and feel comparatively secure for awhile. [5]

The other current, evident in Faulkner's fiction during the late twenties and early thirties, is that of complete disregard for marketability. There can be no question but that he wrote The Sound and the Fury for himself, [6] and for other literary people, at least those conversant with Joyce and/or modern art, and As I Lay Dying, Light in August, and Absalom, Absalom! as well. Phil Stone recounts Faulkner's real bitterness and despair when Sartoris, his best writing to 1929, was received with no higher acclaim, or no greater sales, than his first two books. It was then that Stone encouraged him to write what he wanted to write, money be damned.

That these two impulses in his writing do exist is understandable and interesting, but in no way does this condition lessen the quality of Faulkner's art. Much has been written about the sensationalism of Sanctuary, and the changes made in galley proofs to give Horace Benbow a less important role. [7] There is little question--both in theme and technique--that Sanctuary is much in the mainstream of Faulkner's fiction. The most important point to be made in separating the fiction Faulkner was intending to sell from that he was writing primarily for love is that his narrative method in the marketable writing is nearly always simpler. These stories are told in first or third person; either they progress chronologically, or else transition is carefully provided.

Faulkner seems to have the reader's ability to follow him in mind at all times; he errs on the side of being too explicit rather than too suggestive. Episodes are drastically limited to fit the story shape, even though Faulkner in later use of these same materials finds wider implications.

His practice in Sanctuary was similar. Gerald Langford points out that the earlier version of Sanctuary was written in an experimental narrative method which foreshadows the technique of Absalom, Absalom! Only in the revised version does Faulkner move to the relatively straightforward omniscient narrator, with events proceeding in nearly chronological order, from the beginning of the weekend. There are no stream of consciousness passages, although the character of Temple Drake cries out for them. [8] It seems that chiefly in this respect--of choosing a simpler and hopefully more marketable techniques--was Sanctuary aimed toward a wider audience.

Some further proof that this "commercial style" did exist in Faulkner's concept of fiction is the similarity between his early short stories and those written later. With few exceptions, his short story style is consistent throughout his career--the stories of the thirties are much like those of the forties and fifties. Even though Faulkner liked to say that the story created its own shape--and true as that maxim was for each of his novels--the process of writing short stories was apparently different for him. The random reader of magazine fiction brought to his reading different expectations than the reader of modern novels, and Faulkner was wise enough to try to meet some of the usual expectations. Most of his stories move quickly and easily from conflict to conflict, event to event; use a stable, single narrator; build toward a culminating episode; rely heavily on atmosphere; and make their point in numerous ways.

Such generalization is never possible in describing Faulkner's novels, for each one is distinguished for the masterful harmony between content and form. As Conrad Aiken noted in 1939,

> What immoderately delights him, alike in Sanctuary, The Sound and the Fury, As I Lay Dying, Light in August, Pylon, Absalom, Absalom! and now again The Wild Palms, and what sets him above--shall we say it firmly--all his American contemporaries, is his continuous preoccupation

with the novel as form, his passionate concern
with it, and a degree of success with it which
would clearly have commanded the interest and respect of Henry James himself. [9]

Millgate agrees, pointing particularly to Faulkner's genius in
experimentation with point of view; but he continues to note
the scarcity of first-person narration in Faulkner's fiction,
despite the fact that "the spoken voice is one of the dominant elements in almost all of his books." The answer to
this paradox Millgate sees as being Faulkner's shifting point
of view within a single work:

> What closer inspection reveals is that many of his
> novels have not a single point of view at all but a
> multiplicity of points of view and, further, that
> Faulkner's preference is, in many cases, for a
> multiplicity of types of point of view--first person,
> third person, stream of consciousness, centre of
> consciousness, and so on. [10]

The lesson Hemingway had learned by the time of For Whom
the Bell Tolls was Faulkner's property much earlier; and
perhaps because of his daring in its use, he was able to
reach greater excellence in his organic form, manner being
fully appropriate to content. For the question of point of
view, central as it is to the fiction writer, is but one facet
of the larger question--that of the form and shape of any
work of art as best expressing its full meaning. As Faulkner had phrased it, "The story, the truth he is telling, invents its own style, its own method." [11]

In The Sound and the Fury Faulkner adopts the stream
of consciousness mode, and uses his most dramatic varia-
tions of syntax, prose rhythms, and imagery. The admittedly wide difference between the characters of Quentin and Jason derives mostly from Faulkner's stylistic control of each
section. Given the three interior monologues, probably
chosen because of his interest in the "pure" objective presentation, with the least possible interference by an author.
Given the three sections concluding in a fourth which is less
than omniscient (Margaret Blanchard points out that the fourth
seems to be the reader's section, based as it is on observable happening and only those speculations which might have
been drawn from the knowledge of the first three parts). [12]
Given the artistic problem of Benjy's recall and correlation,
to which the short sentences, leitmotif organization, and

synaesthesia are most appropriate. Then, find Faulkner
faced with his own tour de force: what began as an intriguing way to tell a highly charged story (interior monologue,
whether prompted by Joyce's practices or by Faulkner's
criticism of the more traditional explicator method) became
for the author a means of knowing intimately those characters he had tended to stereotype. Not so much Benjy, for
beyond the obvious use of his idiocy, he serves little purpose in the story; the central conflict between the girl, Quentin, and her uncle would have occurred with or without Benjy.
Faulkner uses Benjy in much the same way Shakespeare used
Ophelia or the blinded Gloucester, as objects to elicit significant feelings from the primary characters. Mrs. Compson feels no love toward Benjy; Caddy and Quentin do. Dilsey gives him her sympathy, while withholding it from Jason,
the forgotten middle child.

So the primary impact of the novel lies in the opposing outlooks of the two "normal" brothers; and in their re-
creation lies Faulkner's highest art. Each character is established as a consistent and predictable persona, each the
"sum of his misfortunes" as Benjy's half-memories of their
childhoods so vividly inform us. Each deserves our compassion. Yet, dating from George Marion O'Donnell's 1939 essay, critics have labeled Quentin the "good" brother; Jason,
the "evil," Snopes-like one. However, in 1944, Faulkner
identified Jason specifically as a "Compson and Sartoris"
when he suggested to Malcolm Cowley that he use the Jason
section in The Portable Faulkner:

> What about taking the whole third section of
> Sound and Fury? That Jason is the new South too,
> I mean, he is the one Compson and Sartoris who
> met Snopes on his own ground and in a fashion
> held his own. [13]

Jason as Faulkner presents him is as believable as any of
the other Compsons. When we meet him, he is a man in his
mid-thirties, dreadfully embittered because for seventeen
years he has been supporting the entire rotting family (Mrs.
Compson, Benjy, the girl Quentin, Uncle Maury, Dilsey and
the other six Negroes). He supports them with no preparation, no training, no breaks. When we meet Quentin he is
himself seventeen, never having experienced much of life, an
anguished romantic. We also read Quentin's section before
Jason's; we are in a sense conditioned to the younger perspective.

We sympathize with Quentin, lulled by the long sonorous lines of his distraught monologue. We sympathize with his loss, although we are never quite sure what it is. We identify with his philosophic concerns--honor, time, woman as symbol--presented so dramatically as they are. Or perhaps, melodramatically. The smashed watch and the jeweler's window filled with discordant times; the grotesque little sister figure leading Quentin into his ironic arrest; the Bland-Quentin fight--all build compellingly to the greatest melodrama of all: a man's suicide. Reading Quentin's pathetically distorted impressions is very different from reading Jason's cryptic insults which follow, but this difference lies to a great extent in the tones of the contrasting sections. One of the greatnesses of the novel is that Faulkner so well manipulates our reactions to these characters--through prose rhythms, diction, and selection of episodes--that we hardly realize that Quentin's concerns are also Jason's; that the problems of honor, time and human delicacy fall with more weight on Jason's shoulders than they ever did on Quentin's.

> (1) 'Damn little time to do anything in, but then I am used to that.'[14]
> (2) 'It never occurred to me she wouldn't keep her promise' [255].
> (3) 'I'm a man, I can stand it, it's my own flesh and blood' [307].

Jason's words. And Quentin's:

> (1) 'Father said that. That Christ was not crucified: he was worn away by the minute clicking of little wheels. That had no sister' [94].
> (2) 'Father and I protect women from one another from themselves our women' [119].
> (3) 'I'm stronger than you.' 'I am not afraid' [215].

Time, women (as the responsibilities of men, as extensions or "proofs" of their personal virtue), and that devout concept of honor that Jason, Sr., tried to undermine--these concerns are near obsessions to both Quentin and Jason. They are Compsons, before any other consideration: "my people owned slaves here when you all were running little shirt tail country stores and farming land no nigger would look at on shares," Jason boasts. And a Compson has certain beliefs: that integrity is more important than success; that men are the heads of their households; that men depend on their

ancestry, the concept of family, for much of their pride;
that men are morally and physically stronger than women,
and must protect them.

If the two sons are motivated so similarly, how then
can we react so differently to them? As I have suggested,
Faulkner deftly manipulates our reactions through the kinds
of language used in each section.

"When the shadow of the sash appeared on the cur-
tains it was between seven and eight o'clock and then I was
in time again, hearing the watch...." The slow sibilants
give a sad tone to all Quentin's reflections, whether he is
thinking of "Shreve's bedsprings and then his slippers on
the floor hishing" or "shabby and timeless patience." Quentin's mourning comes to us through imagery--"Roof of wind,"
"lonely and inviolate sand," "murmuring bones"--no less
than through the subjects of his thoughts. Everything that
happens to Quentin is intensified, refracted as it were
through the anguish that colors his own sight. The cut fin-
ger is of equal importance with the smashed watch--and his
own smashed life; Spoade's terrapin-like progress is equated
with Quentin's own passage toward death, "in a street full of
scuttering dead leaves." And the sentence pattern Faulkner
chooses for much of Quentin's section, strangely like that
of Benjy, is grimly appropriate: simple and compound sentences, many beginning with I and then the barest description of the action. The longer sentences, more heavily imagistic, are often those of his father's words, or Quentin's
echoes of his father's convictions. Accented with short
phrases used like refrains, the long sections of Quentin's
monologue have an indelible rhythm--hesitant and tortuous,
yet building to the more rapid momentum toward the end.
Here all the central images are heightened (Quentin's understated complaint about his mother becomes the "dungeon was
Mother herself" passage); the real and the unreal are as
mixed in Quentin's world as they are in Benjy's, and increasingly, in Quentin's, Faulkner turns to synaesthesia:
eyes "unseeing clenched like teeth" while "hands can see
touching in the mind"; "my nose could see gasoline." Such
couplings lead to Quentin's anguish over smelling "the beating of hot blood," and make his cry against the loud world
somehow more defensible.

As Faulkner presents Quentin, he is nearly always
alone. He has no need to talk with anyone. Faulkner
places him outside the trivia of most human interaction

(when he needs physical help, Shreve does his talking for him) so that his interior monologue can grow in validity as well as in poetic strength. For emphatic contrast, Jason is never alone. Even when he thinks to himself, someone (in the store, the street, his home) is near. Most of Jason's thoughts come to us as fragments of dialogue: Jason, by the nature of his life, is constantly involved.

"Once a bitch always a bitch" is a striking contrast to Quentin's somber lines. Quentin only thought about his mother. Jason has to do battle with her, in order in some way to control the girl Quentin. Shocking his mother--who thinks and lives in layers of platitudes--is best done quickly and vulgarly. Mrs. Compson's spoken language and Uncle Maury's written circumlocution provide wonderful contrast to Jason's humorous and masculine directness--and make even more evident the need for Jason to shock his listeners.

Faulkner emphasizes in Jason's opening speeches the change from Quentin's reflective poetry to Jason's sardonic slang--"gobbing paint on her face," "six niggers," "damn slick-headed jellybeans," "grub," and, one of Jason's most unsympathetic phrases, "I says." On many subjects, however, Jason's diction is normally colloquial; only the girl Quentin and the stock manipulators provoke the abusive language.

So far as Jason uses imagery, Faulkner makes very clear that he speaks from a man's perspective: Quentin's face looked like she had "polished it with a gun rag"; her eyes are "hard as a fice dog's"; her nose, red from crying, "looked like a porcelain insulator." And the self-deprecating humor--depending for its effect on sacrilege and virulence --that certainly is masculine.

Because so much of Jason's section is dramatic in form--the interaction occurring in April 1928 or else recalled by Jason in isolated scenes--the rhythm is crisper, the movement more abrupt. Terseness is economical, too: a great deal happens in Jason's day, even though at the end of it we know much less of him than we do of Quentin at the end of his day. Quentin absorbs all happenings; Jason seemingly reflects them all.

Yet even the most unsympathetic reader can sense that Jason is affected by these experiences. As sensitive to the slights of his world as Quentin was to his, Jason has

to meet those slights and go on living. In that recognition
lies a kind of heroism. Faulkner wrote in 1946 of Jason
that "he assumed the entire burden of the rotting family in
the rotting house." And one is reminded of the author's
praise for Mercutio because he "coped with life, didn't ask
any favors, never whined." Or that for Sut Lovingood who
"had no illusions about himself, did the best he could....
Never blamed his misfortunes on anyone and never blamed
God for them."[15]

Jason is no paragon, of course. Living his life as
he was taught when the isolated, vengeful middle child, Jason reacts in strangely immature patterns of violence and
cruelty. Yet even in the midst of his skirmishes with ironic
fate, Jason longs most for normalcy. The nearly fatal battle with the roadshow roustabout symbolizes Jason's life, in
all its incoherent, bemused struggle.

> Jason glared wildly about, holding the other.
> Outside it was now bright and sunny, swift and
> bright and empty, and he thought of the people
> soon to be going quietly home to Sunday dinner,
> decorously festive, and of himself trying to hold
> the fatal, furious little old man whom he dared
> not release long enough to turn his back and run
> [387].

It looks so simple--"bright and sunny, swift"--and the normalcy of Sunday dinner deludes him for a moment (the lure
of regular meals is for Jason surely the lure of an ordered
existence). Then, again, that "fatal, furious little old man"
confronts him. Only Jason's equally "furious desire not to
die" saved him from this attack, and from all others life
had set up for him. For it is in Jason's ability to hang on,
to exist despite the odds, even to run, that he parallels Dilsey and her children.

That this view of Jason is often overlooked is, perhaps, proof that readers are somehow more interested in
"morality" than in art. Jason is hardly a stereotyped hero,
but then our interest as readers should lie as much in what
Faulkner does with Jason as in what Jason does. Much of
the same problem, of viewing major characters in terms of
moral absolutes, infuses the technically more ambitious As
I Lay Dying, another study in personae. Here Faulkner
works with fifteen voices, separating speeches by characters'
names, almost as if in a dramatic scenario. Darl's speech

is as particular to him as Quentin's was to his character; Vardaman, Jewel, Dewey Dell--all have speech identity. It is interesting, too, that many of the qualities of the Bundrens are direct transfers from the Compsons. Anse's rhetoric sounds much like Mrs. Compson's; Jewel's language is not far removed from Jason's, or Darl's from Quentin's. But for all the similarities, there is a noticeable progression in technique. Faulkner manages to give a nearly chronological plot line instead of returning to the beginning with each character's story. As with his earlier novels, however, the few flashbacks are crucial: without knowing Addie's history and Jewel's desperate effort to earn the horse Anse so easily trades we miss the real lines of tension in the book.

Faulkner's variation within his stream of consciousness method occurred partly because he had been disappointed with the final effect of The Sound and the Fury. That novel was to have been Caddy's story (see note 6), and yet the character of Caddy remains incomplete compared with those of Quentin, Jason, and even Mrs. Compson. So, in Dying, he kept the same kind of approach--characterization through the effects of the person on other, more vocal characters--but reinforced it in numerous ways. If Dying is the story of Addie Bundren and her best-loved child Jewel, as the title and the emphasized relationship suggests, then Darl's role as essential spokesman for the Bundren family is highly appropriate. For Darl is the articulate child (poet as well as clairvoyant); and Addie and Jewel are, by choice, the silent ones. Suiting his treatment to his theme, Faulkner gives Darl eighteen sections, while Addie and Jewel have only one each. Yet, precisely because Addie and Jewel rely on acts instead of on what Addie calls "tricky" words, nearly two-thirds of the action in the book relates to them and their acts (in a wider sense, of course, the entire novel is Addie's act. More specifically, only the episodes of Dewey Dell's sex encounters and Vardaman's fishing do not relate directly to Addie or Jewel). And the character of Darl himself--in all his mocking, hurt perception--is only further evidence of the power of Addie's acts. For Darl, his mother's preference for Jewel was a continual torment; his turn to the abnormal was only a refuge, just as, ironically, the very acts for which he was declared insane were committed out of love for Addie.

Fittingly, then, most of Darl's thought is about Jewel. Jewel is his alter ego, his torment, his masculine pronoun.

Any unidentified <u>he</u> in Darl's sections refers to Jewel.
"Jewel and I came up from the field"--so Faulkner opens
Darl's first monologue, and the novel proper. In the second,
Darl pictures Jewel with his violently loving horse; in the
third he lures Jewel away from Addie's death; in the fourth,
he taunts him with that absence. For Jewel's misery is
Darl's delight, cut off as he has been from Addie's affection
by the taciturn younger boy.

Just as he has in <u>The Sound and the Fury</u>, Faulkner
early sets up the lines of love within the family, but he com-
plicates the picture this time with the views of the neighbors,
of the society that would realistically have had powerful influence in this kind of situation. First he shows clearly how
distraught Jewel is over Addie's imminent death: he is
rough with his beloved horse; his voice is "harsh, savage"
as he insults Tull for being a "buzzard"; he complains bitterly about Cash's building the coffin under her very window
(only Jewel cannot bring himself to say the word <u>coffin</u>):
"let it be private," he cried in anguish. And his vehemence
in his own anguished soliloquy can in no way be misread.
"If there is a God what the hell is He for," he asks, only
to wish, in effect, his own death wish:

> It would just be me and her on a high hill and me
> rolling the rocks down the hill at their faces, pick-
> ing them up and throwing them down the hill
> faces and teeth and all by God until she was
> quiet.... [16]

Faulkner gives us this insight into Jewel's torment early in
the novel; but he also gives us the irony of Addie's best-
loved and best-loving child being misunderstood, by everyone. Here, Jewel is met with his father's admonition:

> 'It was her wish,' pa says. 'You got no affec-
> tion nor gentleness for her. You never had' [19].

Jewel cannot argue with Anse's rhetoric; as Addie had
known, "the lines are too far apart for the same person to
straddle from one to the other." Jewel goes swiftly away
with Darl. He does not say good-bye; the family has beaten
him, just as it has beaten Addie too. Dewey Dell points out
what Jewel's absence will mean to Addie when she asks Darl
why he is taking Jewel (page 27); but Faulkner has preceded
Dewey Dell's accurate reading of the relationship, and of
Darl's savage vindictiveness, with the irony of Cora Tull's

monologue.   Like Anse, Cora is the victim of her own rhetoric, and that of others.   She likes Darl because he <u>says</u>
the right things.   As she reads this particular family scene:

> It was the sweetest thing I ever saw.   It was
> like he knew he would never see her again, that
> Anse Bundren was driving him from his mother's
> death bed, never to see her in this world again.
> I always said Darl was different from those others.
> I always said he was the only one of them that had
> his mother's nature, had any natural affection.
> Not that Jewel, the one she labored so to bear and
> coddled and petted so and him flinging into tantrums
> or sulking spells....
> It was Darl.   He come to the door and stood
> there, looking at his dying mother.   He just looked
> at her, and I felt the bounteous love the Lord again
> and His mercy [20, 23].

Once Faulkner has established these ironies, the reader knows how truly alone Addie is, and waits only for her
wish-punishment to be executed, and perhaps for Jewel to be
vindicated.   The story is, however, not so simple as it might
have been.   Structurally, as is often said, the monologues of
the fifteen different speakers do move chronologically, in sequence despite the fact that the sections of any one character
also form a consistent whole of characterization.   Yet even
beyond this remarkable narrative accomplishment is the
rhythm of the episodes and the recurrence of the several
themes of the novel.   In arrangement, <u>As I Lay Dying</u> works
something like this: the fifty-nine separate sections fall into
seven major divisions, averaging seven to ten monologues
each.   Despite the fact that such speakers as Vardaman,
Darl, and Cash occur throughout, the rhythms of each section differ, as do their purposes.   To achieve such differenti-
ation in the midst of the same composite arrangement called
for real virtuosity on Faulkner's part.

Part I, the longest section with twelve monologues,
opens and closes with Darl's passages.   Darl's sonorous poetic language appears in five of the twelve sections, setting
the tone of this introduction, which also includes monologues
by Cora, Anse, Tull, Doc Peabody, Dewey Dell, and--in
counter-point--Jewel.   Proceeding toward Addie's death, which
does occur in the last passage, all the monologues are somber
and decorous (pages 3-51).   Such long periodic sentences from
this section of description by Darl are common:

From behind pa's leg Vardaman peers, his
mouth full open and all color draining from his
face into his mouth, as though he has by some
means fleshed his own teeth in himself, sucking.
He begins to move slowly backward from the bed,
his eyes round, his pale face fading into the dusk
like a piece of paper pasted on a falling wall, and
so out of the door.
    Pa leans above the bed in the twilight, his
humped silhouette partaking of that owl-like quality
of awry-feathered, disgruntled outrage within which
lurks a wisdom too profound or too inert for even
thought [48].

Part II, only four monologues long (pages 52-70), is
essentially Vardaman's story. The grief-crazed child parallels Jewel in that he can bear his mother's death only through
action. Faulkner fittingly uses short intense rhythms to create the feeling of Vardaman's compulsive acts:

Then I begin to run. I run toward the back and
come to the edge of the porch and stop. Then I
begin to cry. I can feel where the fish was in the
dust. It is cut up into pieces of not-fish now, not-
blood on my hands and overalls. Then it wasn't so.
It hadn't happened then [52].

In despair at his mother's absence, Vardaman runs Peabody's
team, hides, walks four miles to Tull's house, opens his
mother's windows so she can feel the rain, and finally augurs
holes in her coffin (and face) for the same purpose. The
section lurches to its conclusion, with no interference from
Darl at all.

His controlling presence--and rhythm--is once again
evident throughout Part III, pages 71-93; but there are differences. The first seven monologues of this section depict Addie's funeral and the somewhat violent beginnings of the journey, and three of them are Darl's, but Darl is himself confused here in his queries about his own parentage, his own
identity. In language very much like Benjy Compson's, Darl
wonders,

And before you are emptied for sleep, what are
you. And when you are emptied for sleep, you
are not. And when you are filled with sleep, you
never were. I dont know what I am. I dont

know if I am or not. Jewel knows he is, because
he does not know that he does not know whether he
is or not ... [76].

Faulkner reinforces this feeling of Darl's unrest by breaking
his earlier sonorous rhythm; he includes several very short
passages (by both Darl and Vardaman, in the classic one-
sentence monologue, "My mother was a fish"). The closing
monologue is Darl's, but it centers on Jewel's dominant role
in getting the ironic odyssey underway, and Jewel accordingly, in all his bitter grief, comes front stage.

Jewel dominates the central Part IV, although none of
its nine sections are his (pages 94-129). Jewel astride the
painted horse angers both Anse and Darl, who are concerned
about the "propriety" of Jewel's horse, while Addie rots
away. Darl taunts Jewel with the presence of the buzzards,
each comment a personal injury--Jewel loved the woman
whose body is now so defiled. Yet Jewel literally moves the
entire family. The section closes with Darl's account of the
way Jewel won his horse, and his previously repellent pride
in it is consequently justified because of his superhuman labor to earn it. In that, just as in fulfilling Addie's wish,
Jewel had to work against his entire family.

So, poised in our late-acquired knowledge of Jewel's
real bereavement, set for his wild rush to action, we are
ready for Faulkner's relatively rapid progression through the
more dramatic stages of Addie's last journey. Part V (pages
130-174) recounts the "death by water" stage, with Darl's
cowardly evacuation, Cash's sacrifice of his leg, and Jewel's
foolhardy rescue of both coffin and Cash's tools (the compassionate Tull shares in the latter venture). Once the ostensible action has quieted, Faulkner returns to the heart of the
novel with Addie's first and only monologue, by which any
questions about her relationship to Anse and her love for
Jewel are forever answered. Faulkner relentlessly places
Addie's words between Cora's pious inaccuracies and Whitfield's inaccurate pieties. The section closes with Darl
again bringing attention to Jewel and his horse.

Part VI (pages 175-215) opens with Jewel's relinquishing his horse to Snopes for the new team, and closes with
Jewel burned, Cash possibly dying, and Darl crying on Addie's coffin. Darl's verbal incoherence has grown throughout these monologues so that we are not surprised at his setting fire to the barn in an attempt to end the travesty of the

journey (196-198). The fire scene culminates a mockery of action in these nine passages, for four of them are given to Vardaman whose main interest is in counting the buzzards which follow Addie's coffin. Faulkner's sporadic use of Vardaman and his reactions is one of the more successful devices of the narration; used frequently as he was in Parts II and III, Vardaman's grief creates a dramatic image for the emotionally bereft family. During the middle course of the action, Vardaman is presented as fairly stable; but here, drawing near the end, Faulkner uses his childlike interpretations to make sharper their awful irony. It is Vardaman who recounts the aftermath of the fire, with the grieving Darl "out there under the apple tree with her [Addie], lying on her.... The moonlight dappled on him too. On her it was still, but on Darl it dappled up and down" (214-15).

Part VII, the denouement, opens with Darl's penultimate passage, ironically his most rational statement yet. It is Darl who here intercedes for Jewel in his argument with the knife-carrying town man. Darl's sensible monologue is followed by his commitment to the Jackson asylum, and by the most comprehensive statement Cash has yet made (Cash's earlier musing on the beveling and balancing of Addie's coffin places him wholly in the category of man of action: Faulkner suggests that because Cash had an outlet for his grief, he has been tempered by it, not destroyed). Fittingly too, it is Cash who recounts the last of the story, Anse's triumphal return with teeth, wife, and possessions. Cash can stand it; we have already seen all the agony--both physical and mental--he has stood on the journey. And Cash too is Anse's son; he has some loyalty to his father, although we have seen his revulsion to Anse in the scene of Addie's death.

Jewel, on the other hand, acts only to honor his mother. He dominates--indeed, causes--much of the movement of the narrative until Addie is buried; then Jewel nearly disappears from the story. It is as if he had existed only for the purpose of fulfilling her wishes. As she had told Cora,

> 'He is my cross and he will be my salvation.
> He will save me from the water and from the fire.
> Even though I have laid down my life, he will
> save me' [160].

But so far as the Bundren family as family was concerned,

Jewel was an outsider, and could in no reasonable way accommodate Anse's lazy but crippling evil.

The mastery of Faulkner's structure here is clearly evident. No better tribute exists than the fact that most readers are able to read the book as a single story, regardless of these changes in tone, emphasis, and speaker. Like The Sound and the Fury, As I Lay Dying is one of Faulkner's broad comments on life and its verbal distinctions: sane and insane, normal and abnormal, love and hate. That readers could question the moral hypocrisy of Anse returning with teeth, gramophone, and new wife is another tribute to Faulkner's wonderfully imaged conclusions. Of course, loyal and loving husbands and fathers do not behave in his way--but Anse Bundren sounds so pathetic that, like his neighbors, we nearly forget ourselves. Word and act--Faulkner gives us both. But he also gives us, prominently, Addie's scurrilous comments on words:

> We had had to use one another by words like spiders dangling by their mouths from a beam, swinging and twisting and never touching ... [164].
> And I would think then when Cora talked to me, of how the high dead words in time seemed to lose even the significance of their dead sound.... [P]eople to whom sin is just a matter of words, to them salvation is just words too [167-168].

In As I Lay Dying, too, Faulkner has learned to use a "chorus" of outside voices to reinforce our impressions of the Bundren family members. Vernon Tull is the most pervasive and reliable of these figures. In contrast to his wife Cora, Tull sees the struggle over Addie's death wish for what it is, a power struggle within the family. He alone understands Vardaman's malady (it is Tull who physically comforts the boy); he alone understands Jewel's almost primitive necessity to succeed in fulfilling Addie's wish. Interestingly, though somewhat tenuously, Faulkner keeps Tull on stage so that we have the benefit of his perspective even once the journey has begun.

Doc Peabody is another reliable observer, introduced with his vituperative indictment of Anse:

> When Anse finally sent for me of his own accord, I said 'He has wore her out at last.' And I said a damn good thing, and at first I would not

> go because there might be something I could do
> and I would have to haul her back, by God [40].

In his role of sage observer, who both knows and cares
about the families of the county, Doc Peabody is set in contrast to the hypocritical Dimmesdale figure (that Doc's appearance precedes Whitfield's is no accident; we are conditioned even before the anti-climactic rhetoric of the minis-
ter--whose "voice is bigger than him," fittingly--to know
that it is going to be both anti-climactic and rhetoric, a
profanation of Addie's loving spirit).

So that we may better understand Addie's genuine profanation at the hands of her former lover, Faulkner gives us
the obvious foil character of Cora Tull. In early drafts of
this novel, Faulkner presented Cora as vacuous and silly,
but not particularly religious. His addition of Cora's pious-
ly hypocritical cant makes her not only a simple contrast to
Addie, but also a complement to both Anse and Whitfield.
Her language echoes theirs; her opacity parallels theirs; and
in some ways, her lack of understanding seems worse because she too is a woman and might logically have been expected to understand some of the same things Addie had felt.
As Addie had said of her father's words, "I know at last
what he meant and that he could not have known what he
meant himself, because a man cannot know anything about
cleaning up the house afterward" (167-168).

Cora is a definite foil to Addie, but Dewey Dell's
role is not so simple. Faulkner seems to ask us to forgive
her many things because of her age, and perhaps such an attitude has credibility. Dewey Dell, like Steinbeck's Rose of
Sharon, is completely absorbed in her own pregnancy.
Usurped as her emotions are, she has no time to mourn her
mother's dying. Later, desperate in her failure to find the
magic formula for abortion, she sacrifices Darl in order to
silence him. The futile meanness of the latter act, however, convinces us that Dewey Dell is no Addie. In the latter part of the novel, Faulkner is presenting more than adolescent selfishness. Dewey Dell, in her continuing absorption with her own needs and in her misuse of the weakest
members of the family--Vardaman and Darl--is more the
child of Anse Bundren than is any of her brothers. No other
of the children acts intentionally against a sibling.

Addie's isolation is consequently clearer once we
come to know the women in her life. Because Faulkner

levies his indictment through humor in the characters of both Cora and Dewey Dell, their real roles in the novel may be obscured. (He uses near satire for Cora, and Dewey Dell stars in many comic episodes, whether it be eating bananas, carrying cakes, bribing druggists, or having sex.) What he essentially does is to place Cora, wearing her rhetorical halo, and Dewey Dell, parading her complete immorality, in the company of Anse; leaving Addie with only the inarticulate Jewel and the almost disinterested Tull as allies. Doc Peabody was an ally, but as such, could only help her to death.

Addie knew this, of course. That is the reason for her magnificently understated death wish ("getting ready to clean my house") and her equally magnificently understated death wait. She lies there, listening to Cash build her coffin, knowing Dewey Dell cannot be bothered to keep the flies off, knowing Anse will never be hurried into calling Doc Peabody--not that she cares, knowing that somehow the family will keep Jewel from her, even at the very end. But she knows too that the crucible of the act of burying her will test these strangers in her family, that something will happen, that she will have--finally and perhaps for the first time-- been the catalyst for Anse and action.

Addie would settle for motion, for action rather than the pious words she knew all too well. In her death as never in her living, she would move this family. As I Lay Dying is a testimony to an exercise in will, but the will is Addie's, never Anse's.

There is a last bit of irony left to Addie in the novel, an irony that darkens the tone and turns the book even more sharply away from any pretense of comedy. Her only monologue had begun with her memories of teaching, her desperate turn to physical violence in order to reach her pupils "Now you are aware of me! Now I am something in your secret and selfish life" [162]). The irony is that Addie's description of those separate, uncaring students would also describe so accurately her own equally separate and in some ways uncaring children and husband:

> I would have to look at them day after day, each
> with his and her secret and selfish thought, and
> blood strange to each other's blood and strange to
> mine [161-2].

Once Addie has had her own children and has recognized that even physical ties sometimes mean nothing, she concludes that "living is terrible," and readies herself to die. In this respect, As I Lay Dying is not only an indictment of the loaded abstractions Faulkner gives us in the text--fear, sin, salvation, and love. The novel also provides an unrelievedly tragic definition of the word family.

Some of these same devices and themes Faulkner employs again in his 1932 novel Light in August, the novel Brooks sees as the first real study of the community, and man's responsibility to other men.[17] It is true that Light in August is a more ambitious novel in that Faulkner uses at least four separate story lines. But its parallels to both the short stories and the earlier novels are also clear: Faulkner again gives the reader the old legends, those peculiarly integral to the novel's story. The history of the Burden family and the Hightower already seem familiar; only Joe's murder of Joanna--and his own death because of it--is new, and John Cullen among others points out that that story was also common property.[18] Faulkner also uses the panorama of community as both backdrop and character in the manner of the Greek chorus, extending his use of Tull and Doc Peabody--the Armstids, the sheriff, Gavin Stevens, the furniture dealer. It is interesting that Faulkner's censure of community hypocrisy in general (as in Chapter 13) never is sustained in his portraits of individuals; as soon as he draws any single person, he becomes multifaceted and, hence, in some way, sympathetic.

The issue of race also appears, but this time as a means of ridiculing the human culture; the reversal in public opinion--from hating Joanna Burden to wanting revenge for her death--occurs only because of Joe's alleged color. Yet for Faulkner to leave undetermined the truth of Joe's parentage is a masterful touch. Regardless of his color, Joe is a misplaced person; he has chosen alienation over community time and time again--and such alienation has nothing to do with race. For the primary theme here is once again responsibility, with neither Joe Christmas nor Gail Hightower being willing to assume any share of another's burden. Both Joe and Hightower (like Anse Bundren before them) want only peace, want life "complete and inviolable, like a classic and serene vase."[19] Such tranquility is never to be, however, for any man; and so Faulkner gives us Joe's inarticulate acceptance and Hightower's verbalized realization as the real climaxes of the novel. Joe Christmas's story is the more

sensational; and Faulkner, recognizing this, devotes the first
half of the novel to it; but the figures of Christmas and Hightower eventually seem to fuse, as the drama of recognition
becomes Hightower's. (As Carl Ficken notes, Faulkner tried
to open this novel with Hightower's story, and Joe's, rather
than Lena's. [20])

Another similarity is that once again Faulkner used a
woman to illustrate one way life might be successfully lived.
The continuity between Addie Bundren and Lena Grove is
more than accidental. Both care little for social codes; both
look to men and life with men as a way out of stalemate;
both are intrigued with travel (Lucas Burch might well echo
Anse's curse of the road); but Lena is much less bitter (perhaps because she carries a child)[21] as well as much less
aware than Addie. The difference in age and experiences
might account for this, but the primary difference--as always
with Faulkner--is that these are different people. What is
intriguing about the similarities between Addie and Lena is
that Faulkner has borrowed from As I Lay Dying the central
image of Addie ("rim" of all wheels, encompassing all the
journeys and struggles of her family) and has shaped from
that image the structure of Light in August. For the story
of Lena Grove in her never outraged simplicity is used as
more than a frame tale: true, her story does open and
close the novel, but it works much more actively than as a
separate framing device. It surrounds, impinges upon, all
the other stories in the novel. The only one it does not
touch directly is that of Joe and Joanna; Lena is connected
to Christmas through Lucas Burch and Doc and Mrs. Hines,
but she never sees him. [See illustration, p. 192.]

Three concentric circles best represent the design of
the book, with the role of Byron Bunch providing crucial
transition. Byron is not only the townsman who represents
"normal" opinion--a forerunner of V. K. Ratliff, without the
prominence and the humor; he is also the bridge between
both Hightower and Lena, and the rest of the action. As the
novel progresses he also becomes the devil's advocate for
both Hightower and Christmas. Byron becomes the involved
man, the man of action, as his senseless fight with Lucas
Burch so clearly announces. He fights simply because he
should--as Hightower lies for Christmas because he should,
out of pity for all mankind. Indeed, it is Byron who comes
to verbalize Faulkner's stance about endurance, when he
says, almost wonderingly, that "I can bear a hill, a man
can.... It seems like a man can just about bear anything.

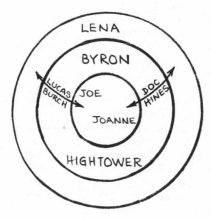

He can even bear what he never done. He can even bear the
thinking how some things is just more than he can bear"
[401].

    For one of the first times in his fiction, Faulkner has
taken his admiration for women and their endurance and extended that admiration to his male figures. Byron, like Lena,
does endure, does in fact persevere. And Byron also has
compassion. For this latter reason, that Byron does understand all people, Lena is not morally superior in this novel
(as Margaret Powers was in Soldiers' Pay or Jenny Du Pre
was in Sartoris). As character, Lena is subservient to Byron because she acts only for herself and her child; she is
not asked to bear the weight of another's misfortune (thus,
her reaction when Byron tells about Hightower is that he
might be able to marry her, not that she might somehow be
able to help him).

    Because of the difference here in the kind of compas-
sion shown by Byron and Lena, and the use made of each
character within the novel, it seems clear that Faulkner is
not opposing Lena and Christmas, or Lena and Hightower.
This latter theory has been advanced by both Carl Benson and
Richard Adams because of the parallels with Conrad's Lena
and Heyst in "Victory."[22] While there may be some suggestion of this influence, there is also the stolid German Lena
("The Gentle Lena") of Gertrude Stein's Three Lives. More
importantly, there is the structure of Faulkner's finished novel. And judging from the total impression of the book, we
see that it is Byron rather than Lena who opposes the attitudes of Christmas and Hightower, and that one of the main

reasons for the recurring dialogue between Byron and Hightower is the full expression of those attitudes. As he was
to do in Absalom, Faulkner here is using each man's reaction to the ostensible "story"--that of Joe Christmas--to
characterize both Hightower and Byron as personae.

Once Faulkner has introduced Hightower as character
(briefly in Chapter Two and more fully in Three), he uses
him primarily as dialogue participant. We see Hightower
only in relation to the news Byron brings; even the one
scene at the grocery exists to stress Hightower's newly
aware state of mind. The conflict between Byron and Hightower begins at once, midway in Chapter Four, as Byron
talks about Lena's search for Lucas Brown:

> Yet Byron can see in the other's face something
> latent, about to wake, of which Hightower himself
> is unaware, as if something inside the man were
> trying to warn or prepare him [74].

Four times in the next ten pages Faulkner mentions that
Hightower's face is marked with "shrinking and denial"; then
he begins to sweat, and he continues sweating until Byron
finishes his story. Then Faulkner gives us the vivid image
of Hightower already rewakened into life, "the sweat running
down his face like tears" as he mourns for the part-Negro,

> 'It is certain, proved, that he has negro blood?
> Think, Byron; what it will mean when the people--
> if they catch.... Poor man. Poor mankind' [93].

The resolution of Christmas' story is here in miniature.
Acted upon by the community which is itself victimized by
conventional beliefs, Joe is to be pitied, and so is all mankind. It will be the dialogue between Byron and Hightower
which will point toward not only the ending of the plotline but
also toward the direction our own sympathies must take.

The vivid flashbacks concerning Joe Christmas occupy
nearly two hundred pages, and bring us closer to the psychology of what Glenn Sandstrom calls "identity diffusion"[23]
than any other literature; but once this story has been told
(by Faulkner's omniscient narrator) he returns immediately
to Byron's narration for Hightower. In Chapter Thirteen,
the conflict between Byron and Hightower is intensified as
Hightower vents his hatred of women, marriage, and man
as dupe. That Hightower's compassion exists for society in

general rather than for man (or woman) in the particular is
clear; it is also, perhaps, to be expected. But even more
interesting is Hightower's blindness about his own life.
Faulkner closes this section with the scene of the old min-
ister mistakenly finding refuge in Tennyson's rhetoric. His
struggle has not yet come.

But from Chapters Sixteen through Twenty, Faulkner
features just that central if undramatic struggle. To fully
record what happens to Hightower, Faulkner must leave the
dialogue format and go to, first, Hightower as active participant in the present-tense story; and, finally, to a mixed
stream of consciousness and omniscient flashback in the stir-
ring penultimate chapter, the section which--aside from Lena's
comic chapter--does close the novel.

This penultimate chapter reinforces the maxim Faulkner had used earlier in reference to Joe: the child as the
father of the man; "Memory believes before knowing remembers." (Mr. Compson said, "Man is the sum of his misfortunes.") Here too Faulkner presents Hightower as child, and
then as adolescent, lured to the seminary and its religion because of its aura of sanctuary. The fallacious dream of
peace begins here.24 Reading the story of Hightower's boyhood, and his bookish notion of love, triggers our recollection of Joe's own isolated childhood, the importance of which
is evident because of the extreme length Faulkner had used
in recounting it--one long chapter devoted to Joe's experiences before he is five; another to the years eight to fifteen; and third and fourth to his first love; another to the
telescoped glimpse of those fifteen lonely years on the road.
It is only after we understand Joe that Faulkner presents the
other two central isolates, Joanna Burden and Hightower.
Because their childhoods have been so much like Joe's, at
least emotionally, Faulkner needs refer only briefly to the
likenesses and we understand.

Faulkner, in his comparatively new role as narrator,
is able here to use image patterns as never before: Miss
Atkins, like Joe's grandfather and Lena Grove, sees life as
a straight and simple corridor. To Joe and Hightower, however, it is an ever-circling road, full of doubt and complexity, a road not unlike the senseless wheel of fortune or the
chess set with its many pawns which figure so prominently
in the novel. Like a pawn himself, Joe is also described
as a toy, a doll. Never master of anyone's fate, Joe must
be sacrificed; such is the nature of the unwitting Percy

Grimm society. But before Joe's death, he has brought
"light" to at least one other character of the book, Gail
Hightower, and, Faulkner implies, to the townsmen who
were involved in his murder.

A plot summary of Light in August diminishes its
force amazingly. Retribution. A culture demanding blood
from a man who sinned at least partly because he had been
taught only to hate (McEachern and Doc Hines are the real
Elmer Gantrys of the fanatical sub-culture). That culture
redeemed by the very death it demanded, even to its own
religious spokesman, Hightower. The strength of the story
lies not so much in the ostensible events, but rather in
Faulkner's manner of telling it. The wide yet beautifully
detailed canvas; the impressionistic shifting of narrators to
help broaden the feeling of dimension (the colored man on
his mule telling of Christmas in the black church, Stevens
hypothesizing as best he can but inaccurately, Byron's mar-
velously paced narration that does so much more than just
give facts); the subterfuge of using what seems to be a narrative device (Byron's telling events to Hightower) when it
is really a thematic one; opening the novel with the purport-
edly climactic action, the fire and the murder--all of these
narrative tactics and the many others illustrate Faulkner's
control of the various storytelling methods, and his sense of
humor in using them. Is there any rule for writing fiction
that by 1932 Faulkner has not already broken? And yet he
is to go even further in 1936 and use as his narrative method exactly Joe Christmas' personal dilemma, his lack of information about the central story. In Absalom, Absalom!
Faulkner gives us four distinct characters bent on re-creating what they too cannot possibly ever "know," the Sutpen
story. Here Faulkner was experimenting with a new means
of characterization, relying not on a man's acts or words
(though to some extent his idiom was bound to be important)
but primarily on his perceptions, the way he looks at life,
to reveal himself.[25] Faulkner's method is evidence again of
not only great skill but also great understanding of human
nature, for in Absalom he also turns once more to an apparently colorful--even shocking--story.

As he had so frequently done before, in Light in August too Faulkner focused attention for at least part of the
book on a grotesque, human-interest kind of story; and then
shifted to a more complicated philosophical problem which
may have been triggered by the slighter though more sensational incident. One example of this device is his emphasis

in Sanctuary on the rape of Temple Drake, all the while he was himself fascinated with the study of Horace Benbow's realization of morality; or in Pylon, as the question of the pilots' life styles is focused first on the matter of the child's parentage, and later on a much wider issue of responsibility for any human being. Even in The Wild Palms, the opening Charlotte-Henry story, with its plot of abortion and "pure" love, is ostensibly more sensational than the convict's fear of all womankind. In all these cases, sex is used as the interest-catching incident, but used primarily as a means of leading both character and reader to a wider, more compassionate understanding of human nature.

Chapter Ten

FAULKNER'S LARGER VISION--
AND THE ROUTE TO IT

Aside from the craftsman's delight in creating effects
that are, in the main, new to his art, Faulkner's evident
satisfaction with writing after <u>Sartoris</u> stemmed primarily
from his ability to use his craft to enhance his ever-matur-
ing vision. In the progression of Faulkner's fiction there is
a decided parallel between the kind of philosophical position
he takes and the method of narration he uses. The more
stable his view, the more direct and understandable his method. Once Faulkner had himself come to realize what Bayard
Sartoris early learned in <u>The Unvanquished</u> (that man can't
possibly fight in the mountains, but has to, nevertheless), he
adopted the clear forthrightness of a Ratliff or Mallison: his
narratives tended to move chronologically once more; they
were told by either a single narrator or by clearly identified
speakers; and they were usually tempered by humor, frequently in both telling and in incident. They were, taken collectively, comedies.

In contrast to his late writing, however, Faulkner's
earlier novels show the marks of his personal search.
There is the outright censure of the personae in <u>Mosquitoes</u>;
Faulkner knows what he does not like, but he fails to create
positive figures to replace Talifero and Fairchild. Then
comes his empathetic period, in which he identifies completely with Quentin Compson, but also with his father and, at
times, with Jason; with Addie Bundren, but also with her
children. What had happened to bring Faulkner to his great
period of compassionate characterization[1] is described in
1957, as he explains that he had learned about people from the
fictional process itself.

> the writer is learning all the time he writes and
> he learns from his own people, once he has con-
> ceived them truthfully and has stuck to the verities
> of human conduct, human behavior, human

> aspirations, then he learns--yes, they teach him,
> they surprise him ... they do things and suddenly
> he says to himself, Why yes, that is true, that is
> so. [2]

The years of, particularly, stream of consciousness presentations had trained Faulkner to empathize with all men, even
the less than noble ones.   His apparent understanding of
characters deepened his portrayal of even minor characters
like the Armstids in Light in August and Mrs. Littlejohn in
The Hamlet.   And since the strong current of non-judgmental
characterization had swept through England and America,
Faulkner's presentations were felt to be effective so long as
they were vivid.   But eventually, each author has to direct
his reader to shades of greatness or evil.   As Faulkner himself realized, it is ultimately not enough to admire endurance,
for many kinds of people endure.   There must be other positive qualities in conjunction with a man's ability to last.

    Part of Faulkner's problem in presenting his total
view was the limitation inherent in a first person point of
view.   Restricted to stream of consciousness or first person, Faulkner could never have used the camera view, the
outside perspective which he felt was so necessary to the
complete view of a character.   For as he was to learn, one
man's view is never "accurate"--indeed, the very foreshort-
ening that occurs when one man looks at an event is the
cause of much of life's tragedy (Percy Grimm's view of Joe
Christmas' crime, Mink Snopes' view of the court decision
in Houston's favor, the reporter's concept of what the last
race meant to Roger Schumann, ad infinitum).   The mixture
of first and third person in nearly all his writing after Sartoris is the technique that allows Faulkner to re-create the
sense of wonderfully individual characters, and yet never
overlook the wider panorama of life from which they have
come.

    One of Faulkner's basic premises is that each man
does come from a matrix of other lives, and correspondingly has his own effect on that milieu: even such seemingly
insignificant men as the Snopes make indelible marks.   And
because man and his fellows and his place are so inextric-
ably joined, most of Faulkner's major fiction centers on that
problem, the issue of one man's rights and, more important
in Faulkner's view, his grave responsibilities.

    That's what I am talking about: responsibility

.... Not just the right, but the duty of man to be
responsible, the necessity of man to be responsible. [3]

As we have seen in Chapter Eight, this thematic emphasis was apparent at least part of the time in Faulkner's
early fiction too, but it was not so clearly expressed as it
was to be later (part of the failure may have resulted from
the relatively conventional narrative methods already discussed). By the time of Sartoris, then, Faulkner praises
Aunt Jenny at least in part because she is responsible for
all the other characters, and censures Bayard for his failure to care. Sartoris is dominantly third person, but much
of the immediacy of the novel springs from the first-person
story telling within the story proper. The vitality of these
family legends makes even more clear the appeal they held
for certain kinds of men--Hightower, Quentin, Bayard--who
live more fully in imagination than in reality.

The Sound and the Fury is the passionate reversal of
omniscient point of view, as the three sons present their
separate accounts of life within the Compson family. The
sections of Benjy, Quentin, and Jason are Faulkner's most
convincing proof that any one man's view is of necessity
false, at least false in the eyes of others. By shifting to
dramatic scenes within these first person narratives, Faulkner does provide the supposedly stable view of an omniscient
observer. This persona probably also controls Part IV (and
might well be a continuation of the unnamed "townsman"
voice of "A Rose for Emily," "Hair," "Death Drag," and
"Idyll in the Desert." A forerunner of Ratliff, the spokesman of these stories is not easily shocked; is pseudo-objec-
tive, humorous, and also deeply compassionate). The importance of this unnamed third person narrator is great, for
it is in the dramatic scenes of the monologues and Part IV,
more so than in Jason and Quentin's monologues, that we find
the most accurate picture of the Compson family (see my essay on this point in The Sewanee Review for Winter, 1971,
554-575).

With As I Lay Dying Faulkner's method is similar,
Darl's sections serving to give the reader some dramatic
vignettes as well as providing a nearly impartial consciousness. Like Benjy and unlike Jason, Darl is more "sensitive" than he is real. Sanctuary, for reasons discussed in
Chapter Nine, reverts to the earlier omniscient narrator
method, but Light in August capitalizes once again on

juxtaposition of the "townsman" narrative voice in the persona of Byron Bunch (and other less important characters) set against the newly-ornate tones of Faulkner's omnipresent speaker. Light in August is Faulkner's "big" novel, and the almost stentorian prose seems to suggest its thematic importance. Man as responsible for other human beings, responsibility as love--Hightower and Bunch both say it and live it, and Joe Christmas searches for it, wordlessly. Faulkner had presented it negatively in Sanctuary, the essential love that is not to be found in either religion (as here, the banalities of Cora, Anse, and Mrs. Compson shift into the violent oppression of McEachern and Doc Hines) or in romantic love (Byron's love for Lena has to become aware before it can hope for realization). Light in August is the symphonic arrangement of what in Sanctuary was only a slender if brilliantly ironic solo, Gowan Stevens' note to Narcissa that he had done a horrible thing, but, at least, he "had injured no one save himself" (126).

With Pylon, Faulkner's most despairing book (or perhaps, as Millgate suggests, only his most rushed one[4]), the combination of omniscient narrator with the first person story of the unnamed reporter works in a different way. Reminiscent in tone and idiom of Byron Bunch, the reporter is yet also a continuation of the Cora Tulls in Faulkner's fiction--he knows too little to be able to really help anyone. He tries repeatedly to be responsible; in fact, the whole novel is a series of happenings which the reporter takes charge of, and yet his interference leads only to death and the abandonment of the child. Rather than use his narrator as surrogate author, as he did with Byron, Faulkner here gives us a protagonist who has more weaknesses than he has strengths. We see the positive attitudes of other characters only as mirror images of the reporter's shortcomings.

The irony in Pylon is both dramatic and conventional. We as readers do know the essential fact--that Laverne is again pregnant--long before the reporter does; therefore we mistrust Roger's motives for wanting to fly the final race. Contrary to the reporter's refrain ("they don't need money"), we know that Roger is desperate for it. But the irony exists as more than a device for duping the reporter. In spite of some inexplicably negative images,[5] he still has our sympathy. In the opening scenes, his dialogues with the editor Hagood depict the latter unfavorably as a man who refuses to get involved; and his bitterly droll account of Laverne and her men (opening, Darl-like, with "She") is well-paced and moving. His understatement works to create horror as well as humor.

Later in the novel, however, the reporter's character changes (such reversal, in both the reporter and editor, seems to be a flaw), and he becomes a rhetorician. His incessant talk keeps him from picking up clues for a just reading of the situation; and Faulkner uses the cutting remarks of both Laverne and Ord to devastate him even after Roger's death. Faulkner also emphasizes another trait of the reporter which dulled his perceptions: he is distraught by his great love for this woman he scarcely knows. Faulkner confirms the foolishness of his obsession by having him think only of Laverne at the time of Roger's death.

So the theme put forward in Light in August changes a little, moving from not just the concept of responsibility and the need to care for others; to an insistence on a responsibility qualified by some awareness of man's condition. Protected as the "baby" by his grotesque mother, the reporter only thinks he knows life. Despite his emphasis on how different the fliers are, Faulkner's message comes through clearly--that the fliers precisely were not different; that any man will risk his life to provide for those he loves. And the social message in what must come closest to being Faulkner's "depression novel" is also clear--trapped by money and authority like Feinman's, the common man takes what he can get, fair or not. Like Steinbeck's Grapes of Wrath four years later, Faulkner was right--beat a humble man down far enough, and he'll thank you for robbing him; while the rest of his society says, quietly, "He ain't my brother."

In this crucial matter of awareness as the way to understanding (the theme that also was to dominate Absalom, Absalom!, The Unvanquished, The Wild Palms, Intruder in the Dust, and Go Down, Moses) Faulkner's treatment of the reporter in Pylon parallels that of Horace Benbow in Sanctuary. Both the reporter and Horace, themselves rational and relatively proud men, are beaten by the very depths (or heights) of a non-rational character's motivations. Pushed far enough out of reasonable circumstances, as both Temple Drake and Roger Shumann were, man reacts only with his emotions: reason, therefore, unaided, cannot fully explain why he does what he does. Part of the effective tension in Pylon results from the discrepancy between Roger's apparently controlled manner and his matter-of-fact attention to business (in contrast to that of the much more volatile Jack) and the real desperation that is evident when he flies (a tension paralleled by the apparently objective, statement-like chapter titles and the hysteric events they record).

There is also an interesting and important change in narrative method in <u>Pylon</u>. In <u>Sanctuary</u> Faulkner kept the reader from knowing why Temple behaves as she does; here, Roger's motivation is explained clearly. The theory has frequently been expressed that Faulkner habitually worked in the detective story genre;[6] while there are some novels that fit reasonably well in that category, more of them do not. Faulkner's characteristic practice of withholding information is probably the best reason for labeling his novels "detective"--that, along with the continuing character of Gavin Stevens--yet Faulkner withholds information from at least some characters in every novel he writes. The device is used, it seems likely, not to create suspense, but rather to increase Faulkner's opportunity for irony. The method has the effect of dooming a conventional plot or character, for if the "good" characters in any ordered society do not understand circumstances, then even their best-intentioned efforts may work negatively. The technique of keeping back information works toward several pervasive effects important to Faulkner's fiction:

(1) It places his characters in the unsatisfying position of having to settle for "doing the best they can."

(2) If men pride themselves on being self-determined, operating under freedom of choice, then even that sense of freedom is misleading since they cannot make the best decisions until they know all the circumstances. But most events require action, not mediation; so that a man must be willing to act with only partial knowledge.

(3) It also helps to free Faulkner from a judgmental attitude toward his own characters. Just when we are sure Faulkner identifies with a character, the character makes the wrong choice (sometimes because he has inadequate information; but, again, sometimes not).

(4) For a society whose members revere fact instead of truth any interference with factual information becomes a crime. Faulkner sometimes uses this high seriousness toward fact for a comic effect, as when he shows that a person may know all the facts and still act insensitively.

He also uses play on this social attitude to create tragedy. And on occasion, most notably in <u>Absalom</u>, he uses the quest for fact as the basis of the entire plot, as well as an important element in all four major characterizations.

One might say that the technique of withholding information becomes, in the late writing, a central method of developing both plot and character. Faulkner's protagonists in these books are frequently men--and women--who know things intuitively, who do not need to accumulate facts in order to make decisions. Chick Mallison and Miss Habersham act entirely on instinct in <u>Intruder in the Dust</u>; Eula Snopes dies simply because Gavin Stevens had no intuition (although in <u>Knight's Gambit</u> he possesses a great deal); Lucius Priest, even when confused, shows much intuition. And Faulkner's fiction is filled with characters--Mrs. Jim Gant, McEachern, Doc Hines, Percy Grimm--who impossibly, irrationally, choose the right direction when they are in pursuit.

Increasingly too in the late stories, the plots will turn as often on the unimportance of fact as on the withholding of it. Empathetic as we are with Ned in <u>The Reivers</u>, we do not know until nearly the end why he has acted as he has; just as in <u>The Mansion</u> Mink Snopes is so surrounded with conditions that he should be unable to leave the prison. He disregards all fact, however; and makes his way unerringly to Flem. Faulkner's brilliant if sardonic play with the issues of fact and truth, knowing and not knowing, becomes almost an objective correlative for the difficulties one man has in understanding another human being. In <u>Pylon</u>, as we have seen, the reporter means well; he makes great personal sacrifice in terms of money, house, job, and emotional attachment; yet even this much concern cannot reach into the circumstances of other men's lives. And in the fiction to come, Faulkner's use of Gavin Stevens nearly always portends the same kind of ineffectual involvement.

Looking at Faulkner's attitudes throughout his writing, it is as if his view had changed from, first, the largely critical in <u>Soldiers' Pay</u> and <u>Mosquitoes</u>; to that which could identify so clearly with the Jewels, Vardamans, Jasons, and Quentins of his world; to that wider perspective that saw the tragedy in Mrs. Armstid's life and her torment in sharing with Lena Grove, as well as the tragedy and torment in the more highly visible lives of Joe Christmas and Gail Hightower; to the even less moralistic attitude of V. K. Ratliff. It is as if through it all Faulkner was himself reaching toward awareness.

For what I have called awareness, Faulkner uses the word, "foreknowledge." Sam Fathers acts more wisely than other men because he draws from his rich communion with the land and its natural knowledge to make his decisions. Of all the hunters, only Sam acts to take the necessary step of finding, and training, Lion, the dog who will help kill Old Ben. And, finally, almost free of social--i. e., man-conceived--restraints and falsity, he is not above asking Boon to kill him.

For Ike McCaslin, the protagonist of Go Down, Moses who tries so desperately to follow in Sam Fathers' footsteps, Boon's act of mercy was the apex of human kinship. Ike himself, however, falls far short of that same nobility, at least partly because he lacks this valuable foreknowledge. In "Delta Autumn" when he is confronted with Roth Edmonds' lover and their son, he is completely shaken; yet his experiences from the old ledgers should have prepared him for that eventuality. As the other scenes in Moses prove, Ike understands very little except hunting; he exists only for those two weeks in the hunting camp, with the men. Ike's life has been one of withdrawal, of searching for "peace," and we have earlier seen Faulkner's definition of that state. Even his relinquishing the land is a negative act, for he may say that "the earth was no man's but all men's," yet he acts only to make McCaslin and not himself take the responsibility. Had he wanted to somehow share his wealth, dividing it would have been simple enough. Giving it back to the McCaslin family only increased the present inequity (as Roth's lover points out to him, and as Lucas Beauchamp had observed[7]).

In The Wild Palms, Faulkner had also indicated a man lacking essential awareness. Harry Wilbourne, as male, could have controlled Charlotte (several points in the novel give him opportunity) yet he too adopts the rhetoric of rationalization. There are fine-sounding reasons for every mad thing he and Charlotte do; and as the story runs into her inevitable death, Faulkner creates for Wilbourne two scenes of opposition: one, as McCord sends them off to the mines; a second, as the old doctor calls him a butcher.

Indeed, part of the vitality of "Old Man," the counterpoint story in The Wild Palms, results from the fact that the convict is only too aware of what may happen to a man. He acts almost entirely in reaction to the strong forces of the woman and her sex, and comes back to prison gladly in

Faulkner's comic treatment of a man much too aware of what lies ahead in the married world. [8]

The ability to foresee, to judge accurately both other men and the unpredictable circumstances of life, is clearly presented as a virtue in many other of Faulkner's novels, most notable in this period The Hamlet and The Unvanquished. Ratliff is able to stay with Flem Snopes as long as he does precisely because he does understand both Flem and his townspeople. His real error, which comes at the end of the novel, is only that of respecting Will Varner too highly. Because Ratliff believes that Varner never made a worthless buy, he is ready to purchase the Old Frenchman's Place from Flem. Such duping, as Faulkner handles it here, is comic, and--were it not for the Armstid part in the debacle--would not darken the roughly humorous, Twain-like atmosphere of the whole novel.

In The Unvanquished, however, Faulkner uses the quality of foreknowledge with a more serious intent. Bayard Sartoris is aware of the dangers in both the distraught yet still desirable Narcissa and the ritual-governed code of the South. He has to look beyond the immediate necessity for honor, and act in the larger interests of the family, as well as of himself. Alone, Bayard makes his decision, although Faulkner characteristically involves Aunt Jenny as champion after the fact. It is interesting that the title term had originally referred to the scrappy Rosa Millard in her mule duplicity--the slight Southern grand dame beating the Yankees out of 200-odd head of stock--but that Faulkner in shaping the novel from the stories transferred the approbation of "unvanquished" to Bayard and his much larger decision. Rosa Millard was acting within the circumstances of her life; Bayard--by going to meet Redburn unarmed--was creating his own circumstances.

Faulkner's emphasis on the endurance of the land--which is to dominate Go Down, Moses and later stories--also occurs in The Unvanquished, as Bayard and Ringo make their "living map ... against which the most brilliant of victories and the most tragic of defeats are but the loud noises of a moment" (3). The odor of verbena also symbolizes the strength of a man's land, and provides a rationale for the Southern indomitability (and that of Narcissa as well). But here too Faulkner develops the voice of restraint and concern in the person of Bayard, both in his own acts and in his telling the story of Sutpen's rebuilding:

> Father said, 'Are you with us or against us?'
> and he said, 'I'm for my land. If every man of
> you would rehabilitate his own land, the country
> will take care of itself' and Father challenged him
> to bring the lamp out and set it on a stump where
> they could both see to shoot and Sutpen would not
> [256].

Repeatedly Faulkner leaves the rhetoric that does, at times, slow some of the later novels (rhetoric included at least partly because the problem once more is that of characters' being caught by false words) and proves to us how true what he is saying is. We see clearly Bayard's refusing to duel, Sam Fathers' staying at the hunting camp once Jobaker was dead, Roth Edmonds' bitterness over his lover's infant son (vividly proved in his killing of what Ike knew had to be a doe). In method as in theme, Faulkner returns us to the concrete, to the single (usually human) episode that sparks the wandering argument, just as Nancy Mannigoe's murder brought Temple Drake back to reality. That the concrete episodes, the dramatized scenes, are proportionately fewer here than in books like As I Lay Dying and even Mosquitoes is not necessarily a fault; rather Faulkner's method here once again becomes an adjunct to his theme. The culture of the Sartoris' family after the War--indeed, the culture of the South--is shaken; it questions everything it has known and once accepted; and questioning takes words. And, it seems that Faulkner does not resent the words themselves so much as he resents their insulating quality. For the evil in Faulkner's later characters lies precisely in their ability to insulate themselves. Both Roth Edmonds and Ike have denied what Roth's lover has told the latter--that emotion (whether love or hate) lies at the heart of man's existence, and that even "suffering and grieving is better than nothing" (186). Roth refers to Ike as a dead man, and we see from Roth's own violence--like that great portrayal of Rider's grief in "Pantaloon in Black"--that he is trying to remain safe, but that he too is lost to his feelings.

"Go Down, Moses," Faulkner's epilogue story to the book, presents this theme most vividly as Mollie and Miss Worsham live through their grief over Samuel Worsham Beauchamp by living it. They have found release. Gavin Stevens, much as he tries to find solace through his money gift, does not. Go Down, Moses affirms in total once again that man's life is not designed for peace, but that, as Harry Wilbourne finally learned at the end of The Wild Palms, "between grief and nothing I will take grief" [324].

Faulkner's novels of the late thirties and early forties seem to fit into a larger pattern, just as his novels in the late twenties and early thirties had worked together as a kind of unit. From Sartoris through The Sound and the Fury, As I Lay Dying, Sanctuary, and Light in August, he was presenting, first, the importance of family love and cohesion, and then widening his concept of family, as in Sanctuary and Light in August, to include at least community, and by implication all mankind. The next group of five novels also presents a mosaic of parallel themes. The issue of man's responsibility for other men is central to the 1935 Pylon, but in this novel Faulkner treats the theme ironically. Even when the spirit is willing--and flesh too--a combination of both external circumstances and man's own depravity or ignorance manages to defeat even the best intentions. Absalom, Absalom! repeats the same kind of ironic pattern, but with much greater intensity, perhaps because its focus is again that specific culture which Faulkner himself understood so thoroughly.

While the narrative method of Absalom is the grandly dramatic extension of both such narrator-dominated stories as "Idyll in the Desert" or Pylon, it seems to be closest thematically to Light in August. Faulkner's ostensible canvas again is the racist behavior of the South, the prejudice that eats into all the good and simple souls of the Bible belt. Most of the townspeople are obsessed in much the same way Percy Grimm is; and Faulkner proves their blindness repeatedly in the course of the novel. The town can accept Sutpen's use of the wild niggers, but it is horrified by his physical intimacy with them; and it is angered when he tries to assume a respectability that can never be his, as he marries Ellen Coldfield. Yet, to further condemn the people of the town, Faulkner goes on to show that once Sutpen did marry Ellen, the town abandoned her; she is left to her eventual death in the cruel and vicious world of Sutpen's Hundred. Faulkner sets up the characteristics of intolerance (pride masked by hypocrisy) and the denial of any genuine responsibility to condemn not only the people of Absalom but also Sutpen himself, Henry--truly his father's son, and Rosa Coldfield. And he uses the black blood of Charles Bon as objective correlative, as focal point to show these characters' real attitudes (sans rhetoric).

Again Faulkner has clarified his method, and by erasing questions, has deepened his irony: in Light in August, no one knew whether or not Joe Christmas had any black blood.[9] In <u>Absalom,</u> the heinous fault of Sutpen's first lover was precisely that she did have. When Sutpen disowns her, and their son, for this crime, we immediately know how warped his own ideas have become. No matter how commanding and admirable he may be in some scenes of the novel, we can never forget the flaw that will eventually bring Wash Jones to kill him.

As incrementation on his theme, Faulkner repeats this flawed character in the persona of Henry. Any sympathy he might have created for the weak brother's "protection" of his sister is destroyed when we realize all too clearly that Henry kills Charles Bon not to prevent incest but rather miscegenation. Bon himself says it, as he taunts his former friend and roommate, " 'I'm the nigger that's going to sleep with your sister.' " Henry's insane coldness as he rides with Bon up to the mansion's door, only to shoot him then, proves the complete irrationality of his responses. Faulkner's deep condemnation lies in the fact that Henry's father, and his culture, and even his sister would all accept his murder of his own half brother as "reasonable."

But perhaps the most selfish use of all the inhuman social codes Faulkner has presented in <u>Absalom</u> occurs with the character of Rosa Coldfield. Incapable of any feeling for others, a parasite on society, she has worn mourning for forty-three years. Like Hightower, her life too revolves on that single moment of shock--Sutpen's insult. She has never tried to understand him or the conditions under which he was living; she has only reverted to the code for woman's behavior (the Drusilla sub-plot in <u>Unvanquished</u> is an elaboration on the implications of Rosa's ladyhood). Yet in her own passive way, in telling her story to Quentin, she has managed to finish the Sutpen dynasty, killing both the loyal Clytie and Henry; and to further burden the already distraught Quentin (and this too, Faulkner suggests, maliciously; for the Compson family had early befriended Sutpen). In the sinister proper evil of Rosa Coldfield lies the real damnation of the South. Her acts, like those of Percy Grimm, are the function of cold reason. She <u>knows</u> she is right.

Faulkner's portrayals of Clytie and Wash are even stronger since they are set against such characters as Rosa. Like Dilsey, Clytie does the best she can; but her unquestioning loyalty to both Henry, her own half brother, and the proud Sutpen legend, places her far above Faulkner's stereotypical Negro. And Wash, although white, in the process of questioning his own beliefs, comes to a kind of nobility, and also gives Faulkner the tone and stance for some of the characters in Go Down, Moses.

This 1942 novel (along with its companion book Intruder in the Dust) is Faulkner's fullest treatment of the life of the Southern Negro in relation to the Southern white. To continue his theme of the Negro endurance, stemming from their belief in the basic moralities, he creates the McCaslin family, with its genealogy both white and black. In almost every juxtaposition of legitimate white heir with unacknowledged black, the black is more stable, more just. "The Fire and the Hearth" establishes Mollie and Lucas Beauchamp as moral barometers for the clan--Mollie knows what will happen to her own family, including Nat and George, should Lucas' money fever get out of hand; just as Lucas correctly reads Ike's relinquishing his land. In "Go Down, Moses," Faulkner proves that Mollie's fears were legitimate, as he shows the effects of the fast, grasping culture on Mollie's grandson: the only stability Sam remembered was Mollie's hearth, with its constant fire. Powerful as it is, to the blacks as well as to whites like Edmonds, the Beauchamp fire--"constant, steadfast"--cannot temper everyone's life. Mollie's very real physical involvement in other people's lives (caring for both the white and black babies, walking in to see Stevens out of concern over her grandson) puts her in marked contrast to Uncle Ike and his withdrawal from human involvement. As a point of comparison, too, Faulkner uses scenes of bereavement, and it is surely significant that only Rider and Mollie feel genuine grief over the loss of another person; and that only the black Eunice feels enough shame for her lover's incestuous relationship to commit suicide. Faulkner's fondness for the proud Lucas is also evident in his continuing with him as one protagonist for Intruder in the Dust, and the spirit evinced so indomitably at the conclusion of the later novel perhaps springs from Lucas' earlier surety because in his blood, black and white were in harmony (104).

Rather than reading Go Down, Moses as a number of stories somehow clustered around "The Bear," one must instead see "The Bear"--particularly with its otherwise turgid fourth section--as only another component of the total McCaslin story. Faulkner's inclusion of Part IV in the story links it with the other five episodes in this dominant theme. Even without that section, however, the reader makes the extension from Sam Fathers to the old buck and Old Ben as emblematic of the stability of wilderness (and fire and hearth); but the fourth section provides closer thematic correspondence and much more character development for Ike.

Go Down, Moses is an important book for the Faulkner canon because it gives him his first opportunity to identify how warmly he viewed the stability and tradition of the Negro culture (the same emphasis occurs a few years later as Nancy sacrifices her life to keep the Stevens' family together, and to save Temple from herself). Surely there could be no misinterpretation, reading this book; the sequence was, as Faulkner himself said, "held together by one family, the Negro and the white phase of the same family, same people."[10]

It comes as no surprise that Faulkner also dedicated Go Down, Moses to Mammy Caroline Barr. It is truly his testimony to the Negroes he loved.

Chapter Eleven

THE LAST BOOKS

In the progression of Faulkner's attitudes of which we have been speaking, his firm belief in the basic goodness of most Negroes is a constant. What comes to change is his juxtaposition of black against white. There are relatively few Negro characters in the later fiction; but even if there were, one senses that Faulkner had come to accept nobility as a condition of all mankind, regardless of color. In The Town, The Mansion, The Reivers and A Fable, essentially the same statement is repeated: "people are really kind, they really are capable of pity and compassion for the weak and orphaned and helpless."[1] And in these novels it is the ignoble or victimized white men (or women) who become protagonists--Mink Snopes, Eula and Linda Snopes, the runner and the corporal of A Fable, Miss Corrie. Faulkner's choice of protagonists seems to substantiate his comment in 1932 that a man goes through a continuum of attitudes about his fellowmen:

> There is the first stage when you believe everything and everybody is good. Then there is the second, cynical stage when you believe that no one is good. Then at last you come to realize that everyone is capable of almost anything--heroism or cowardice, tenderness or cruelty.[2]

From this third perspective, Faulkner also moved further, to finding his examples of both honor and baseness among all kinds of people. (The variety among the almost mindless executioners in A Fable is one example of Faulkner's conglomerate evil.)

He also moved further out in widening his former belief in man's power to endure. Increasingly in his late fiction, endurance alone is inadequate. As much of A Fable's dialogue implied, man must also hope; he must "believe in belief," even if his belief is only in death (33). He must

have foundation, ritual, roots. The aspersions Faulkner
casts on organized religion by having men of God commit suicide or at least question their own faith are secondary;
they are ineffectual men because they do not act--they talk.
In the comparative silence of the three women of his fable,
Faulkner shows their virtue in action--they find their half-
brother, fight off the hostile crowd, ask for and receive his
body, and take it home. The chapters devoted to them are
much less turgid than those written about the quandaries of
the general or even the runner. And Faulkner clearly gives
his comment on "honor" in the ludicrous scenes where the
general demands that the whole regiment be shot, or in his
sending a company of men to find the iron-handled cooking
spoon.

In A Fable, Faulkner uses the innocent spiritu-
alism of the peasants to stress his belief in heart over
mind, emotion over intellect. The general is suspect from
the start because he is committed to "facts" and "mind" instead of heart. The clairvoyant "idiot" Marya is treated
throughout with sympathy, and pictured as serenely noble.
Like Faulkner, Marya understands these wretched, maimed
men; and like the later Faulkner, she can still smile.

A Fable has often been criticized as being unneces-
sarily difficult in style. Perhaps it was an ill-conceived
book, which might better have been an essay. But in terms
of Faulkner's own philosophy, A Fable underlay nearly all
his later writing, particularly The Mansion and The Reivers.
The theme of society's judging a man and/or his act is here
central, in both the definition of "mutiny" and the town's reaction to the thirteen men and the three women. And the
use of the "stranger," the character who stands apart and is
consequently judged, both foreshadows later characters and
affirms Bayard Sartoris, Lucas Beauchamp, and Charles Mallison, who were all "intruders" in "man's enduring anguish
and his invincible dust" (218). Rather than being a complex
philosophical book, A Fable once again repeats Faulkner's
pervasive ideas, that man sins against other men only by using them for his own ends (293); that enduring gives one
some start in his mad but sometimes humorous race with
and for life (310); and that there is virtue in "simple unified
hope," just as there is power in the "dream of simple man"
(294). The book also includes some vivid images of life's
power to endure, in the three-legged racehorse and the half-
charred runner.

Admittedly, A Fable is one of Faulkner's weakest novels, not because of its themes or structure but rather because of the sketchiness of its characters. There are fragments of vitality, moments of drama, but for the most part Faulkner's characters are only spokesmen for their ideas (then, too, there are so many men important to the novel that we cannot know enough about them to empathize). His failure with much of A Fable makes evident the truth of Faulkner's own theory, that great characters were bound to make a great book.

In Faulkner's later fiction it might be said that there are few such great characters. The Quentin and Jason Compsons are gone, as are the Joe Christmases. Instead Faulkner is left with people who are not inherently dramatic (we have seen the way he purposely avoided letting Hightower and Bunch dominate Light in August, yet by the fifties he intentionally chooses Ratliff and Gavin Stevens as narrators). Not only are many of Faulkner's late protagonists somewhat bland, they also share many of the same qualities (can we now, then, formulate a "Faulkner hero"?)

(1) They share a strong sense of identity. Chick Mallison, Eula, Lucius Priest, Temple Drake, Mink Snopes, Ratliff, Marthe--none ever asks for help. Each makes decisions and acts on them, usually with little regard for self. They seldom if ever complain. They are unusually honest, with others and themselves. Part of Eula's (and Linda's) attraction for men, Stevens included, is that complete personal honesty.

(2) They are frequently responsible for others as well as themselves. Lucius feels his authority over Boon and Ned, the real need that he take care of them. Chick's weight of concern for family, Miss Habersham, and Lucas becomes a genuine physical burden. Marthe, at nine, is responsible for her retarded older sister and a newborn infant. Even Temple feels responsible for Gowan and Bucky, as well as Nancy. And Faulkner explains the change in Eula by the time of The Town as being one result of her caring for her child.

> she had that child. I like to think that the claim
> that the child, the helpless child ... makes on any-
> one, no matter how selfish they might have been
> .... [S]he knew that this child must be defended
> and protected.[3]

Similarly, Faulkner explained that Eula's suicide was also for Linda, "for the sake of that child."[4]

(3) They are relatively healthy mixtures of idealism and realism. Unlike Quentin, they know what life is like; yet they still work toward goals. Mink knows it will cost him his freedom and life, yet he lives to kill Flem (for his double lapse from a humane code of family honor). The young Mallison acts to exonerate Lucas, despite the opposition of family and society. The corporal's decision to die in A Fable is based not only on his idealistic belief in the protest against war, but also on his real understanding of human nature ("But what of the ten?"). As Richard Hauck describes this attitude, "a character accepts his fate and makes it the choice of his will."[5]

(4) Along with these qualities, they share the traits that Faulkner had described in Go Down, Moses as belonging to the best of hunting men: "the will and hardihood to endure and the humility and skill to survive" (191). While only the poorest of the Snopes had such primitive physical conditions to live in, each of Faulkner's later protagonists has come to realize what a jungle man has made of his civilization (see A Fable, 31), and yet has the control to laugh at himself and it. The wry humor of the later books is evidence of this attitude.

(5) The best of Faulkner's protagonists also have roots in a body of tradition, which is sometimes synonymous with the physical land. Joanna Burden's father had said it first, that "a man would have to act as the land where he was born had trained him to act."[6] Faulkner's respect for the power of community has often been noticed; in his later fiction as well he describes characters' relationships with the very land, almost as a means of explaining their behavior. The juxtaposing of the dialogue scenes in Requiem for a Nun with the descriptions of Mississippi village life and law is one example of this use of material. His exoneration of Percy Grimm; his comparison of the young convict with the forceful "old man" Mississippi River; and his aligning Harry Wilbourne with the dessicated wild palms--these stances show Faulkner's own feelings about man's rapport with nature, as also do his more obvious treatments of the theme in Big Woods and Go Down, Moses. The poignant scene in A Fable of Marthe sowing seed in her timeless "ritual" also establishes the tranquil tone of the novel's conclusion (the corporal too had been a "natural" farmer). Again, Faulkner's

reverence for the hunt--like Hemingway's--derives chiefly
from the fact that it was also a ritual (indeed, the ritual
gave it the only meaning it had), "the best game of all,"
"the ancient and unremitting contest according to the ancient
and immitigable rules."[7]

This identification with the land, especially in Faulkner's last writing, appears to transcend even the inherent
bond within families. The tie of father and son, and mother
and child, which Faulkner had used in nearly every novel,
comes to be of secondary importance. Perhaps this shift occurred partly because many of the later protagonists were in
themselves childless--Ratliff, Gavin, Marthe, Miss Reba--or
were themselves children; perhaps because Faulkner had realized that it was truly an unnatural person who did not sacrifice for his own child.

A more dramatic situation, therefore, was sacrificing
for mankind in general. In a closing image of A Fable, he
quite directly has Marthe move from her sorrow as a be-
reaved mother (her role as older half-sister) to that as a
partner of the land:

> France, England, America too by now probably were
> full of women who had given the lives of their sons
> to defend their countries and preserve justice and
> right: who was she to demand uniqueness for
> grieving? He was right: it was the farm, the land
> which was immune even to the blast and sear of
> war. It would take work, of course, it might even
> take years of work.... [T]heir palliation and their
> luck was the work they faced.... More still: re-
> storing the land would not only palliate the grief,
> the miniscule integer of the farm would affirm that
> he had not died for nothing and that it was not for
> an outrage that they grieved, but for simple grief:
> the only alternative to which was nothing, and be-
> tween grief and nothing only the coward takes noth-
> ing [349-350].

The repudiation of peace and tranquility as man's natural condition is once again set against the more normal connotation
of grief--something to be avoided. But change and motion
bring death and a natural grief, and only the land, finally,
endures, except in the memories of other human beings. The
characters Faulkner chose to immortalize in his writing are
generally the "memorable" ones, whether memorable for

noble acts, evil ones, or foolhardy ones. They are those
who move just a cut out of the beaten traces, if only for
an instant. Legends grow around acts, never around rhetoric.

Similar as Faulkner's later protagonists are, no
reader would deny that there is a great difference between
the effect of A Fable and the other books published during
the ten years he was writing it (Intruder in the Dust and
Requiem for a Nun) and the last three books, The Town,
The Mansion, and The Reivers. Once again, the difference
results not from any change (or even modification) in
themes, but from Faulkner's method in handling his materials.

The heavy seriousness of A Fable is reflected in not
only the many allegorical elements, but also in the set
pieces of dialogue among characters whom we see only as
spokesmen for ideas, never as normal, living people; and in
the unusually cumbersome style. Nowhere does Faulkner use
the balanced sentence, complete with colon and antithetical
element, so frequently as here. Though having more narrative focus and plot, Intruder in the Dust and Requiem for a
Nun are similarly marred by the staged pseudo philosophical
dialogue. Even though Gavin Stevens, the man chiefly responsible for the circumlocution in these two books, is central also to The Town and The Mansion, Faulkner has under-
cut Stevens' ponderous tone by using multiple narrators--and
of these, V. K. Ratliff in himself is able to change the solemn tone. By using Ratliff's cool and earthy sarcasm,
Faulkner gains both a seeming objectivity and humor. And
because Ratliff is by trade a story teller (one who farms not
land but people), he can include many more "stories" in the
fabric of the novel. Even though most of the stories told do
relate thematically to the books, they shift texture and tone,
and often provide outright comedy. In short, the presence
of the novel differs tremendously. Quentin Compson no longer shadows the scene, weighted down with his flat irons.
Instead Ratliff picks his teeth.

The later novels also represent a turn back to Faulkner's earlier methods, of letting the concrete scene or episode present its own meaning, without the paraphrasing comment of an omniscient narrator. It is interesting that in A
Fable Faulkner used several apparent "objective correlatives"
--the locket, the basket, the burning coat, the spoon--with-
out creating any of the sense of immediacy one supposes he

was after. Yet by the time of The Reivers, he trusts the entire novel to one episode, told without allegory; in itself, entire, an objective representation of the progress to honor.

The structural and tonal simplicity of the last books has already been well defended by Millgate in his 1967 essay, when he claims that "Faulkner may have felt in writing the more conventional of his final novels that he had in fact found not a retreat or a respite from, but actually an answer to, those very problems which had earlier led him into more evidently adventurous paths."[8] His use of multiple narrators does create the sense of man in relation to other men, just as his emphasis on town and the spirit of the land makes impossible viewing a character as isolated. Millgate concludes,

> one has to see Faulkner's major emphasis [particularly in these late novels] as falling not so much on the individual in isolation as on the individual in his relation to other human beings. Faulkner, indeed, seems 'traditional,' rather than 'modern,' in his insistence on questions of right conduct, and it might well be argued that the major themes in his work, taken as a whole, are essentially social in character [191].

It must also be considered, in studying Faulkner's later novels, that these books were written less often from the single anecdote or interesting character approach than from a sense of commitment to a project. Of the Snopes trilogy, Faulkner said that he had "thought of the whole story [all three books] at once like a bolt of lightning lights up a landscape and you see everything but it takes time to write it, and this story I had in my mind for about thirty years."[9] Faulkner admits feeling a great urgency to finish his trilogy.

Internal evidence suggests too that Faulkner's art had shifted a little from being an almost completely lyric process to relying on a greater variety of sources. The truth of Faulkner's comment about his use of other books for stylistic studies as well as plots and characters is evident particularly in his fiction from the mid-thirties on (see Appendix III).

THE LAST BOOKS

Several entire books have been written about Faulkner's trilogy, and rightfully so. The Hamlet, The Town, and The Mansion provide remarkably apt conclusions to (or extensions of) several of Faulkner's major themes throughout his writing. They also, in their various arrangements of structure and point of view, enable him to re-create the seething ferment of the rich Mississippi life. And they too provide a stage to display fully his favorite character, Ratliff.

Considering that the Snopes trilogy had been conceived in 1925, and The Mansion was not published until 1959, one might be tempted to venerate Faulkner's total accomplishment on purely a time basis (the comparison between Mink's waiting thirty-eight years to finish his task, and Faulkner's thirty-odd years in progress might well be made). The Hamlet does contain the wry and wily Ratliff, the magnificent Eula, the unbelievably shrewd Flem, and the general milieu. However, there are crucial changes in these three characters before the next two books of the trilogy: Ratliff grows more benevolent. The egotism which causes him to compete against Flem has mellowed (Mrs. Littlejohn first questions Ratliff's motives when he interferes with Ike). By The Town, Ratliff has become protector, not avenger. Flem too goes through several stages as his education progresses, the most reprehensible being his fanatical respectability. Eula's death and De Spain's leaving town both result from Flem's use of the Christian ethic, convenient for the first time in his eighteen years of cuckoldry. The greatest change in these three characters, however, occurs in Eula Varner Snopes. In The Hamlet she takes on the bovine qualities of Lena Grove; her sensuality so dominates her character that the reader is aware of no other trait. By the time of The Town, however, Eula has become a discrete and loving woman, sacrificing happiness with the man she loves to keep her daughter's life pleasant. Unlike the suicide of Quentin Compson, Eula's suicide represents complete abnegation of self, as Faulkner shows so well in her last meeting with Stevens, where Eula does not in any way suggest what she plans. She asks for no pity, no admiration, no help. Eula--and Linda after her--epitomize Faulkner's women: aware and self-reliant, they see life truly and see it whole. Their acts cut through the words that surround them.

Were the Snopes trilogy simply the execution of Flem
Snopes' rise to wealth and respectability, it would be a
comparatively slight story, of interest only for its comic or
regional elements. But, under the apparent guise of describing the Snopes' progression, Faulkner has again por-
trayed his two compelling themes--that a man will endure
anything, if his purpose is strong enough; and that a woman
will suffer anything, if her love is great enough. The
abundance of satisfying man-woman relationships in the trilogy (not the least of them being between Ratliff and Valli-
nova) makes it one of Faulkner's most optimistic panoramas,
yet the basic conflict for at least two of the books is the
timeless theme of man's education at the hands of women.
Gavin Stevens becomes Faulkner's protagonist, and for good
reason--all of life, all of humanity (and especially Eula and
Linda) is a cause of wonderment to him. Hauck describes
him as "the character who best articulates the common values of the educated readers of Faulkner ... Stevens is a
hopeless failure when it comes to evaluating situations and
deciding on courses of action that will with any certainty
prove 'moral.' "10

Yet, Stevens is likeable. He is without vanity, is
not puffed up; he too loves. His naiveté alone would be unbelievable (it would also pose some narrative problems), so
Faulkner involves as co-narrators Stevens' nephew Chick
Mallison (whom he had admired so thoroughly in Intruder)
and the eternally beloved Ratliff. Chick's view provides the
direct impressions of a boy; Gavin Stevens', in contrast,
seems further from direct action. Speech gets in his way.
Correspondingly, Faulkner uses Ratliff to show that it is not
Gavin's age--since he and Ratliff are nearly the same--so
much as his stance toward reality that is askew. There is
too much courtly gentleman in Stevens, too much tendency
to prove, always logically, that the best will happen. Stevens seems to represent the whole energy of hope, always
blithely expecting the best. So important is Stevens to The
Town and The Mansion--in his self-designated role of protector of the town--that the trilogy might better have been
labeled "The Education of Gavin Stevens."

In fact, within the three books Faulkner has provided
for numerous educations. The Hamlet is the story, primarily, of Ratliff's. Doomed to match wits with Flem throughout his career, Ratliff first takes on the task of matching
and, hence, containing Flem because of his affection for the
Varners. But the contest becomes one of simple pride; and

then, later, one of genuine responsibility for others. In an early scene, Ratliff first cajoles and then warns the men of Frenchman's Bend (see page 223). On the occasion of the Texas horse sale, he suffers terribly when Flem refuses Mrs. Armstid her $5--but at the same time he denies his complete involvement to Bookwright (the only character who has consistently been with or ahead of Ratliff during the novel). By the time of The Town, he and Stevens have made a pact, that they together will hold the town against the Snopes; and the victory at the end of The Mansion is that, ironically and with Flem's own help as he tries to attain an image of respectability, they have done just that. The seemingly pessimistic ending of The Hamlet, in which Flem has bested both Bookwright and Ratliff and so moves on to better worlds, has truly been only an interim. (By finding gullible buyers for the Frenchman's Place, Flem has also alienated himself from Will Varner; and so is in a much weaker position than he was as Will's apprentice.) And as Hauck points out, of Ratliff and others, "Most of the characters who are fooled in The Hamlet are not deceived by an opponent's ploy. They are almost invariably deceived in the way Jody is: by the machinations of their own imagination" (182). By the end of the trilogy, human kindness has, at long last, triumphed over the use, and misuse, of other men and women. But in the meanwhile, Stevens, under Ratliff's tutelage, has found his own way of understanding; and in the constant counterpoint of Ratliff and Stevens, Faulkner has picked up and elaborated Addie Bundren's maxim about words. Ratliff is a great man, a great student of humanity, because he is a listener. Stevens is--or, unfortunately, becomes--another great Southern talker.

Admittedly, as is now common knowledge, Faulkner was trying very hard to incorporate the typically Southwestern humor stories into The Hamlet. Pat Stamper, the wild Texas horses, the whole Houston story--these episodes are truly a story teller's dream, and yet to make of them a successive novel was difficult. So Faulkner had to establish continuing characters to observe and in some cases tell the random stories: the greatness of the Snopes trilogy lies at least partly in the authenticity of these characters, Ratliff and Flem in all three books; Chick Mallison and Stevens in the latter two.

Another sort of greatness lies in the fact that Faulkner was once again able to choose the best narrative method for conveying various parts of the trilogy, and not necessarily the same narrative method for each novel.

The Town has the simplest structure. As both Stephen Mooney and Millgate have pointed out, the juxtaposing of the three story tellers--Mallison, Ratliff, and Stevens--enables Faulkner to create a sense of the town itself.[11] In these three Faulkner gives us the sedate conservative upperclass with the earthy peasant voice, and the uninitiated young boy, the latter meant, so Faulkner says, to represent the comparatively naive town itself ("So when I say 'we' and 'we thought' what I mean is Jefferson and what Jefferson thought," page 3). In a technique which combines the titled As I Lay Dying sections with the questioning monologues of Absalom, Faulkner manages to involve the reader as well as include great amounts of material from both present happenings and past. A new sense of continuity evolves too out of the semblance of interrupted dialogue which Faulkner gives by having one narrator answer or repeat what the previous narrator had said as conclusion--each of the three thus seems to be continuously involved in the main story being told, here, Flem's unscrupulous quest for respectability, and Eula's resulting death.

Faulkner has here used the device of having Charles Mallison narrate not only the opening and closing chapters, but also some of the most emotional sections, so that his comparatively unaware view might come closer to objectivity. Again characteristic of Faulkner, many of the Stevens' episodes are of little use so far as fact is concerned; for Stevens' logical deductions and pages of ratiocination only deter the story. Even while we come to know Stevens intimately, we react at times like Ratliff with his "No no, no no, no no. He was wrong. He's a lawyer, and to a lawyer, if it ain't complicated ... you don't believe it" (296).

The Mansion continues this three-way narration in only one of its three books, the second, "Linda," which is really an extension of the Eula story from The Town. Here Faulkner's method works for the same reasons it did in The Town: it is important that we see Stevens' rationalizations, both through his own eyes and those of the two men who have the most compassion for him.

In Book I of The Mansion Faulkner tries his best to re-create Mink Snopes in a first-person narrating role. Important as this presentation is to our understanding of Mink, and any eventual sympathy with him, the voice which results may not be much different from that of Tull or even, in places, of Ratliff himself. Faulkner does give Mink earthier descriptions of women than any other of his characters, and his simple trust in <u>They</u>, a kind of Greek Fate, also comes through well. Book I, "Mink," opens with two chapters narrated by Mink, and closes with one; in between is one section given to Ratliff and another told by Montgomery Ward Snopes, interesting in that this inside look at the Snopes clan by another Snopes points up the great differences in the men of the clan, [12] as well as--by comparison with Montgomery Ward--elevating the much simpler (and prouder) Mink.

But with the concluding book, the story of Flem, Faulkner goes back to an omniscient (and unnamed) narrator. As he had in <u>The Sound and the Fury</u>, Faulkner did not presume to make Ratliff an extra-conscious observer. No longer was the dodge of a "different" mind, like that of Darl or Vardaman or Benjy, necessary. The greatest of all omniscient narrators, Faulkner himself, was willing to become involved in this story. He points morals. He has compassion for all his characters. He backs and fills so that he can tell stories as yet unheard, and at times slows the book a bit too much. But because he moves from Mink to Linda to Flem and Gavin and Ratliff, he must be omniscient. So <u>The Mansion</u> ends with the same method Faulkner has used throughout <u>The Hamlet,</u> and once again for the same reason, there were too many fragments of tales, too much material to be included easily as being the experiences of a single narrator.

The structural problem in the Snopes' trilogy--unlike that of <u>The Reivers</u>--was simply too great a quantity of plots, people, and themes. As Faulkner himself discussed it,

> Unless a book follows a simple direct line such as
> a story of adventure, it becomes a series of
> pieces. It's a good deal like dressing a showcase
> window. It takes a certain amount of judgment and
> taste to arrange the different pieces in the most ef-
> fective place in juxtaposition to one another. [13]

Arranging the pieces is the problem that Faulkner met and solved so well in <u>The Hamlet.</u> Because it is so simply Ratliff's story, there is no need for the subtle shifts in view point of <u>The Town</u>. But because Faulkner includes so many stories which are almost uniformly more colorful than Ratliff's own life or part in them, he must structurally emphasize Ratliff. The book opens with Flem's trading a job in Varner's store for his ambivalent protection against his barnburning father. But immediately Faulkner involves Ratliff,

the shrewd observer, who even in this initial stage of Snopes
infiltration, is "not laughing" (15).   By page 28 Ratliff has
himself established the contest, to see which man--he or
Flem--is a worthy counterpart to Will Varner (the refrain,
"That ain't been proved yet," recurs throughout the novel).
As the chapters move ahead, filled with the anecdote and
episode Faulkner's unnamed narrator tells so well, Ratliff's
motivation for his contest with Flem is justified further.
Ratliff asks Tull.

> 'Ain't none of you folks out there done nothing
> about it?' ...
> 'What could we do?' Tull said.   'It ain't right.
> But it ain't none of our business.'
> 'I believe I would think of something if I lived
> there,' Ratliff said.
> 'Yes,' Bookwright said.... 'And wind up with
> one of them bow ties in place of your buckboard
> and team' [72].

Faulkner has early positioned Ratliff as the avenger and
Bookwright as the man of caution.   He returns to Ratliff's role later in Part 2 of Chapter II, with Ratliff--
already bested by Flem's use of the idiot Ike--repeating his
challenge, followed by that quintessential statement of what
he has already learned about the Snopes:

> I just never went far enough, he thought.   I quit
> too soon.   I went as far as one Snopes will set
> fire to another Snopes's barn and both Snopeses
> know it, and that was all right.   But I stopped
> there.   I never went on to where that first Snopes
> will turn around and stomp the fire out so he can
> sue that second Snopes for the reward and both
> Snopeses know that too [89].

The understood ethics of the human race are not the
ethics of Flem Snopes (although they are of Eck, Wallstreet
Panic, and some of the younger Snopes).   The story of "the
usurpation of an heirship" continues, with Flem arriving by
the end of Book I on the very throne where Will Varner had
begun the novel.   The symbolic "rise" has already been ac-
complished in ninety-two pages; what gives the novel its interest is not the factual plot line--we know Flem is indomit-
able--but rather Faulkner's embroidery and extension of those
facts.   The story telling itself in The Hamlet is superbly
timed, filled with rich detail and character.   Yet the real

strength of the novel is the way Faulkner extends Flem's comparatively simple acts of chicanery, to use them--and the town's reactions to them--to explore man's social conscious-ness (and hence his humanity) thoroughly. The tension be-tween Flem's amoral acts and Ratliff's reactions to them is the heart of the book. Each episode of The Hamlet empha-sizes that tension.

Book II, devoted as it is to Eula Varner's story, is the least obviously related section of the novel. Ratliff is the implicit on-looker and admirer, although his lusty bach-elorhood has been confirmed several places before. He mourns for the waste of Eula on Flem (Venus and the crip-pled Vulcan), but the length of Book II may be questioned in the context of The Hamlet. It can, however, be justified in relation to The Town, where Eula's fidelity to De Spain and her sacrificial suicide dominate the plot. Faulkner seems to realize that he needs to make explicit the relationship between Flem's acquiring Eula and his battle with Ratliff, for he closes "Eula" with the surreal scene of Flem being given an-other throne, having this time vanquished the Devil. So armed with a beautifully sensual wife, Faulkner implies, Flem will be unbeatable. Again, Flem's trading on Eula's infidelity eighteen years later bears out this assumption.

Book III of The Hamlet returns us to Ratliff's more direct involvement, with his reaction to Eula's marriage, and her dowry. That Flem had been given The Old Frenchman's Place in payment for taking Eula only reaffirmed Ratliff's be-lief that the property had value. The rest of the novel builds to his own purchase of the salted land, his final lesson from Flem, that even his trust in Will Varner was mistaken. From the end of The Hamlet through the next two books, Rat-liff goes it alone. He has earned the right to.

In the same way, Lucius Priest goes through his in-itiation in The Reivers. Indeed, it is as if Faulkner had felt the need to simplify. In this novel he leaves the confusion of the Snopes tribe and the allegory of A Fable and turns once again to the McCaslin family; he uses a single episode instead of the composite of adventures. The themes, how-ever, are the same. Lucius learns how to endure, and--more positively--to cope, to meet whatever conditions exist, not just to suffer them but to use them to his own advantage. Faulkner here defines intelligence as "the ability to cope with environment ... to accept environment yet still retain at least something of personal liberty."14 Just as he uses the mule as the natural image for a body "still free, still cop-ing," so the acts of Ned McCaslin, Lucius, and--in a more limited way--Boon Hogganbeck all reflect that spirit.

Ever since Faulkner made his now-famous statement that he was going to write his golden book and then break the pencil, critics have been trying to locate such an encompass-ing collection. It was unfortunate in many ways that Faulk-ner's death followed so closely the 1962 publication of The Reivers, for it became his last novel perhaps unintentionally. In critical opinion, The Reivers was a slight book, further evidence of what was taken to be Faulkner's slower momen-tum already evident in The Town and The Mansion. Although many writers have now defended the book, few seem to be-lieve that Faulkner had fulfilled his aim, that The Reivers was "the golden book of Yoknapatawpha County." Internal evidence, however, suggests that it was; and that Faulkner clearly intended it to be (and see Appendix III).

The story, as in Go Down, Moses, centers on the various branches of the McCaslin family, with the laurels almost evenly divided between Ned and Lucius, the latter be-cause he realized the race had become more important than his own Virtue; the former because his whole seemingly wild exploit was undertaken to save Bobo Beauchamp, his kinsman. As Faulkner described Ned's herculean efforts during those long sleepless days,

> Ned had carried the load alone, held back the
> flood, shored up the crumbling levee with whatever
> tools he could reach--including me [Lucius]--until
> they broke in his hand [304].

Under stress, or perhaps one might more accurately say, given a purpose, Ned sheds his lazy nigger façade and be-comes another Ratliff figure, capable of using cajolery, guile, and just plain trickery to serve his ends. He quickly allies himself with Miss Reba (and in this novel she too is a paragon of shrewdness and compassion).

Faulkner further develops the admirable traits of the black culture by first juxtaposing the dignity of Uncle Par-sham Hood with the mean Butch and the foolish Boon; and in a more impressive scene, by using Parsham as Lucius' pro-tector and bedfellow. Lucius' continual references to his grandfather whenever he speaks of Uncle Parsham reinforce the implied comparison: Lucius feels a kinship with Uncle

Parsham; he has only hatred for the crude Butch, and in at least one instance for the equally violent Boon.

Lucius venerates not only the stability of the black culture but also its ethics. (As Faulkner presents it, Uncle Parsham maintains his dignity at least partly because his culture allows him, expects him to be dignified.) The traditions of human relationships are once again at the heart of the novel. Lucius continuously compares his own actions with an abstract code of behavior (similarly, Otis' role in the book is to remind everyone how base an adolescent really can be; by comparison with Otis, Lucius seems hardly to have erred at all). So conscious is Lucius of the justification for his acts (not stealing the car, but the acts after Ned had brought the horse) that when his father is about to whip him, he can decide for himself

> If after all the lying and deceiving and disobeying and conniving I had done, all he could do about it was to whip me, then Father was not good enough for me. And if all that I had done was balanced by no more than that shaving strop, then both of us were debased [301].

The grandeur that touched Lucius' exploits and his learning, about both Virtue and Non-Virtue, stemmed partly from the common recognition that men are "the poor frail victims of being alive" (174), and that as such victims they could still be such indomitable characters. The sheer physical endurance of Ned, Boon, and Lucius is admirable, but one must add to it various skills, mental agility, and most of all compassion. As Lucius comes sadly to recognize, situations like Miss Corrie's, and mentalities like Butch's, are a part of life; but life need not mirror only the crudities:

> ... hated myself for listening, having to hear about it, learn about it, know about it; hating that such not only was, but must be, had to be if life was to continue and mankind be a part of it [174].

Much like Chick Mallison in Intruder in the Dust and The Town, Lucius Priest also gains an initiation into the most humane level of experience, that order which teaches a man that he can bear anything and also that he can never judge another human being. All the play on the word whore, spoken or unspoken, in The Reivers only points to the distinction Faulkner makes repeatedly, in nearly every episode--

that the "wrong" people, those who are not operating under the moral social code (Corrie and Reba in their promiscuity; Boon, Ned, and Lucius in their various thefts) are the virtuous. Using the timeless dichotomy of virgin and whore to objectify the distinction, Faulkner proceeds to question justice in the abstract, and to condemn all of those (including his readers) who have judged Ned before they know why he was involved in the horse race (here again Faulkner relies on his familiar technique of withholding information from both readers and characters).

The questioning of absolute terminology is reflected in the title itself. Just as The Reivers suggests robbery and plunder, so it also may imply a judicious escape, as in Soldiers' Pay Faulkner had used the verb. On the one hand, viewed factually, Ned, Boon, and Lucius were criminals, guilty on at least two major counts; yet by their acts they were saving Bobo from a life of terror and perhaps even death at the hands of an extortioner. Elsewhere in Faulkner's novels, and here too in the persona of Butch, we have seen the summary though always factual ministration of the orthodox law; like Faulkner, we now view it as something to work around instead of with. But more frightening than the legal procedures proper is the social code that condemns people with no understanding of their circumstances, that accepts the one-word label, like whore or thief or black, as the total character.

In the same way, even the terms Virtue and Non-Virtue, which Lucius bandies about in the opening of the novel, may be open to question. For Faulkner shows through the progress of the novel that people respond not to verbal abstractions but to other people: Corrie decides to become an honest woman not because she hates the sound of the word whore but because she wants Lucius to think well of her. And Lucius similarly behaves as he does tangential to not only Corrie but Uncle Parsham, Lycurgus, and Ned. Initiation, education--all man's learning can be only a humane process; as Ackerman said to Goethe, "One learns only from those one loves." For finally, The Reivers is Faulkner's definition of love, his concrete representation for that state of a man's heart once he realizes "you don't love because: you love despite; not for the virtues, but despite the faults."[15] Faulkner has brought us full circle: Margaret Power's selfless giving of her womanness in Soldiers' Pay is scarcely different from Miss Corrie's similarly physical sacrifice in The Reivers. What has changed is that Faulkner has himself grown from being an adequate story narrator to "a master of deliberately ambivalent serious humor."16

Chapter Twelve

"THE END OF SOMETHING"

And so Faulkner evolves, not so terribly different a person than he was when he began writing--a gentle, compassionate man, able to draw superbly human characters whom he is also able to love no matter what they are capable of doing. Faulkner's is not a judgmental attitude because he appreciates every person, not only the great ones.

Compassionate men are not, however, always great writers. In order to become successful fiction, the large vision of the man of empathy must be shaped and timed to tell a moving story effectively. No writer of this century created better-crafted novels than Faulkner; but Hemingway ran a close second. The power of economical writing, the countless successes of le mot juste: the novel as the New Form of Conrad and Ford's dream became a reality through the writing of Hemingway and Faulkner. Jay B. Hubbell, in his recent Who Are the Major American Writers? points out that interest in these two writers is higher now (1972) than in any other American authors. [1] David Pownall notes in his bibliography of critical essays published during the past fifteen years, over seven hundred essays on Faulkner, five hundred on Hemingway (and another five hundred on Joyce). [2] We have only to consider that each man won the Nobel prize twenty years ago (ten years before their respective deaths) to gauge the international impact of this writing.

The position of Faulkner and Hemingway seems incontrovertible (as Hubbell notes, fully aware of how fragile literary reputations in America are, "Perhaps we can now be sure that Frost, Eliot, Faulkner, and Hemingway belong in the rare company of Melville, Thoreau, Emily Dickinson, Henry James, and Mark Twain" [337]). Yet there are signs that contemporary fiction writers are restless. Hemingway's philosophy of life already has cost him readers in this generation (the stoic acceptance of life as it is, with man existing only to meet it, jars at least obliquely with the

watchword of "seize the day"). But a more significant kind
of reaction is that to technique. The surreal elements, the
comedy, the fast tempo and sometimes senseless activity of,
particularly, the Black Humorists like Pynchon, Heller and
Vonnegut seem to represent a turning away from the concept
of the well-made novel as the zenith of narrative method.
Arthur Mizener recently pointed out that "the fundamental
purpose of a fiction--to evoke a particular emotion--and its
means--a set of carefully selected concrete particulars" have
been the same for both poetry and fiction of this century.
But as Mizener continues, parenthetically,

> This theory of literature has dominated the twenti-
> eth century; whether it is true or not may be a
> question.[3]

The interest in Norman Mailer's journalism, or Truman Capote's re-creation of "fact," also presumes a different method of shaping external realities into story. And the writers
of "silence" like Samuel Beckett and Camus, though extending Hemingway's natural emphasis, also suggest different
methods of evoking responses. The novelistic theory of
Robbe-Grillet; the books of Butor and Marguerite Duras may
suggest great changes from practices in modern American fiction. W. M. Frohock suggests, however, that even these
writers have been greatly influenced by Faulkner, particularly in his withholding of information and his reliance on
myth.[4] And Robert Humphrey maintains that, had it not
been for Faulkner's use of stream of consciousness, the
technique might well have remained esoteric. But Faulkner
combined the method with "significant external action," plot,
and therefore enabled stream of consciousness to enter the
mainstream of fiction.[5]

Because of Faulkner's awesome variety, in both subject and technique, he seems less likely to be trapped by
changes in the direction of future fiction, even if those
changes are radical. The black humor characters may have
had their antecedents in the behavior and language patterns
of Jason Compson and Jewel Bundren; surreal elements were
represented frequently in Faulkner's stream of consciousness
scenes, or such places as Chick Mallison's watching the
people stream out of town; or Joe Christmas' remembering
his buttons; or Quentin's breaking his watch. Man's role as
singular and alienated was perhaps presented first, not by
Camus in The Stranger but by Faulkner in Sartoris (and the
affinities between Meursault and Bayard may be one reason

Camus himself produced the play version of <u>Requiem for a Nun</u>).

Because of his versatility, then, in some ways Faulkner's accomplishment seems further reaching than that of Hemingway. Hemingway's writing, however, perfectly shaped as it is, reaches the reader more quickly, with little loss of effect no matter on what level it is read. In Hemingway's fiction, the hawk remains a hawk: literal levels are sometimes as satisfying as the effects he achieves with his "fifth dimension" prose. And for the hurried modern reader, Hemingway's pace may be more suitable than Faulkner's. Endurance in modern American letters may in the long run depend on readability.

Stylistically, no reader can fault Hemingway. As Ford Madox Ford wrote in his preface to <u>A Farewell to Arms</u>,

> Hemingway's words strike you, each one, as if they were pebbles.... They live and shine, each in its place.... The aim, the achievement of the great prose-writer is to use words so that they shall seem new and alive because of their juxtaposition with other words. [6]

Hemingway himself was delighted with this emphasis. As he wrote in 1961, "From my very first novel ... I never for a moment doubted that I was the pioneer of a new era."[7] And, regarding his literary reputation, "the public has always tended to exaggerate my importance--and underestimate my significance."[8]

As craftsman, Hemingway broke the wood of artificial prose into an immediately dynamic, yet suggestive, medium.[9] To retain the effect of simplicity and ease while writing so capably about love and death, and man's identity in relation to each, was never easy; and as we have seen, critics often misinterpreted the very effects he was struggling to achieve. But as Mark Schorer wrote in 1954, Hemingway has been responsible for writing "the very finest prose of our time. And most of it is poetry."[10]

If we can accept Hemingway as the lyric poet of American fiction, then we must not malign him for that other characteristic of the lyric poet--the use of self and personal emotion as subject, the tendency to create evocations of

mood instead of adventure stories, and the necessity to repeat themes when one's vision remains stable. Robert Penn
Warren speaks to this quality in Hemingway:

> he is essentially a lyric rather than a dramatic
> writer, and for the lyric writer virtue depends up-
> on the intensity with which the vision is rendered
> rather than upon the creation of a variety of char-
> acters whose visions are in conflict among them-
> selves....
>   Hemingway is a peculiarly personal writer, and
> for all his apparent objectivity ..., his work, to
> an uncommon degree, forms a continuous whole.[11]

Warren's point was substantiated with the publication of The
Old Man and the Sea, the novel that paralleled The Sun Also
Rises in so many ways, even structurally. With critical attention focused on Santiago, many readers thought they had
found a new direction to Hemingway's philosophy, but only his
cast of characters had changed. As Joseph Waldmeir wrote,
the work was very much a part of the Hemingway canon,
based as it was--and as his other novels had been--on Hemingway's "Religion of Man." As Waldmeir said emphatically,
"Hemingway did not turn religious to write The Old Man and
the Sea. He has always been religious."[12]

   Even this perspective, finding the unified vision
throughout Hemingway's work, had its negative side. The
concept of Hemingway as having one or two basic ideas was
a popular one, and usually damning. But Warren continues,
"The history of literature seems to show that good artists
may have very few basic ideas.... [T]he ideas of the artist
are grand simply because they are intensely felt, intensely
realized." Anaïs Nin agrees that the lyric vision has this
strength of intensity, is "closer to the laser light, more intense, more effective, and the reaches of its intensity are
concentrated."[13]

   Had Hemingway lived to complete his trilogy--the land,
sea, and air novels--perhaps he might have outdistanced all
of these objections. For an epic poet creates a broad canvas, and usually a more varied one. It seems likely that
Hemingway the lyric writer might well have become Hemingway the epic poet (and perhaps he did reach that category in
writing For Whom the Bell Tolls), had his own fates been
willing. As it was, he became America's greatest lyric
writer, whose "significance" is apparent wherever fiction is
written, or read.

To Faulkner instead went the designation of "epic writer." Both Valéry Larbaud and André Malraux used the term early in the thirties,[14] and established the range for Faulkner's vivid story telling, marked with its own kind of subtlety, and effecting its own kind of quiet resolution. Because Faulkner's range is so broad, and his characters are so numerous, his perspective appears to be more objective; he seldom sacrifices one character to the glory of another. Consequently, we tend to believe his impartiality, his pose as "only" a story teller.

While many of the same points can easily be made about Hemingway's and Faulkner's fiction, there are these important differences, and others. Since Faulkner is less the lyric poet and more the epic story teller, his style reflects his overall structural pattern. Consequently, while Hemingway could create the central image for an entire fiction in a single paragraph, Faulkner took much more time, and space. His stories came to mean chiefly through the telling, and usually <u>only</u> through the entire telling. One can excerpt from Hemingway's fiction, but doing so with Faulkner's is usually unsatisfactory. Part of the difficulty lies with what Frank Baldanza sees as Faulkner's giving syntax "a dominating rhythmic importance," a rhythm which serves to hold the reader within a "vibrant continuum whose dimensions and textures and climate are as rigidly controlled as they are vividly evoked."[15] Amazing as it seems, Faulkner's writing in its complete forms can be justified in a word-by-word analysis, just as can Hemingway's despite the many long and complex sentences. One is reminded of Pound's very apt comment about Henry James,

> he is seldom or never involved when a direct bald statement will accurately convey his own meaning, <u>all</u> of it. He is not usually, for all his wide leisure, verbose.[16]

The application to Faulkner's writing is evident.

There also seems to be an important difference in each man's attitude toward his readers. In one sense, Faulkner shares more with his listeners/readers. His protagonists are seldom completely formed; they are often in a state of becoming, and the experiences of the fiction are the very experiences that form their lives. (Hemingway's characters are more frequently already set, and the experiences show only how firmly directed they are.) As Richard Adams phrases it, Faulkner (like Hawthorne) repeatedly emphasizes the theme of "individual development.... The point of the best fiction generally turns on the protagonist's development into maturity [regardless of age]. The outcome of the typical crisis depends on the ability of the central character ... to accept, assimilate, and exercise the responsibilities of a father of a family and a grown-up citizen in a community."[17]

Because Faulkner's focus is often the process itself, his narrative method often enables him to trace subtle changes in the persona's attitude, even while he is telling the often dramatic events that precipitate the maturity in question. Important as the concern is to style, Van Nostrand sees it as also modifying Faulkner's use of myth. Faulkner seldom used any myth entire, in its usual version; he instead used it to show "the way the character had to act out his personal version of it," and it is this "tortuous cerebral process" that dominates Faulkner's fiction. Faulkner's poetry, continues Van Nostrand, lies in the various and distorted repetition of fragments, a process which continues until a new, whole realization of one's self emerges."[18]

This kind of interest leads to not only differences in method, but also to what Michel Gresset sees as, thematically, a "conservative" order of the world. Faulkner's county very simply "rests on the individual and on the family and on the community, in a progressive opening up to the cosmos."[19] In contrast, Hemingway's world, more often, rests only on the individual. One of Faulkner's primary themes, therefore, becomes a man's responsibility to other men, whereas for Hemingway, man's responsibility frequently is directed mainly toward himself. Consequently, we tend to think of the "Hemingway hero" as being quintessential in the fiction; while with Faulkner we think more often of a variously peopled world. The mirror is wider; it catches us in more postures, and seems to reflect more clearly.

Whatever their eventual reach, in their interest in craft, Hemingway and Faulkner consistently echo each other. This comment was made regarding a poem which was heavily rhetorical:

> Put the passion in it, but sit on the passion. Don't try to say to the reader what you want to say, but make him say it to himself _for_ you.[20]

The speaker this time was Faulkner, but it could well have been Hemingway, or Pound. For all three recognized the necessity for the concrete, the scene or detail that brought an abstraction to life, that affirmed again and again that " 'Language is just the smoke that rolls away from what a man has done.' "[21] Faulkner mistrusted "rhetoric" just as Hemingway mistrusted "tricks." And, as we have seen, each man did respect the other, because for each, writing was his reason for living. As Ray B. West concluded twenty years ago,

> The twentieth century called for revaluation, for a re-examination of the moral and aesthetic principles upon which both American life and American art had been established. Ernest Hemingway and William Faulkner, each in his own way, represent the vanguard of such revaluation in American fiction; and, different though they may seem in many ways, their similarities outweigh the differences. If it becomes increasingly difficult to see them as experimenters--as the avant-garde, it is above all because their values have become accepted and incorporated into one tradition.[22]

Contemporary American fiction. Projected forward, hurled, by a few Nick Adams stories, three virtuoso interior monologues, an old man with bleeding hands--all shaped with the deft caress of the great writer. For Faulkner, his efforts reached into mythic patterns; for Hemingway, his writing brought to life many poignantly memorable characters. And there is no question that both Hemingway and Faulkner wrote to lead their readers to an honest vision, a situation that attempted to evoke a feeling of the real world, somehow ordered and shaped, but never frozen. For both, the craft of writing became the means to understand their confusing worlds. And for Faulkner, it also became the means to love.

Appendix I

HEMINGWAY AS POET

What is perhaps most interesting about Hemingway's poems is not so much their quality but their chronology. Hemingway wrote poems, apparently, throughout his life, most frequently in his Paris days and earlier, and then again after World War II; but also during the later twenties and thirties. As Philip Young mentioned in his inventory of the Hemingway manuscripts, "more than once the author announced that he intended to bring out a book of poems."[1]

Hemingway's earliest poems prove conclusively that he knew of and admired Imagist poetry. His 1921 "On Wedding Gifts" represents perfectly the dictum of making every word count--indeed, here, for surprise effect, even the punctuation mark becomes a word:

> Three traveling clocks
> Tick
> On the mantelpiece
> Comma
> But the young man is starving.[2]

Just as Williams was doing in his poems of the twenties, Hemingway here drew in his reader through his stark, identifiable details, only to change direction abruptly in the last line. The shift in direction works also to amplify the earlier lines of the poem.

His "Riparto D'Assalto," a somewhat longer poem first published in Poetry and then in 3 Stories & 10 Poems, follows the same pattern. Beginning with the detailed description of soldiers riding in a cold truck, Hemingway gives us their physical discomfort, their sex-oriented reveries, and then the ride itself,

> Damned cold, bitter, rotten ride,
> Winding road up the Grappa side.[3]

It is only after another passage of these kinds of details that, in the last line, he tells of the men's deaths ("where the truck-load died").

"Riparto" is an Imagist poem not only in its use of seemingly factual detail, but also in the poet's apparently objective attitudes toward the soldiers (a "truck-load" is hardly a sentimental description). Such a tone characterizes many of Hemingway's "tough" poems--"Ultimately," "The Age Demanded," "Captives," "Champs D'Honneur"-- but it is successful only when he lets the poem stand on its own imagery instead of adding the "tags" that name the emotion he is trying to create. "Mitraigliatrice," which depends entirely on the comparison between typewriter and battlefield, is a stronger poem, consequently, than "The Ernest Liberal's Lament."

There seem to be two major difficulties about Hemingway's poems, whenever they were written. His tendency to fall into easy end-rhyme patterns spoils much of his phrasing elsewhere in the line (see "Chapter Heading," "Soul of Spain," and especially "Second Poem to Mary" where the tone is nearly destroyed with the jingling rhymes). Even more destructive, however, is Hemingway's tendency to use his poems--as he seldom did his fiction--as vehicles for personal vituperation. Whether it is his satire on the Lausanne Conference, his "blood is thicker than water" verse to his brother Bill, or his "The Lady Poet with Footnotes," Hemingway uses word play (sometimes rhyme, sometimes repetition) and purposely unpoetic diction and imagery--and at times flat statement instead of imagery. These elements are evident in the satiric poem, "Valentine" (Collected Poems, 28), dedicated to hostile critics:

> Sing a song of critics
> pockets full of lye
> four and twenty critics
> hope that you will die
> hope that you will peter out
> hope that you will fail....

Profanity or sexual references (as here) often carry the weight of the satire, as in "They All Made Peace--What Is Peace?"

> ...
> Lord Curzon likes young boys.

So does Chicherin.
So does Mustapha Kemal. He is good looking too.
 His eyes
Are too close together but he makes war. That is
 the way he is. [4]

  The best example of these early vindictive poems is
"The Soul of Spain," filled with the anal humor and naughty
word choice of an adolescent. Set against the insults to his
brother Bill and Gertrude Stein is the definitely complimentary
passage to Ezra Pound, although Pound might understandably
have not cherished the "monument" Hemingway creates for
him. Parts II through VI of the poem foreshadow Hemingway's parody of Anderson to come in The Torrents of Spring.
The titles of each section are themselves jokes (Part IV is
of a literal story; Part V puns on the idea of following itself). Language within each section also varies widely, from
the forced rhyme at its worst ("The wind blows/ and it does
not snows look at the bull with his bloody nose") to the simp-
listic pseudo-Anderson mockery ("We got on a train and went
somewhere else") to the echoing word repetition of Stein
("Short knives are thick short knives are quickshort knives/
make a needed nick"). The effect of "The Soul of Spain" in
total is much funnier than that of many of Hemingway's other
satiric poems, simply because there is such variety in each
section, and because the juxtaposition works successfully.
(Hemingway's usual strategy regarding structure is very much
in the mainstream of Imagist practice. His longer poems
are nearly all montage or pastiche. His short ones build
from or to a controlling image. Regardless of length, juxtaposition is used instead of formal transitions.)

  Hemingway's most effective early poems, it seems to
me, are his straight social protest poems like "T. Roosevelt," in which the Hemingway identity does not become involved (the weight of the details about Roosevelt conveys the
author's feeling about him) and his recollection poems, the
best of which is "Along with Youth" (Collected Poems, 26).

  A porcupine skin
  Stiff with bad tanning,
  It must have ended somewhere.
  Stuffed horned owl
  Pompous
  Yellow eyed;
  Chuck-willow-widow on a biassed twig
  Sooted with dust.

> Piles of old magazines,
> Drawers of boys letters
> And the line of love
> They must have ended somewhere.
> Yesterdays tribute is gone
> Along with youth
> And the canoe that went to pieces on the beach
> The year of the big storm
> When the hotel burned down
> At Seney, Michigan.

This poem not only echoes the nostalgic tone of many of the stories in In Our Time and passages from later Nick Adams stories; it also works well as a set of separate images, piled one on the other, and relying for its final effect on the concluding image. (One might wish the title line--not powerful in itself--had been omitted in the body of the poem.)

Part of the problem in dealing with Hemingway's poems is their unevenness. A passage like "Smoke smarts my eyes, / Cottonwood twigs and buffalo dung / Smoke gray in the teepee--/ (or is it my myopic trachoma)" immediately precedes this quite effective description (Collected Poems, 19):

> The prairies are long,
> The moon rises
> Ponies
> Drag at their pickets.
> The grass has gone brown in the summer....

Hemingway often has good single lines, or even a passage that coheres; but sustaining a mood or an image in poetry seems difficult for him. Part of his difficulty seems to come from the kicky rhyme that he falls into. Another problem is his self-conscious pose--Hemingway the poet, an attitude that less often appears in his fiction. For whatever reason, the fact is that Hemingway frequently includes asides and irrelevancies in poems that would never be allowed in his fiction.

Interestingly, the same elements noticeable in the poems of the twenties appear again in the poems from the middle and late forties. There are the good single lines, some of which are distillations of his fiction during this period:

> The days between flying are months.
>
> all of us need to be alone
>
> Sitting now here in the room
> Waiting to go to the battle.
> A man without his children or his cats.

Some of Hemingway's best poetry appears, finally, in the
two poems to Mary, but unfortunately each poem is comparatively long, and the good lines are obscured by other less
effective passages. The opening of "To Mary in London" is
quite lyric:

> I, loving only the word
> Trying to make with a phrase and a sentence
> Something no bomber can reach
> Something to stand when all of us are gone
> And long after....

as is his simple description of her,

> ... she will come,
> Opening softly with the in-left key,
> Saying 'May I come in?'
> Coming small-voiced and lovely.... [5]

The "Second Poem to Mary," in its longer and more stri-
dent lines and its reliance on word play, undercuts its interesting opening ("Now sleeps he/ With that old whore
Death"). [6] Even though this is the poem in which Hemingway says it plainly ("But now, for a moment, there is only
love and compassion. Knowing how to endure. And only
love and/ compassion"), he leads into that passage too indi-
rectly. The reader is lost in the pseudo-sophisticated verbal dexterity:

> You may go now, all of you. Go as quietly as possible.
>   Go as far as possible. You may even take possible
> with you, if you can find him....
> Today no one uses slang because clarity is of the utmost
>   importance.
> Fucking, alone, is retained, but is only used as an adjec-
>   tive.
> Sweating-out is retained.
> It means that which one must suffer without the possibility
>   of changing the result or the outcome.
> Those of us who know walk very slowly, and we look at
>   each other with infinite love and compassion.

The irony of Hemingway's less-than-successful poems is that he stops presenting and tells, or he stops presenting and glories in his own cleverness with words. It is both surprising and disappointing that the medium which is by nature the most suggestive mode of writing became for Hemingway only his alternative mode. For other writers, prose was the genre for "getting it all down," and from prose they would choose and polish the gems of their poems. Perhaps since Hemingway had already polished his prose to the point of brilliance, his poetry was all that remained to catch his "easier" writing. Hemingway appears to have used his poems as he did much of his non-fiction, as a more clearly personal outlet rather than an artistic one; and the quality of both the poems and the non-fiction suffered as a result.

Appendix II

FAULKNER AS POET

Faulkner's two books of poetry and the other uncollected poems are interesting on several counts. Technically, they range from free form image poems to formal sonnets; from direct lines like "now slaps her white behind to rosy fire" to the more self-conscious "The race's splendor lifts her lip." Thematically, they foreshadow many of the themes of the later novels. The range of both poetic devices and subject matter in Faulkner's poems is perhaps the clearest evidence of the young writer's search for effective methods; and his equally wide range of success in the poems also suggests how integral method was to his best presentation of theme.

Because Faulkner's poems were often not published when they were written, dating his styles exactly is difficult. Genrally, however, the iambic couplets of The Marble Faun (1924) can be dated 1919, with most of the poems of the 1933 A Green Bough being written in the early and middle twenties. The poems which appeared in the 1932 Faulkner issue of Contempo were, for the most part, not included in the second book; Faulkner's concept of the unity necessary in any collection--whether of short stories, poems, or novellae--was even here demanding that some poems be omitted. It seems that Garrett and Richardson are right in placing most of Faulkner's poetry before 1925, when he turned to prose with the Times-Picayune sketches and Soldiers' Pay.[1] That he wrote poems occasionally the rest of his life seems likely, but his devotion to his role as novelist also is evident. What apparently happened to Faulkner was, quite simply, that he found a more satisfying and, artistically, a more effective mode for expressing himself. As he explained so poignantly in that seminal 1925 essay, "Verse Old and Nascent," he had found poetry and loved it; he had then been excited by the innovation of Housman, Aiken, Frost, and H. D.; but then he had felt the incompleteness of their expression and had turned again to the fuller statement of the Romantic poets (and to their more traditional poetic forms). The devices of the free-form Imagists were too restricting; just as the life-view of Eliot's The Waste Land and Pound's Mauberley were too bleak. Perhaps it is the tone of the most influential contemporary poems that irritated Faulkner the most:

> Is there nowhere among us a Keats in embryo, someone who will tune his lute to the beauty of the world? Life is not different from what it was when Shelley drove like a swallow southward from the unbearable English winter.... Here is the same air, the same sunlight in which Shelley dreamed of golden men and women immortal in a silver world.... Is not there among us someone who can write something beautiful and passionate and sad instead of saddening?[2]

That Faulkner's own life-view was such as he describes is evident, and of even more significance to his aesthetic theory is his description of these "golden men and women." When a writer's interest is primarily characterization, poetry is often a difficult vehicle. (Browning had chosen one tack, and Robinson, another; but their experiments, though successful as poems, were hardly presentations of fully developed, complex people. Faulkner's poems indicate that he knew the work of each poet, but to suggest the difficulties, imagine a character like Joe Christmas as protagonist of a poem.)

Many of Faulkner's poems do indicate this interest in character, by doing little more than describing a man or woman; they sometimes tell a fairly involved narrative as well. Seldom does the poem exist to express abstract generalization. Just as seldom does Faulkner use the I persona; even when an I appears in a poem, another character is usually the center of interest. In short, Faulkner's poetic impulse seldom took the most direct route for a writer of modern lyrics. Even his poems were structured as dramatic interchanges, with characters other than the poet-persona providing the "confessional" element.

Some of his best writing in the poems seems to occur in Faulkner's characters. In "Twilight" (X) he describes

> The dream that hurt him, the blood that whipped him
> Dustward, slowed and gave him ease.

In XI, a love scene, he uses physical detail to catch the yearning innocence of the heroine, "Young breasts hollowed out with fire.... [A] small white belly yielded up." His ready use of personification ("spring is quick with child, and sad"; "Dogwood shines so cool and still, / Like hands that, palm up, rigid lie") may also stem from his tendency to equate everything with human beings. Even descriptions of nature are often used, as they are in his fiction, to supplement or contrast the emotion of the character within the poem; in "Visions in Spring" these lines are used to reflect the protagonist's melancholy,

> Soft hands of skies
>
> Delicately swung the narrow moon above him
> And shivered the tops of trees....

Nature descriptions in their own right also pervade Faulkner's poems. The number of "spring" poems would suggest that he uses the theme of nature's renewal to represent his own dauntless hope. Five of the six poems in the Faulkner issue of Contempo are spring poems, and all contain good lines:

> Winter is gone, snow but an old wives tale:
> Winds have forgotten it....

From "April,"

> Some ways are white with birches in a hood
> Of tender green. A sunset weaves
> A tapestry upon some silent wood
> Calmly quiet, and the leaves
> Clothe the half-clad trees in solemn gold.

Images like these also prove the poet's own real love of his countryside in spring--urban poets even in the twenties were less sensitive to such traditional subjects.

In the innovative twenties, the risk of writing about these conventional poetic subjects in fairly conventional forms was insurmountable. Reviewers and the few readers his poems had labeled them imitation Romantic, and ignored Faulkner as poet.[3] Yet, as Garrett points out so convincingly, Faulkner's strengths are many, given what he was trying to accomplish within the medium of the poem.

Reading The Marble Faun as a closely-related sequence of poems, as Garrett does, is satisfying for a number of reasons. Most apparently, the book is a pastoral cycle, a series of poems related through subject, sound, poetic devices, and a common rhythm and form. Judging the poems as poems can be done more fairly when one understands the traditions in which Faulkner was working. [4] The somewhat obscure meaning of the book is also clarified when the sequence is read as a study of the Prufrock-like character of the faun, caught and "marble-bound" in his own conflict between awareness and innocence. Faulkner contrasts him with the "quick keen snake," and opens his first poem, "If I were free, then would I go;" and so he does, eventually, to follow the vital Pan. His quest is to experience the vivid life, the joys of nature; compared with which man's intellectual stalemate is cold, dull marble. Brought to life in his joy at nature, the faun does attain movement ("All day I run before a wind, / Keen and blue and without end"), falling finally to rest upon the earth's "Beating heart that's never old."

The last poem of the sequence proper seems to contain a satisfying resolution, as the faun is finally warmed and vitalized by the sun ("I am sun-steeped, until I / Am all sun, and liquidly / I leave my pedestal and flow / Quietly along each row"); but the Epilogue reverts to the cold imprisonment of his earlier condition ("My heart knows only winter snow"). Bound by the poetic convention as he was, Faulkner's wish fulfillment of coming to life is more effective than the stasis he actually describes in the cycle. His response to the beauty of changing seasons, representative of all change, is still effective even though some of it is written in nostalgic poetic diction.

Less unified as a collection but more interesting as poetry, A Green Bough shows Faulkner attaining what is to be his more pervasive rhythm. The longer line and structures of incrementation here allow him to move in the lengthier patterns of his later prose. Rather than a two- or three-line image, Faulkner in many of these poems uses a whole stanza to build a single effect. Poem II, which focuses on a woman playing the piano while her lover watches, musing, has as refrain "Play something else" (and while the music continues, so do his thoughts):

> It is as though he watched her mount a stair
> And rose with her on the suppleness of her knees
> Saw her skirts in swirling line on line,

> Saw her changing shadows ripple and rise
> After the flexing muscles; subtle thighs,
> Rhythm of back and throat and gathered train.
> A bursting moon, wheels spin in his brain.
> As through a corridor rushing with harsh rain
> He walks his life, and reaching the end
> He turns it as one turns a wall....[5]

The images echo of <u>Light in August</u>, but more important here
they reflect the sensual, almost sinister tone of the poem as
the lover forces a confrontation which the woman seems to
fear. Unlike a Browning monologue, however, Faulkner
handles the scene in third person, with both characters moving through their lines, saying scarcely anything, but moving. The tenor of the scene is conveyed mainly through the
images of contortion and fire ("He sees his brain disinte-
grate, spark by spark"). The ending of the poem presents
sexual imagery, the stair setting, and the suggestion of personal torment all coalesced in one brief scene:

> He stands and watches her mount the stair
> Step by step, with her subtle suppleness,
> That nervous strength that was ever his surprise;
> The lifted throat, the thin crisp swirl of dress
> Like a ripple of naked muscles before his eyes.
> A bursting moon: wheels spin in his brain,
> And whirl in a vortex of sparks together again.
>
> At the turn she stops, and trembles there,
> Nor watches him as he steadily mounts the stair.

This kind of complexity in characterization is new in
Faulkner's poems (achieved also in I, III, IV, VII, and
XXV). The wider line helps him to more freely present
tangential and more nearly ambivalent details. The quat-
rains and sonnets that follow in <u>A Green Bough</u> are in total
effect much less successful, although several of these poems
are certainly also superior work.

In brief, I must agree with Garrett when he says,

> If there is continuity in Faulkner's verse there
> is, as in his prose, a restless experimentation,
> and an attempt to achieve, within the limitations
> which he demanded for verse, new variations on
> the oldest themes. The final effect is not one of
> 'immature romanticism.' It is rather one of

strenuous effort to create a poetry which, had it
been continued, might have been a sophisticated
lyric strain in contemporary verse. 6

Judging from Faulkner's poems--the adaptations from Verlaine and Sappho (and Eliot and Housman), the image poems,
the ironies--he did know and understand the modernist mode.
Faulkner's aim, however, even as a comparatively young
artist, went beyond the possibilities of the single poem. Because his intention was so broad, the lyric poem did not sat-
isfy him. Instead he created his own poems in his novels,
but they were epics rather than lyrics.

Appendix III

SOME CORRESPONDENCES

Much of Faulkner's writing in the last fifteen years of
his life seems to have come more from memory than from
actual or contemporary experience. We have seen that he
drew on many local or regional tales--or at least types of
these stories--throughout his writing. Increasingly in his
later novels, he appears to have been influenced as much by
what he read[1] as by what he had heard, or had himself in-
vented.

Beginning with <u>Absalom, Absalom!</u> in 1936, there is
a noticeable use of elements which other authors had used
with some success. Clifton Cuthbert's 1933 <u>Thunder Without Rain</u>[2] had explored the situation of incest between an
older brother and his sister. Peter and Mary, who live with
their widowed, drunken mother, are lovers while Mary is
still in school; but she eventually marries Peter's college
roommate who is dark-skinned. Years pass; Peter becomes
a priest. After many affairs, Mary searches for and finds
Peter, attempting to resume the former relationship. Peter
murders her with a knife. Overwritten as the book is (with
Peter's apprentice years in a butchershop foreshadowing the
ending murder scene), Cuthbert's dramatic (and empathetic)
presentation of incest is effective. Faulkner's frequent use
of the possibility of incest may stem in part from his early
identification of Quentin with it, but the important difference
in his use of incest in <u>Absalom</u> is its comparative lack of
significance. No one really cares if Charles Bon and Judith
are children of the same father. The social crime that has
horrified countless cultures is as nothing to the South that
sees all relationships in terms of literal black and white.
By using incest ironically, to call attention to the real sin
of miscegenation, Faulkner has taken the reader far beyond
his expectations.

Other elements in <u>Absalom</u> are reminiscent of Cuthbert's early thirties novels. The community attitude that

whatever Sutpen did was his business recalls a strong scene
in Cuthbert's 1931 Joy Street where a young bootlegger slips
out of a poker game just before a man is knifed, instead of
trying to prevent the act:

> We walked all the way up to the corner without
> saying anything. I was thinking about Buono stand-
> ing in front of the Jew with the knife held up in the
> air. I wondered what had happened after that. I
> saw a picture of the Jew lying on the floor in the
> corner with Buono's knife sticking out of his chest.
> I didn't like to think of that though. There seemed
> to be no need of thinking of that.... It was lucky
> Santoro had yelled to me to follow him out just
> then [44].

Repeatedly in Faulkner's later novels, the issue of man's responsibility to others is central, as is the supposedly rumi-
nating protagonist who manages to escape most reality.

Faulkner's signed collection of books is also rich in
the tales and fiction of his native South West. Not only the
Sut Lovingood stories but books like those by Roark Bradford, James Branch Cabell, James Street, and Emmett Gow-
en (his 1932 Mountain Born) probably only confirmed Faulkner in what he was already writing--the "down home" idiom
stories like "Idyll in the Desert" and "Hair." Gowen's story
teller Fate Shannon must have taken lessons from Twain in
that his timing in his tales is excellent; as he says, he
"plays them out."[3] In Mountain Born also we find the figure
of Old Ben, in this case the patriarch of a human clan rather than a bear.

Some of the most interesting correspondences between
Faulkner's novels and the writing of another contemporary
occur in comparing his Snopes trilogy with T. S. Stribling's
The Forge, The Store, and The Unfinished Cathedral (1931,
1932, and 1934). Only these three books of the many which
Stribling had written were among the signed and dated books
of Faulkner's collection.[4] Taken collectively, the influence
of Stribling's writing is important because his trilogy provided a pattern, a scaffolding for a multiple event and multiple character chronology. They too charted the rise, and
fall, of an ambitious man. And they also emphasized the
role of the women--lovers and daughters alike--who, being
female, met certain obstacles men would not have had.
(This latter interest dovetailed nicely with Faulkner's

apparent preoccupation with young women as characters in his later novels, explicable since his own child was then a maturing woman. A Fable was also dedicated to Jill.)

Stribling's patriarch is Jimmie Vaiden, a thundering old pioneer who (like Will Varner) "followed the casualness of Nature."[5] He had many children, but his youngest daughter is, like Eula, a sensual charmer. His son, Miltiades Vaiden, is the protagonist of the trilogy, the man of ambition who forgets charity in his quest for status. Incest, marriage for money, the use of his friends, robbery, personal cruelty--Milt stops at nothing to gain his ambition. Yet the novels focus more often on the family relationships than on Milt's financial chicanery.

Once jilted by the beautiful Drusilla Lacefield, Milt returns to her after his own wife has died, only to marry not Drusilla but her equally beautiful daughter Sydna. For twenty-two years, "Uncle" Milt had been Sydna's "silent, almost unseen protector"; unbelievably, they marry and prosper. Despite all the scandal, Milt does become respectable--president of the bank, KKK, American Legion, Methodist. His only son, however, a white Negro, is mistakenly hanged by a mob; Handback, his business rival, shoots himself (Handback's relationship with Gracie resembles Eula's with De Spain); Milt has no legitimate sons, only a daughter who, in her own illegitimate pregnancy, threatens to mar his final respectability. But a husband is found, and Marsan does produce a son.

The ultimate "justification" for Milt's life--his tomb and church, newly built--also fails him in the final book, The Unfinished Cathedral. An assassin, the son of an old enemy, dynamites the church and Milt is crushed by a falling column. Like Flem Snopes, Milt has effectively brought his death on himself, as the result of earlier injuries to other human beings. Also like Gavin Stevens, Milt is motivated often by his response to women: Sydna as daughter of the woman he had loved many years parallels Linda Snopes, as does his granddaughter Marsan in her own independent spirit.

Stribling's trilogy depends on plot rather than on the motivation of its characters, and many of the things that happen are far from convincing. There is no question that Faulkner's stories of the Snopes rise to power took different directions because Faulkner was working from the characters he had created: consequently the total effect of The Hamlet, The

Town, and The Mansion is quite different from that of the
Stribling series.   Part of Stribling's trilogy is also set during the Civil War, and the racial issues tend to dominate the
novel.   Jimmie Vaiden dies in the arms of his octoroon
daughter Gracie, but even in death he will not acknowledge
her; in fact, he insults her.   Faulkner's trilogy does not
cover nearly so many years; and his tone differs considerably since the race issue and the Civil War are barely mentioned.

For The Reivers, the literary source (even if ironically) becomes Lucius Apulius' The Golden Asse.[6]   This merry
tale of an adventurer who goes to any lengths to be with his
beloved sorceress has its parallel in Boon's theft of the car
to reach Miss Corrie; and, like Apulius who turns himself into a jackass instead of a wise owl, Boon's carriage also
fails to deliver Miss Corrie.   It too changes shape, dissolves
into the less noble horse.   In the course of The Reivers proper
also, Boon has no sexual fulfillment.

Numerous catastrophes occur in each book, and the
tone is certainly ironic and comic; and yet the real impact of
The Reivers is much gentler than Boon's story in itself.   In
this contrast of tones, the novel also mirrors the earlier
golden book, for it also built to the tender Cupid and Psyche
story, the greatest of love stories.   The love story of Faulkner's Lucius, who is also a "priest," and Miss Corrie, bears
some resemblance to the Cupid and Psyche story.   Both Corrie and Psyche are made to perform seemingly impossible
tasks.   Psyche succeeds because she has the aid of super-
natural powers and creatures.   Corrie, virtually unaided,
fails in all but spirit.   Even Lucius' return to his family is
a kind of echo of Apulius' return from the animal kingdom,
in that he receives a message and benediction from the highest priest, his grandfather; much later, to complete the initiation which is the novel's "story," he is taken by his Isis
(Everbe Corintha) to see the infant, his namesake.

The final comparison which might be made between
Faulkner's method and that of Apulius' is that each wrote
simply, in the vernacular.   As Robert Graves explained, a
learned priest like Apulius wrote his popular tale chiefly because "the popular tale gave ... a wider field for description
of contemporary morals and manners ... than any more respectable literary form."[7]   Once again it seems that Faulkner is experimenting with form: here using a literal "fable"
--in his own vernacular--to make explicit the truths expressed throughout his other writing.

In idiomatic language rather than formal style, the story is also told by Lucius himself, parts of it set in a "robbers' cave"; and contains much sympathetic commentary about animals' lives (it also contains much criticism of modern man's life). At one point in The Reivers Faulkner refers specifically to a "Milesian mode," and the opening section of the novel is devoted, somewhat strangely unless one recognizes Apulius, to discussions of Virtue and Non-Virtue, with the theme of the novel being the discovery of Virtue in the midst of apparent Non-Virtue. Apulius would have been pleased with Faulkner's golden book.

NOTES

PREFACE

1. Letter from Hemingway dated October 18, 1924, as quoted in Edmund Wilson, The Shores of Light (New York: Farrar, Straus and Young, 1952).

2. Lion in the Garden, eds. James B. Meriwether and Michael Millgate (New York: Random, 1968), 71. Hereafter cited as Lion.

3. Islands in the Stream (New York: Scribner's, 1970), 103. Hereafter cited as Islands.

4. Pound, Literary Essays of Ezra Pound (Norfolk, Conn.: New Directions, 1935), 10.

5. As quoted by Arthur Mizener in The Saddest Story; A Biography of Ford Madox Ford (New York: World, 1971), xix, quoted from Robie Macauley in "The Dean in Exile: Notes on Ford Madox Ford as Teacher," Shenandoah (Spring 1953), 44-48. Of interest also is John Paterson's The Novel as Faith: The Gospel According to James, Hardy, Conrad, Joyce, Lawrence, and Virginia Woolf (Boston: Gambit, 1973).

6. The Lyrical Novel (Princeton, N.J.: Princeton University Press, 1963), 273. "The direct portrayal of awareness becomes the outer frontier where novel and poem meet." More recently, Marion Montgomery made the point that "the revolution in fiction has been in the direction of the lyric.... [T]he revelation of psychological and emotional states replaces action" in much modern fiction ("Emotion Recollected in Tranquility: Wordsworth's Legacy to Eliot, Joyce, and Hemingway," The Southern Review, VI, no. 3 [July 1970], 711).

7. Everyman His Own Poet (New York: McGraw-Hill, 1968), 2; and see also Paul Hernadi's Beyond Genre: New Directions in Literary Classification (Ithaca, N.Y.: Cornell University Press, 1972).

8. Hugh Kenner's The Pound Era devotes many pages to a summary of James' importance during the years of Imagism (Berkeley: University of California Press, 1971). Jay B. Hubbell also confirms the rising influence of James in the early twenties ("1922: A Turning Point in American Literary History," Texas Studies in Literature and Language, XII, no. 3 [Fall, 1970], 481-92).

9. "The Art of Fiction," in Theory of Fiction: Henry James, ed. James E. Miller, Jr. (Lincoln: University of Nebraska Press, 1972), 33. Emphasis added. See also Hemingway's mock journal in which he couples James' death with WWI, "Ernest Hemingway," in Selden Rodman's Tongues of Fallen Angels (Norfolk, Conn.: New Directions, 1974), 51-61.

10. Introduction to Nightwood; The Selected Works of Djuna Barnes (New York: Farrar, Straus, Cudahy, 1962), 228. That the situation has changed little in 25 years is evident in Sharon Spencer's comment in Space, Time and Structure in the Modern Novel that "newer, more ambitious, more daring and often more 'realistic' types of novels are consigned to obscurity, or are never published, simply because the public has never been taught to read them" (New York: New York University Press, 1971), xiv.

11. Introduction to New American Story, eds. Robert Creeley and Donald M. Allen (New York: Grove Press, 1965), 3-4.

12. William J. Handy, Modern Fiction; A Formalist Approach (Carbondale: Southern Illinois University Press, 1971), 15ff.; see also David Madden, The Poetic Image in 6 Genres (same publisher, 1969).

CHAPTER ONE

1. John Dos Passos, Occasions and Protests (New York: Henry Regnery, 1964), 5.

2. A Second Flowering (New York: Viking, 1973).

3. Ernest Hemingway, Cub Reporter: Kansas City Star Stories, ed. Matthew J. Bruccoli (Pittsburg: Pittsburg Press, 1970), 4.

4. The Best Times (New York: New American Library, 1966), 142.

5. "A Few Don'ts by an Imagiste," Poetry, I, no. 6 (March 1913), 200-1.

6. "Imagism," Poetry, I, no. 6 (March 1913), 199.

7. "Vorticism," Fortnightly Review, XCVI (Sept. 1, 1914), 469.

8. Literary Essays, 9.

9. "Some Reflections on Ernest Dowson," Egoist, I (March 1915). This section of quotations given by Christian Stead in The New Poetic (London: Hutchinson University Library, 1964).

10. Literary Essays, 114.

11. "Author's Introduction to The Wedge," The Collected Later Poems of William Carlos Williams (Norfolk, Conn.: New Directions, 1950), 4.

12. The New Poetic, 96.

13. Henri Bergson, Introduction to Metaphysics, trans. T. E. Hulme (Indianapolis: Liberal Arts Press, 1955, reprinted from 1912), 27-28. See also John B. Vickery's comments in The Literary Impact of the Golden Bough (Princeton: Princeton University Press, 1973).

14. Pound/Joyce, ed. Forrest Read (Norfolk, Conn.:

New Directions, 1967), 44, 65, 193.

15. _Confucius to Cummings_, eds. Ezra Pound and Marcella Spann (Norfolk, Conn.: New Directions, 1964), 327.

16. _Ibid._ For complete discussion see Eric Homberger's "Pound, Ford and 'Prose': The Making of a Modern Poet," _Journal of American Studies_, V, no. 3 (Dec. 1971), 281-93.

17. _Ibid._

18. _The Critical Attitude_ (London, 1915), 28.

19. "On Impressionism," _Poetry and Drama_, II, no. 2 (June 1914), 175.

20. "Literary Portraits XXXV: Les Jeunes and 'Des Imagistes,' " _Outlook,_ XXXIII (May 9, 1914), 636.

21. _Imagism_ (Norman: University of Oklahoma Press, 1950), 113.

22. _Saddest Story_, 255.

23. "Ford Madox Hueffer," _The New Freewoman_, I, no. 13 (Dec. 15, 1913), 251. As recently as this decade, Kenneth Rexroth described Ford's poems as "the high point of British Imagism" (_With Eye and Ear,_ New York, Herder and Herder, 1970, p. 44.)

24. _Letters of Ford Madox Ford,_ ed. Richard M. Ludwig (Princeton, N.J.: Princeton University Press, 1965), 127.

25. _Novelist of Three Worlds; Ford Madox_ Ford (Syracuse, N.Y.: Syracuse University Press, 1962), 57.

26. "Joseph Conrad: A Portrait," _the transatlantic review,_ II, no. 4 (1924), 456.

27. See Kenner's _The Pound Era,_ 246-47.

28. George Wickes, _Americans in Paris_ (New York: Doubleday, 1969), 106. See also Wickes' essay "Sketches of the Author's Life in Paris in the Twenties," in _Hemingway in Our Time,_ eds. Richard Astro and Jackson

J. Benson (Corvallis: Oregon State University Press, 1974), 25-38.

29. World War I and the American Novel (Baltimore: Johns Hopkins Press, 1967), 40.

30. The Flesh and the Word; Eliot, Hemingway, Faulkner (Nashville, Tenn.: Vanderbilt University Press, 1971), 2-4.

31. The Age of Surrealism (Denver: Swallow Press, 1950), 29.

32. "The twentieth century brought with it a tremendous force for making change: a new science, a new psychology, a new way of living, new ideas of many kinds, and new literary impulses and techniques. It followed that there would be marked changes in literary fashion and in critical standards. There would be a second American literary renaissance comparable in importance to that which in 1837 Emerson had heralded in 'The American Scholar' " (Texas Studies, 1970, 481).

33. The New Poetic, 98.

34. Winifred Bryher, The Heart to Artemis (New York: Harcourt, Brace and World, 1962), 153.

35. Reflections on a Literary Revolution (Washington, D.C.: Catholic University of America Press, 1960), 1.

36. Imagism, 214.

37. Gorham Munson, "A Comedy of Exiles," The Literary Review, XII, no. 1 (Autumn 1968), 47, 49, 56.

38. Epiphany in the Modern Novel (London: Peter Owen, 1971), 18.

39. The Art of James Joyce; Method and Design in Ulysses and Finnegans Wake (New York: Oxford University Press, 1964), 55ff.

40. Ezra Pound, Pavannes and Divagations (Norfolk, Conn.: New Directions, 1958), 50-51.

41. The Middle Distance; A Comparative History of American Imaginative Literature, 1919-1932 (New York: Free Press, 1971), 88.

42. William Seward, My Friend Ernest Hemingway (New York: A. S. Barnes, 1969), 66.

43. The Autobiography of Alice B. Toklas (New York: Harcourt Brace, 1933), 261-62.

44. The Flowers of Friendship; Letters written to Gertrude Stein, ed. Donald Gallup (New York: Knopf, 1953), 164.

45. Ernest Hemingway, "My Own Life," New Yorker, II (Feb. 27, 1927), 23-24.

46. A Moveable Feast (New York: Scribner's, 1964), 15.

47. The Uncollected Prose of Ernest Hemingway, ed. Clinton Burhans (East Lansing: Michigan State University, 1967), 692. See also A Moveable Feast, p. 28, and "A Lost Book Review: A Story-Teller's Story," Fitzgerald-Hemingway Annual (1969), 71-74.

48. Ernest Hemingway and the Little Magazines: The Paris Years (Barre, Mass.: Barre Publishers, 1968), 40. See also James R. Mellow's Charmed Circle, Gertrude Stein & Company (New York: Praeger, 1974).

49. K. L. Goodwin in The Influence of Ezra Pound (London: Oxford University Press, 1966) says, "On arrival in Paris Pound was largely occupied with helping Joyce, Eliot, and Hemingway" (p. 41). See also Harold Hurwitz's "Hemingway's Tutor, Ezra Pound," Modern Fiction Studies, XVII, no. 4 (Winter 1971-72), 469-482 and Jackson J. Benson's introduction to Hemingway In Our Time, 1974, 1-12.

50. Uncollected Prose, 691.

51. As quoted by Charles Norman in Ezra Pound, rev. ed. (London: Macdonald, 1960, 1969), 275.

52. The Writer's Art of Self Defense (Minneapolis: University of Minnesota Press, 1969), 24. Stanley Cooperman too finds a close relationship between what he

calls Hemingway's "cinematic tautness" and Pound's "ideogram" (p. 40).

53. Glenway Westcott, letter to Eric Homberger, 1970, printed in Homberger's Ezra Pound; The Critical Heritage, (London: Routledge and Kegan Paul, 1972), 215.

54. Morley Callaghan, That Summer in Paris (New York: Coward-McCann Co., 1963), 30. As Karl Shapiro also notes in To Abolish Children, "Pound occupies a strange chair in poetic history ... he is a Henry Ford, a man who got the bugs out of the poem.... Ezra Pound wanted to saturate America with great poetry of every clime and age. And in a way he too succeeded" (Chicago: Quadrangle Books, 1968), 243.

55. The Collected Essays and Occasional Writings of Katharine Anne Porter (New York: Delacorte Press, 1970), 119, 40. Hurwitz [see note 49] concludes, in fact, that Pound's chief value to Hemingway was "not so much in showing him how to do it but in helping to convince him that it was worth doing" (Modern Fiction Studies, 482). See also Frederick J. Hoffman, The Twenties (New York: Viking, 1955), 163-86ff.

CHAPTER TWO

1. Alan Levy, "Ezra Pound's Voice of Silence," The New York Times Magazine (Jan. 9, 1972), 14-15, 59-68.

2. "Small Magazines," The English Journal, XIX, no. 9 (Nov. 1930), 700.

3. "Ernest Hemingway," in Writers at Work; The Paris Review Interviews, ed. Malcolm Cowley (New York: Viking, 1963), 235.

4. Ibid., 236.

5. "A Man's Credo," Playboy, X, no. 1 (Jan. 1963), in Burhans' Uncollected Prose of Ernest Hemingway, 254.

6. Joseph Conrad: A Personal Remembrance (Boston: Little, Brown, 1968), 225.

7. Literary Essays, 10.

8. Green Hills of Africa (New York: Scribner's, 1935), 26, 27.

9. "Joseph Conrad: A Portrait," the transatlantic review, II, no. 6 (1924), 698.

10. Uncollected Hemingway, 258 and 261.

11. Writers at Work, 226. As Pound had written in 1925 (March 26 to R. P. Blackmur), "At the start a man must work in a group; at least that seems to be the effective modus; later in life he becomes gradually incapable of working in a group. But in any case no one man can do everything, or be the whole of a milieu" (The Letters of Ezra Pound, 1907-1941, ed. D. D. Paige, New York: Harcourt, Brace and World, 1950, p. 199).

12. the transatlantic review, 697.

13. Pound writing as Daniel Chaucer, "Stocktaking," Ibid., II, no. 4 (1924), 398.

14. Uncollected Hemingway, 255, 261. See also "Emerson, Thoreau, and Hemingway: Some Suggestions About Literary Heritage," by Donald J. Greiner, Fitzgerald-Hemingway Annual, 1971, 247-261; and C. Hugh Holman, "Hemingway and Emerson," Modern Fiction Studies, I, no. 3 (Aug. 1955), 12-16.

15. "Vorticism," Fortnightly Review, 463.

16. "Ezra Pound and George Antheil: Vorticist Music and the Cantos," American Literature, XLIV, no. 1 (Mar. 1972), 52-73.

17. "Small Magazines," The English Journal, 699-700. Emphasis added.

18. As Pound wrote in Guide to Kulchur, p. 51: "The ideogrammic method consists of presenting one facet and then another until at some point one gets off the dead

and desensitized surface of the reader's mind, onto
a part that will register" (London: Faber and Faber,
1938).

19. Introduction to Men at War (New York: Crown Pub-
     lishers, 1942), 12.

20. That Summer in Paris, 103.

21. James Joyce and His World (London: Thames and Hud-
     son, 1967), 123.

22. Writers at Work, 226.

23. Ibid.

24. Guide to Kulchur, 89.

25. The best single study is Clinton Burhans' "The Complex
     Unity of In Our Time," Modern Fiction Studies, XIV,
     no. 3 (Autumn 1968), 313-328. See also Nicholas
     Joost, Ernest Hemingway and the Little Magazines;
     Julian Smith, "Hemingway and the Thing Left Out,"
     Journal of Modern Literature, I, no. 2 (1970-71),
     169-182; and Richard Hasbany, "The Shock of Vision:
     An Imagist Reading of In Our Time," in Ernest Hem-
     ingway: Five Decades of Criticism, ed. Linda W.
     Wagner (East Lansing: Michigan State University
     Press, 1974).

26. Uncollected Hemingway, 261. Hemingway's phrasing
     here is reminiscent not only of Pound and Ford but
     also of Joyce, who had said, according to Frank Bud-
     gen, that he wanted readers "to understand always
     through suggestion rather than direct statement"
     (James Joyce and the Making of Ulysses, Bloomington:
     Indiana University Press, 1960, p. 21). So far as
     The Sun Also Rises itself was concerned, Hemingway
     referred to it as "the most moral book he had ever
     written" (conversation with Fraser Drew, "April 8,
     1955 with Hemingway: Unedited Notes on a Visit to
     Finca Vigia," Fitzgerald-Hemingway Annual, 1970,
     113).

27. Carlos Baker, Ernest Hemingway: A Life Story (New
     York: Scribner's, 1969), 179.

28. The Sun Also Rises (New York: Scribner's, 1926), preface page. All further references to this book occur in the text.

29. As Hemingway's columns on bullfighting substantiate, the lure of the matador is irresistible, for both sexes; see pp. 90-108, By-Line: Ernest Hemingway, ed. William White (New York: Scribner's, 1967).

30. Poetry, 205.

31. Lillian Ross, "Profiles: How Do You Like It Now, Gentlemen?" The New Yorker, XVI (May 13, 1950), 60.

32. Literary Essays, 50.

33. Poetry, 205.

34. See The Flesh and the Word.

35. Hemingway's interest in Brett as character--much like his later fascination with Pilar--seems genuine. As he wrote in a 1956 column (By-Line, 461): "I have always considered that it was easy to be a man compared to being a woman who lives by as rigid standards as men live by."

36. Stanley Edgar Hyman, Standards: A Chronicle of Books for Our Time (New York: Horizon Press, 1966), 31.

37. Ihab Hassan, "Hemingway: Valor Against the Void," The Dismemberment of Orpheus (New York: Oxford University Press, 1971), 80ff.

CHAPTER THREE

1. Emily Stipes Watts, Ernest Hemingway and the Arts (Urbana: University of Illinois Press, 1971), 3.

2. Ibid., p. 18, and see especially Chapters I and V.

3. Besides Pound's impressive essay on Vorticism (Fortnightly Review, 1914), see also Hugh Kenner's discus-

sion in <u>The Pound Era</u>, where he quotes Pound describing words as "electrified cones," 238ff.

4. "How I Began," <u>T. P.'s Weekly</u> (June 6, 1913).

5. "Small Magazines," <u>The English Journal,</u> 704.

6. <u>Death in the Afternoon,</u> 100.

7. "On Writing," <u>The Nick Adams Stories</u> (New York: Scribner's, 1972), 248.

8. <u>Green Hills of Africa,</u> 21.

9. <u>Ibid.</u>, 27.

10. <u>Uncollected Hemingway,</u> 254.

11. <u>Ibid.</u>, 255: "Too many modern novels teach no lesson and serve no purpose."

12. <u>Death in the Afternoon,</u> 2.

13. Cowley's comment on the CBC radio broadcast, aired 1970. Ihab Hassan also has this high praise for <u>In Our Time</u>: "Story and vignette, sound and sight, blend perfectly, enclosed by the same deep stillness. It is the stillness of terrible truth, and it helps to make the collection the best written by an American in our century" (<u>The Dismemberment of Orpheus</u>, 96).

14. Quoted in <u>The Shores of Light</u>, 122. Letter dated Oct. 18, 1924.

15. "Night Before Landing" also suggests the same pre-battle tension (<u>Nick Adams,</u> pp. 137-143). In the 1925 collection, two of the earlier vignettes were titled and used as stories proper, "The Revolutionist" and "A Very Short Story." Names and places in the latter were changed for the 1925 publication.

16. "Three Shots," one of Hemingway's early Adams stories, is also a study of fear (<u>Nick Adams Stories</u>, 3-6), as is "A Day's Wait."

17. <u>In Our Time</u> (New York: Scribner's, 1930), 11.

18. <u>Nick Adams Stories</u>, 243.

19. <u>Writers at Work</u>, 233. See Sheldon N. Grebstein's <u>Hemingway's Craft</u> for much insight into his creation of movement (Carbondale: Southern Illinois University Press, 1973).

20. <u>Uncollected Hemingway</u>, 255.

21. Seward quotes Hemingway's remark made in October, 1957, pp. 24-25.

22. Philip Young's recent comment that the Nick stories in <u>Men Without Women</u> are not arranged chronologically, is, of course, correct. As the title of the collection suggests, <u>Men Without Women</u> is not a Nick Adams book but rather a group of stories about random, struggling men (<u>Nick Adams Stories</u>, v). See also Arthur Waldhorn's <u>A Reader's Guide to Ernest Hemingway</u> (New York: Farrar, Straus and Giroux, 1972).

23. <u>The Short Stories of Ernest Hemingway</u> (New York: Scribner's, 1938).

24. <u>Writers at Work</u>, 226.

25. <u>LE</u>, 401.

26. "Preface" to <u>Short Stories of Ernest Hemingway</u>, v.

27. "Notes on Life and Letters," <u>Esquire</u> (Jan. 1935), 159.

CHAPTER FOUR

1. Hemingway's Foreword to <u>Green Hills of Africa</u> has a nearly belligerent tone: "The writer has attempted to write an absolutely true book to see whether the shape of the country and the pattern of a month's action can, if truly presented, compete with a work of the imagination." See also Ch. 5. James Schroeter writes convincingly about the importance of <u>Green Hills</u> in "Hemingway via Joyce," <u>The Southern Review</u>, X, no. 1 (Jan. 1974), 95-114.

2. "How Do You Like It Now, Gentlemen?" New Yorker, 43. See also Green Hills, 70-72.

3. Death in the Afternoon, 2.

4. As reported in Carlos Baker, Ernest Hemingway; A Life Story, 229, 271, 277.

5. According to Baker (p. 314), Hemingway in 1937 wanted the Morgan story published in an omnibus volume with selections from his NASA dispatches from Spain, and other war-related stories. "It was clear that he wanted the book to document in some fashion his recent reconversion to social consciousness."

6. To Have and Have Not (New York: Scribner's, 1953), 148. Hereafter cited in text. Of some interest also is Hemingway and Jake, by Vernon (Jake) Klimo and Will Oursler (New York: Doubleday, 1972).

7. The Snows of Kilimanjaro and Other Stories (New York: Scribner's, 1955), 122.

8. Joseph Waldmeir, "Confiteor Hominem: Ernest Hemingway's Religion of Man" in Ernest Hemingway; Critiques of Four Major Novels, ed. Carlos Baker (New York: Scribner's, 1962), 148.

9. "Carlos Baker on Ernest Hemingway" in Talks with Authors, ed. Charles F. Madden (Carbondale: Southern Illinois University Press, 1968), 75.

10. Pound praised Joyce (review of Portrait of the Artist, May, 1918, in Future) for his "swift alternation of subjective beauty and external shabbiness, squalor and sordidness. It is the bass and treble of his method."

11. See Beongcheon Yu's excellent essay "The Still Center of Hemingway's World," Phoenix, XII (Spring 1968), 15-44. in which he stresses the many differences between A Farewell to Arms and For Whom the Bell Tolls. One such difference is that "Henry is the victim of illusions whereas Jordan is beyond them."

12. The Flesh and the Word, 138-151.

13. "The Art of Fiction," 299, 300.

14. Talks with Authors, 81.

15. "On Writing," Nick Adams Stories, 246. Hemingway would surely have agreed with D. H. Lawrence's definition of imagination, given his 1929 "Introduction to These Paintings": "The reality of substantial bodies can only be perceived by the imagination, and the imagination is a kindled state of consciousness in which intuitive awareness predominates." (In Phoenix: The Posthumous Papers of D. H. Lawrence, ed. Edward McDonald, London: Heinemann, 1936, 559.)

16. "Vorticism," Fortnightly Review, 466.

17. Linda Wagner, Denise Levertov (New York: Twayne, 1967), 92-95 and 138-140.

18. "Vorticism," 466.

19. "Hark to Sturge Moore," Poetry, VI, no. 3 (June 1915), 140.

CHAPTER FIVE

1. Uncollected Hemingway, 253. Hemingway declares then, "I do most of my work in my head. I never begin to write until ideas are in order." See Baker's Life Story for specific accounts of the way each novel came to be written; and also Hemingway's Paris Review interview, p. 233 in Writers at Work.

2. Baker, 208.

3. See Hemingway's March 18, 1937 dispatch (By-line, 258).

4. The Fifth Column in The Fifth Column and Four Stories of the Spanish Civil War (New York: Scribner's, 1969), 80. Hereafter cited in text.

5. "The Denunciation," Ibid., 100.

6. For positive views of this relationship, see "A Clean, Well-Lighted Place," The Sun Also Rises, and To Have and Have Not. Part of Cantwell's malaise in Across the River, in contrast, may rise from his difficulties in some of these same relationships.

7. Hemingway states this admiration directly in his introduction to Men at War, 11-12.

8. Somewhat reminiscent of "Turn About," Faulkner's 1934 war story, this part of "Night Before Battle" also includes some references to the drunken Baldy writing for a Mississippi paper, and having trouble telling his story "straight."

9. The Spanish Earth (Cleveland: J. B. Savage, 1938), 46.

10. The Short Stories of Ernest Hemingway, 79.

11. "Nobody Ever Dies," Cosmopolitan (March 1939).

12. Uncollected Hemingway, 254.

13. That Hemingway in 1939 turned to Spanish women for his heroines is understandable. Dorothy Bridges was a disaster; throughout his work no major female character had been well drawn, except Brett Ashley, and she was consistently misread. By using, first, Maria and then Pilar, and finally the Italian Renata, Hemingway was both protecting himself from charges of unreality by his largest reading public, the American; and he was also freeing himself of one obstacle in creating mature women characters--his feeling for his mother. The farther he was culturally from the white, middle-class America of "Soldiers' Home" and the Nick Adams stories, the more easily he could forget the stereotypes he found there. It is interesting to note that Hemingway much earlier had created a character in the Maria mode, "Littless," the young and loving sister in "The Last Good Country" (Nick Adams Stories, 65-131).

14. See Alan Holder's essay, "The Other Hemingway," Twentieth Century Literature, IX (1963), 153-157, in which Holder points out, rightly, that contrary to stereotype Hemingway has had great sympathy for many of his heroines from the beginning of his writing career:

women are often for Hemingway those " 'whom things are done to'. . . .
> that she can be more sinned against than sinning, that she has legitimate demands which his males either ignore or refuse to meet."

There is also the biographical connection between Pauline's nickname, Pilar, and his choice of that name to designate his tough gypsy. Pilar also names the shrine at Zaragoza, his cruiser, and his daughter ("Pilar Cézanne") in a 1927 New Yorker parody, "My Own Life" (Feb. 1927, 23-24).

15. Men at War, 9.

16. Baker, 337.

17. Chaman Nahal, The Narrative Pattern in Ernest Hemingway's Fiction (Rutherford, N.J.: Fairleigh Dickinson University Press, 1971), 132.

18. Nick Adams Stories, 247, 248.

19. The Sun Also Rises, 11.

20. Mystery and Manners (New York: Farrar, Straus and Giroux, 1970), 113.

21. Baker, 340. Hemingway's characteristic exuberance with writing which pleased him is evident too in his 1948 comment to William Seward, as he expressed wonder at " 'how the hell any son of a bitch could write that well;' " then adding " 'That isn't conceit. It's knowing my trade' " (My Friend Ernest Hemingway, 36).

22. "Notes on Life and Letters," Esquire (Jan. 1935), 159.

CHAPTER SIX

1. Across the River and Into the Trees (New York: Scribner's, 1950), 233. Hereafter cited in text.

2. As Hemingway had written in his 1946 introduction for Treasury for the Free World (New York: Arco Pub.

Co., 1946), "We have come out of the time when obedience, the acceptance of discipline, intelligent courage and resolution were most important into that more difficult time when it is man's duty to understand his world rather than simply fight for it" (xiii).

3. Horst Oppel points out that Renata is used as an agent of castigation and purgation; she effects health in Cantwell, and brings him to his happy death ("Hemingway's Across the River and Into the Trees," Hemingway and His Critics, ed. Carlos Baker, New York: Hill and Wang, 1961, 221).

4. See Baker's discussion of Renata as Venus, and her use in Across the River (Life Story, 476-477.)

5. Baker, 471ff., 476.

6. Quoted by Rodman in Tongues of Fallen Angels, p. 55.

7. Baker, 488-494.

8. My Friend Ernest Hemingway, 36.

9. Writers at Work, 231.

10. Ibid., 222.

11. In a letter to the Editors of Life, August 25, 1952, p. 124.

12. Uncollected Hemingway, 262.

13. Quoted in Baker, Life Story, 504.

14. Ezra Pound, Instigations (New York: Boni and Liveright, 1920), 246.

15. The Old Man and the Sea (New York: Scribner's, 1952), 16. Hereafter cited in text.

16. William A. Gass, Fiction and the Figures of Life (New York: Knopf, 1970), 95-96.

17. See Waldmeir's discussion of Santiago's relationship with God in "Confiteor Hominem," 144-149.

18. Hemingway is himself the "strange" old man, in private conversations. His use of the adjective here has the connotation of joke as well as of allusion. See Lillian Ross's profile, p. 49. In fact, even the mako sharks had been described by Hemingway as "strange" in that they were superior to other kinds of shark ("Out in the Stream," Esquire, August 1934, 19).

19. See "Hemingway's The Old Man and the Sea" in Handy's Modern Fiction, 94-118.

20. Islands in the Stream (New York: Scribner's, 1970), 326. Hereafter cited in text.

21. William Faulkner, The Unvanquished (New York: Vintage Books, 1938), 19.

CHAPTER SEVEN

1. Lawrence Bowling, "William Faulkner, The Importance of Love," The Dalhousie Review, XLIII (Winter 1963), 474. See also Herman E. Spivey, "Faulkner and the Adamic Myth: Faulkner's Moral Vision," Modern Fiction Studies, XIX, no. 4 (Winter 1973-74), 497-506.

2. Cleanth Brooks, "Faulkner's First Novel," The Southern Review, VI, no. 4 (Oct. 1970), 1061.

3. As comments by both Faulkner and Hemingway show, he at first rebels against the surveillance, but a mature man's attitude is more accepting. Anthony Bailey's recent In the Village echoes Faulkner's sentiments. As Bailey says, "contact is what the village is all about.... It behooves us to know people.... Responsibilities form a reinforcing mesh" (New York: Knopf, 1971).

4. Lion, 72. See Malcolm Cowley's comment on Hemingway and Faulkner as "countrymen," conservative in their morality because of their ties with the soil (The Faulkner-Cowley File, 1944-1962, New York, Viking, 1966, 151-152).

5. Faulkner in the University, eds. Frederick L. Gwynn

and Joseph L. Blotner (Charlottesville: The University of Virginia Press, 1959), 5. Hereafter cited as University.

6. Bowling, "The Importance of Love," 474.

7. Faulkner at West Point, eds. Joseph L. Fant, III and Robert Ashley (New York: Random, 1964), 76.

8. Sherwood Anderson, Letters, eds. Howard Mumford Jones and Walter B. Rideout (Boston: Little, Brown, 1953), 89.

9. William Faulkner, "Sherwood Anderson," The Dallas Morning News, April 26, 1925; pt. III, p. 7. Faulkner's portrayal of Anderson as Fielding Dawson in Mosquitoes also proves the younger writer's understanding.

10. University, 10.

11. Letters [see note 8], 393.

12. Sherwood Anderson's Memoirs; A Critical Edition, ed. Ray Lewis White (Chapel Hill: University of North Carolina Press, 1969), 238.

13. Faulkner at West Point, 84.

14. Lion, 145 and 267.

15. See Joyce W. Warren's "Faulkner's 'Portrait of the Artist,' " Mississippi Quarterly, XIX (Summer 1966), 121-131.

16. William Faulkner, Mosquitoes (New York: Liveright, 1927), 243.

17. "A Note on Sherwood Anderson," Essays, Speeches & Public Letters, ed. James B. Meriwether (New York: Random, 1965), 8.

18. Joseph Blotner, Faulkner; A Biography (New York: Random, 1974), p. 47 in Notes and p. 1547.

19. Blotner, p. 51 in Notes. See also Noel Polk's "William Faulkner's Marionettes" in A Faulkner Miscellany,

ed. James B. Meriwether. Jackson: University Press of Mississippi, 1974, pp. 3-36.

20. Blotner, p. 418.

21. Letters, 118.

22. Lion, 34.

23. University, 47.

24. Lion, 18.

25. Carlos Baker defends the so-called "one-dimensional" Hemingway characters by pointing out that because readers may have ignored method, they thereby misread the figures presented: "Hemingway is not much of a character analyst.... He doesn't, in Henry James fashion, go in and out ... and under and over the motivation of his characters. That's what they want him to do and what Hemingway himself would never conceivably do--expound at length on the motivation" (Baker on Hemingway in Talks with Authors, 81).

26. William Faulkner, "On Criticism," Double Dealer, VIII (Jan.-Feb. 1925), 83-84.

27. Literary Essays, 46.

28. Faulkner at West Point, 57; see also University, 19.

29. "On Writing," Nick Adams Stories, 247.

30. Quoted in Ivan Kashkeen, "Letters of Ernest Hemingway to Soviet Writers," Fitzgerald-Hemingway Annual (1971), 202. Letter to Kashkeen, August 19, 1935.

31. Lion, 177.

32. Occasions and Protests, 276.

33. University, 19. Somewhat similarly, Faulkner preferred the Old Testament to the New because in the former he had "the pleasure of watching what these amazing people did." "One is about people.... The New Testament is philosophy and ideas" (Lion, 112).

34. <u>Faulkner at West Point</u>, 82.

35. <u>University</u>, 277.

36. <u>Lion</u>, 53.

37. <u>Lion</u>, 54.

38. <u>University</u>, 282.

39. <u>Lion</u>, 251.

40. <u>Lion</u>, 224.

41. "Joseph Hergesheimer," in <u>William Faulkner: Early Prose and Poetry</u>, ed. Carvel Collins (Boston: Little Brown, 1962), 102-103.

42. <u>University</u>, 277.

43. "American Drama: Inhibitions" in <u>Collins</u>, 96.

44. <u>Lion</u>, 55 and 32. Faulkner had much company in his skepticism about plot-oriented fiction. Pound had early written, "Life, for the most part, does not happen in neat little diagrams and nothing is more tiresome than the continual pretense that it does" (<u>Literary Essays</u>, 400). And in 1925, Anderson had described what he called "the poison plot" of America's short stories: "Everyone knows there are no plot stories in life itself and yet the tradition of American short story writing has been built almost entirely upon the plot idea. Human nature, the strange little whims, tragedies and comedies of life itself, have everywhere been sacrificed to the need of plot" (As quoted in Roy Lewis White, "A Critical Analysis," <u>Readers and Writers</u>, I, no. 6 [April 1968], 36).

45. <u>Faulkner at West Point</u>, 73.

46. "William Faulkner: The Problem of Point of View," <u>Patterns of Commitment in American Literature</u>, ed. Marston La France (Toronto: University of Toronto Press, 1967), 181.

47. <u>University</u>, 65.

48. Richard P. Adams, "The Apprenticeship of William Faulkner," <u>Tulane Studies in English,</u> XII (1962), 128-29.

49. "Sherwood Anderson," <u>The Dallas Morning News</u>.

50. <u>Essays, Speeches, & Public Letters</u>, 174.

51. <u>University</u>, 39.

52. The correspondences between Pound's theories and those expressed by Alain Robbe-Grillet in <u>Pour un Nouveau Roman</u> (trans. Richard Howard, New York: Grove Press, 1965) are striking. The best critical discussion of this "new" current in fiction is Spencer's <u>Space, Time and Structure in the Modern Novel.</u>

53. Cleanth Brooks, "Faulkner as Poet," <u>The Southern Literary Journal,</u> I, no. 1 (Dec. 1968), 18. As Brooks writes, "he needed the kind of context which would allow him to set up a real tension between his own more purely 'literary' tendencies and his sense of a solid and believable world."

54. Or, as Faulkner phrased it in his <u>Paris Review</u> interview, the "thesis" he was "always hammering at" was "that man is indestructible because of his simple will to freedom" (<u>Lion</u>, 241).

55. As given in <u>Lion</u>, 81, and elsewhere, the list rated Thomas Wolfe first and included Caldwell, Dos Passos, and himself, before Hemingway. See Baker, 461, for Hemingway's reaction to the remark, and Blotner, 1231-35, for a complete description of the situation.

56. Blotner, 1308; see also 1334 and 1351.

57. <u>University</u>, 143-44 and 149. Cowley's comparisons in <u>The Faulkner-Cowley File</u> are apt, as Cowley stresses the fact that the two men "resembled each other in many fashions, great and small. Both of them had sharp eyes for landscape; both liked to go barefoot as boys and even as young men; ... both were hunters by devoted avocation. Both loved the wilderness, lamented its passing.... Both returned in their work to many of the same themes" (159-60).

58. Ibid., 144.

59. Ibid., 149.

60. See Baker 234, 439, 503, and 532.

61. Quoted in Blotner, 1191-92.

62. University, 150.

63. Philip Young and Charles W. Mann, The Hemingway Manuscripts, An Inventory (University Park: Pennsylvania State University Press, 1969), 121-122.

64. The value of this long-lived friendship is attested to in many places, among them O. B. Emerson, "Bill's Friend Phil," Journal of Mississippi History, XXXII (May 1970), 135-145; Stark Young, "New Year's Craw," New Republic, XCIII (Jan. 12, 1938), 283-284; H. Edward Richardson, William Faulkner: The Journey to Self-Discovery (Columbia: University of Missouri Press, 1969), 201; W. R. Ferris, "William Faulkner and Phil Stone," South Atlantic Quarterly, LXVII, no. 4 (Autumn 1969), 536-542.

65. Faulkner's going to New Orleans initially occurred because he "had heard of The Double Dealer and the people there for years" (University, 231).

66. John McClure, "New Poems of Ezra Pound," Double Dealer, III, no. 17 (May 1922), 269.

67. "Modern Isms," Ibid., 227.

68. "Lewellyn Jones, "Have We a Literary Capitol?" Double Dealer, II, No. 8-9 (Aug.-Sept. 1921), 98.

69. And see Joost, 21-31.

CHAPTER EIGHT

1. University, 116-117. See also Faulkner's 1933 introduction to The Sound and the Fury, quoted in James Meriwether, The New York Times Book Review (Nov. 5, 1972), 6-7.

2. <u>Lion</u>, 55; <u>Writers at Work</u>, 226-228.

3. "Turns and Movies," <u>The Mississippian</u> (Feb. 16, 1921), 5. Aiken's interest in psychology and his own experiments in fiction (the stream of consciousness in the 1927 <u>Blue Voyage</u>, for one) would also have interested Faulkner.

4. Quoted in <u>William Faulkner: Early Prose and Poetry</u>, 60.

5. <u>The Marble Faun</u> and <u>A Green Bough</u> (New York: Random, 1924 and 1933), 18-19.

6. "An Examination of the Poetry of William Faulkner," <u>Princeton University Library Chronicle</u>, XVIII (Spring, 1957), 134.

7. That Faulkner knew some of Pound's theories is suggested from his use of the terms <u>vorticist, vortex, impersonality</u>; and his use of Pound's concluding line to his "Metro" poem, "wet black bough." One of Faulkner's objections to Hemingway's prose is his readiness to use again and again "that method [of] which his preceptors said, 'This is a good method' " (<u>Lion</u>, 107). It is interesting also that Faulkner himself owned a copy of Aiken's 1927 <u>Modern American Poets</u>, from which collection Aiken omitted Sandburg, Pound, and Masters because, according to his Preface, "The work of these three poets interests me in the mass ... but disappoints me in the item" (New York: Modern Library, 1927), vi.

8. "Turns and Movies," 5.

9. "Verse Old and Nascent: A Pilgrimage," in <u>Early Prose and Poetry</u>, 114-118. See also <u>University</u>, 201.

10. See especially Richard Adams' essay (<u>Tulane Review</u>) and Frederick L. Gwynn, "Faulkner's Prufrock--and Other Observations," <u>The Journal of English and Germanic Philology</u>, LII, no. 1 (Jan. 1953), 63-70.

11. <u>The Dial</u>, LXXV, 480-483. For more information on this subject see Carvel Collins' "The Pairing of TSATF and AILD," <u>Princeton University Library Chronicle</u>, XVIII (Spring 1957), 114-123.

12. Once again, see Adams, and also his discussions of the importance of Melville, Hawthorne, Balzac, and many other writers to Faulkner (Tulane Review).

13. Ibid., 129.

14. John Faulkner, My Brother Bill (New York: Trident Press, 1963), 212.

15. William Faulkner, New Orleans Sketches (New Brunswick, N.J.: Rutgers University Press, 1958), 37-40.

16. William Faulkner, Soldiers' Pay (New York: Liveright, 1926), 150. Hereafter cited in text.

17. See Millgate, Achievement, 63-64; and Brooks, "Faulkner's First Novel," Southern Review, 1061.

18. See Millgate, 72; and Joyce Warren, Mississippi Quarterly, (1966), 121-131.

19. Thomas L. McHaney, "The Elmer Papers: Faulkner's Comic Portrait of the Artist," A Faulkner Miscellany, 37-69. McHaney attributes this innovation to Faulkner's interest in Bergson.

20. William Faulkner, Sartoris (New York: New American Library, 1964), 284. Hereafter cited in text. See also p. 285, where Faulkner describes Jenny's real glory, in her "spare and erect and brusque and uncompromising and kind" manner, "looking after the place which was not hers and to which she had been transplanted when her own alien roots in a far-off place ... had been severed violently; running it with tireless efficiency." Comparison throughout with Flags in the Dust will be helpful, the reissue of Sartoris which replaces the original pages cut by Faulkner's agent (New York: Random, 1973).

21. See Alan Friedman, The Turn of the Novel (New York: Oxford University Press, 1966) and Robert M. Adams, Strains of Discord: Studies in Literary Openness (Ithaca, N.Y.: Cornell University Press, 1958).

22. Olga Vickery, "The Making of a Myth: Sartoris," Western Review, XXII (Spring 1958), 209-210.

CHAPTER NINE

1. Whereas Joyce's jokes were wide in scope and applica-
    tion, Faulkner often played upon a word or phrase
    more unobtrusively. One thinks of his early recur-
    ring use of impersonal (Margaret Powers is the only
    "impersonal" heroine in American literature), vortex,
    and thing, perhaps drawing from the then aesthetic
    vocabulary in very avant-garde writing. Later use of
    "Hemingway" phrases carried on the tradition of pri-
    vate joke (see Thomas L. McHaney, "Anderson, Hem-
    ingway, and Faulkner's The Wild Palms, PMLA,
    LXXXVII, no. 3 (May 1972), 465-474.

2. Percy Lubbock, The Craft of Fiction (New York: Vik-
    ing, 1957), 62.

3. "All the Dead Pilots," These Thirteen (New York: J.
    Cape & H. Smith, 1931), 82.

4. Cleanth Brooks, William Faulkner, The Yoknapatawpha
    Country (New Haven, Conn.: Yale University Press,
    1963), 103-115.

5. James Meriwether, The Literary Career of William
    Faulkner (Princeton, N.J.: Princeton University
    Press, 1961), 167.

6. As Faulkner wrote in an untitled essay (University of
    Virginia Library, Faulkner Collection), "One day I
    seemed to shut a door between me and all publishers'
    addresses and book lists. I said to myself, Now I
    can write. Now I can make myself a vase like that
    which the old Roman kept at his bedside and wore the
    rim slowly away with kissing it. So I, who had never
    had a sister and was fated to lose my daughter in in-
    fancy, set out to make myself a beautiful and tragic
    little girl."

7. See Gerald Langford's Faulkner's Revision of Sanctuary
    (Austin: University of Texas Press, 1972).

8. See Brooks, Country, 127-138, where he discusses
    what Faulkner has done instead.

9. Conrad Aiken, "William Faulkner: The Novel as Form,"
    William Faulkner: Four Decades of Criticism, ed.

Linda W. Wagner (East Lansing: Michigan State University Press, 1973), 139.

10. Millgate, "The Problem of Point of View," 182.

11. Lion, 204.

12. Margaret Blanchard, "The Rhetoric of Communion: Voice in The Sound and the Fury," American Literaature, XLI, no. 4 (Jan. 1970), 556.

13. The Faulkner-Cowley File, 16.

14. William Faulkner, The Sound and the Fury (New York: Vintage, 1965), 292. Hereafter cited in text.

15. Lion, 251.

16. William Faulkner, As I Lay Dying (New York: Vintage, 1930), 15. Hereafter cited in text.

17. Brooks, Country, 47-74, where he also defines the novel as a comedy.

18. John Cullen, Old Times in the Faulkner Country, in collaboration with Floyd C. Watkins (Chapel Hill: The University of North Carolina Press, 1961), 89ff. See also William Faulkner of Oxford, eds. James W. Webb and A. Wigfall Green (Baton Rouge: Louisiana State University Press, 1965).

19. William Faulkner, Light in August (New York: Modern Library, 1932), 453. Hereafter cited in text.

20. "The Opening Scene of William Faulkner's Light in August," Proof 2 (1972), 175-84. J. F. Kobler compares the structure of the novel with that of Keats' "Ode on a Grecian Urn," in which the urn itself appears--like Lena--to open and close the art object ("Lena Grove: Faulkner's 'Still Unravished Bride of Quietness,' " Arizona Quarterly, XXVIII (1972), 339-54).

21. Faulkner's admiration for pregnant women seems genuine. In an early "Frankie and Johnny" story (University of Virginia Faulkner Collection) he describes the unmarried, pregnant Frankie lying awake: "Frankie lay thinking of all the other girls throughout the world,

lying with babies in the dark. Like the center of the
world, she thought; wondering how many centers the
world had: whether the world was a round thing with
peoples' lives like fly-specks on it, or whether each
person's life was the center of a world and you
couldn't see anybody's world except yours.... She
felt as impersonal as the earth itself; she was a strip
of fecund seeded ground lying under the moon and
wind and stars of the four seasons,... and that now
was sleeping away a dark winter waiting for her own
spring with all the pain and passion of its inescapable
ends to a beauty which shall not pass from the earth."

22. See Adams, Tulane Studies, and Carl Benson's "Thematic Design in Light in August," The South Atlantic
Quarterly, LIII (1954), 540-555.

23. Glenn Sandstrom, "Identity Diffusion: Joe Christmas
and Quentin Compson," American Quarterly, XIX
(Summer 1967), 207-223.

24. As Faulkner spoke about peace in his comments at the
University of Virginia (University, 67), it seems to be
unattainable, at best: "Maybe man is incapable of
peace.... Maybe there's no such thing as peace,
that it is a negative quality.... [M]aybe peace is only a condition in retrospect, when the subconscious
has got rid of the gnats and the tacks and the broken
glass in experience and has left only the peaceful
pleasant things--that was peace. Maybe peace is not
is, but was."

25. Millgate points out that Absalom is not an historical
novel; it is more concerned "with the act of historical
interpretation in and of itself" (" 'The Firmament of
Man's History': Faulkner's Treatment of the Past,"
Mississippi Quarterly, XXV (Spring 1972, supplement),
26. See also Joseph W. Reed, Jr., Faulkner's Narrative (New Haven, Conn.: Yale University Press,
1973).

CHAPTER TEN

1. One wonders that James Gindin did not have more to say

about Faulkner in his recent Harvest of a Quiet Eye:
The Novel of Compassion (Bloomington: Indiana University Press, 1971). Gindin defines this sort of
novel as one characterized by "the concreteness, the
emotional depth, the uncertainty of articulation or
definition, and the irresolution of most human experience" (359).

2. University, 96; see also 108.

3. Lion, xiv.

4. Millgate, Achievement, 142-144.

5. See pp. 100ff of Pylon (New York: Modern Library,
   1935, 1967). Hereafter cited in text. The parallel
   with Prufrock and similar ineffectual Waste Land men
   is the obvious reason for some of these scenes, although the novel would have been better realized had
   Faulkner not forced the characters in those directions. Clifton Cuthbert's Thunder Without Rain, a
   1933 novel which Faulkner owned and had signed, may
   have given him the idea for the Eliot tone. It uses
   two lines from The Waste Land as epigraph, and tells
   the story of hopeless love which is also incestuous,
   doomed religion, and murder (see Appendix III).

6. See Julian Symons, Mortal Consequences, A History--
   From the Detective Story to the Crime Novel (New
   York: Harper and Row, 1972); Warren French,
   "William Faulkner and the Art of the Detective Story,"
   The Thirties, ed. Warren French (Deland, Fla.:
   Everett Edwards, 1967), 55-62; W. M. Frohock,
   "Faulkner in France: The Final Phase," Mosaic, IV,
   no. 3 (1971), 125-134.

7. See pp. 39-40, Go Down, Moses (New York: Random,
   1942). Hereafter cited in text.

8. See University, 178. For an excellent discussion of
   Absalom as "a novel about why novels get written,"
   see John Middleton's "Shreve McCannon and Sutpen's
   Legacy," The Southern Review, X no. 1 (Jan. 1974),
   115-124.

9. University, 72.

10. <u>Ibid.</u>, 4.

CHAPTER ELEVEN

1. William Faulkner, <u>A Fable</u> (New York: New American Library, 1954), 261. Hereafter cited in text. This stance was also the basis for Faulkner's children's book, <u>The Wishing Tree</u>, for in it St. Francis tells Dulcie, "I'll give you each one of my birds. And if you'll feed it and care for it, you'll never make a selfish wish, because people who care for and protect helpless things cannot have selfish wishes" (New York: Random, 1964, p. 77).

2. <u>Lion</u>, 32.

3. <u>University</u>, 116-117.

4. <u>Ibid.</u>, 195.

5. Richard Boyd Hauck, <u>A Cheerful Nihilism</u> (Bloomington: Indiana University Press, 1971), 70.

6. <u>Light in August</u>, 241.

7. <u>Go Down, Moses</u>, 192.

8. Millgate, "The Problem of Point of View," 181.

9. <u>University</u>, 90.

10. Hauck [see note 5], 169.

11. Millgate, <u>Ibid.</u>, and Stephen L. Mooney, "Faulkner's 'The Town': A Question of Voices," <u>Mississippi Quarterly</u>, XIII, no. 3 (Summer, 1960), 117-122.

12. See Joseph Gold, "The Normality of Snopesism: Universal Themes in Faulkner's <u>The Hamlet</u>," <u>Wisconsin Studies in Contemporary Literature</u> (Winter 1962), 25-34.

13. <u>University</u>, 45.

14. William Faulkner, The Reivers (New York: Vintage, 1962), 121. Hereafter cited in text.

15. University of Virginia Faulkner Collection. Conclusion of Faulkner's essay "Mississippi."

16. Hauck [see note 5], 168.

CHAPTER TWELVE

1. Jay B. Hubbell, Who Are the Major American Writers? (Durham, N.C.: Duke University Press, 1972).

2. As compiled by David Pownall, Articles on Twentieth Century Literature: An Annotated Bibliography, 1955-1970 (Milwood, N.Y.: Kraus Reprint Co.).

3. Arthur Mizener, Twelve Great American Novels (New York: New American Library, 1967), 126.

4. W. M. Frohock, Mosaic, 1971.

5. Robert Humphrey, Stream of Consciousness in the Modern Novel (Berkeley: University of California Press, 1968), 113, 121.

6. Ford Madox Ford, Introduction to A Farewell to Arms (New York: Modern Library, 1932), ix-xx.

7. Uncollected Hemingway, 253.

8. Ibid., 254.

9. For parallel careers, consider those of Glenway Westcott and Morley Callaghan. See especially Wallace Stegner, "Rediscovery: Westcott's Goodbye Wisconsin," The Southern Review, VI, no. 3 (July 1970), 674-681, and Victor Howard, Morley Callaghan (Toronto: Copp Clark Pub. Co., 1969).

10. Mark Schorer, "Mr. Hemingway and His Critics," New Republic, CXXXI (Nov. 15, 1954), 20.

11. Robert Penn Warren, "Ernest Hemingway," Selected

Essays (New York: Random, 1958), 117, 85.

12. Joseph Waldmeir, "Confiteor Hominen," 149. John Mc-
    Cormick, The Middle Distance, agrees (p. 55).

13. Anaïs Nin, The Novel of the Future (New York: Mac-
    millan, 1968), 78.

14. As quoted by Maurice Coindreau in The Time of Wil-
    liam Faulkner (Columbia: University of South Caro-
    lina, 1971), 79-80.

15. Frank Baldanza, "Faulkner and Stein: A Study in Styl-
    istic Intransigence," Georgia Review, XIII (Fall 1959),
    274. See also Warren Beck, "William Faulkner's
    Style," in William Faulkner: Four Decades of Criti-
    cism, ed. Linda Wagner (East Lansing: Michigan
    State University Press, 1973), 149.

16. Ezra Pound, Instigations, 128.

17. Richard Adams, Tulane Review, 144.

18. A. D. Van Nostrand, Everyman His Own Poet, 177.

19. Michel Gresset, "Psychological Aspects of Evil in The
    Sound and the Fury," Mississippi Quarterly, XIX,
    no. 3 (Summer, 1960), 153.

20. University of Virginia Faulkner Collection, Faulkner's
    letter to Joe Brown, 1/24/45.

21. Ibid., "Love" (story).

22. Ray B. West, Jr., The Short Story in America, 1900-
    1950 (Chicago: Henry Regnery, 1952), 106. Of great
    interest in any discussion of these two authors is
    William Barrett's Time of Need, Forms of Imagina-
    tion in the Twentieth Century (New York: Harper and
    Row, 1972).

APPENDIX I

1. The Hemingway Manuscripts, An Inventory, x.

2. As quoted by Baker in Life Story, 82.

3. The Collected Poems of Ernest Hemingway (New York: Haskell House, 1960), 22. Hereafter cited in text.

4. "They All Made Peace--What Is Peace," reprinted in Louis Zukofsky, "Comment, Program: 'Objectivists,' 1931," Poetry, XXXVII (Feb.,1931), 270-271.

5. "To Mary in London," Atlantic Monthly, CCXVI, no. 2 (Aug. 1965), 94, 95.

6. "Second Poem to Mary," Ibid., 96-100.

APPENDIX II

1. George P. Garrett, Jr., "An Examination of the Poetry of William Faulkner," Princeton University Library Chronicle, XVIII (Spring 1957), 124-135. H. Edward Richardson, William Faulkner, The Journey to Self-Discovery.

2. In Collins, 118.

3. See Harry Runyan, "Faulkner's Poetry," Faulkner Studies, III, nos. 2-3 (Summer-Autumn 1954), 23-29; Morris U. Schappes, "Faulkner as Poet," Poetry, XLIII, no. 1 (Oct. 1933), 48-52; William Rose Benet, "Faulkner as Poet," The Saturday Review of Literature, IX, no. 41 (April 29, 1933), 565; and Peter Monro Jack in The New York Times Book Review (May 14, 1933), 2.

4. See Garrett, 124-125.

5. The Marble Faun and A Green Bough (New York: Random, orig. pub. 1924 and 1933), p. 14. For poems not included in these books, see Contempo, I, no. 17 (Feb. 1, 1932) and Collins, Early Prose and Poetry.

6. Garrett, 134.

APPENDIX III

1. George Garrett, "The Influence of William Faulkner," Georgia Review, XVIII (Winter 1964), 419-427.

2. Clifton Cuthbert, Thunder Without Rain (New York: William Godwin, 1933) and Joy Street, 1931. See also Ilse Dusoir Lind, "The Design and Meaning of Absalom, Absalom!" Four Decades, 276, for a comparison of Absalom with the Oedipus trilogy.

3. Emmett Gowen, Mountain Born (Indianapolis: Bobbs-Merrill, 1932), 45. See Mark Twain's essay, "How To Tell a Story," How to Tell a Story and Other Essays (New York: Harper, 1897).

4. As listed in Joseph Blotner, William Faulkner's Library; A Catalog (Charlottesville: University Press of Virginia, 1964).

5. T. S. Stribling, The Forge, The Store, and The Unfinished Cathedral (New York: Doubleday, Doran, 1931, 1932, and 1934), The Forge, p. 1.

6. According to Blotner, Faulkner owned the 1923 edition of The Golden Ass of Lucius Apulius, an edition which was reviewed in the July 1924 issue of The Double Dealer. See also Ben M. Vorpahl, "Moonlight at Ballenbaugh's: Time and Imagination in The Reivers," The Southern Literary Journal, I, no. 2 (Spring 1969), 3-26. For a summary of references to his own earlier fiction, see William Rossky, "The Reivers: Faulkner's Tempest," Four Decades, 361.

7. Robert Graves, Introduction to his translation of Lucius Apuleius' The Golden Ass (New York: Farrar, Straus and Young, 1951). For more discussion of literature which was probably important in Faulkner's writing see Joseph Brogunier, "A Housman Source in The Sound and the Fury," Modern Fiction Studies, XVII, no. 2 (Summer 1972), 220-224; Cecil D. Eby, Jr., "Ichabod Crane in Yoknapatawpha," Georgia Review, XVI (1962), 465-469; Randall Stewart, "Hawthorne and Faulkner," College English, XVII (Feb. 1956), 258-262; and Richard Adams, Tulane Review.

INDEX

In order to hold this index within the confines of
a reasonable length, I have chosen to list all
characters from a novel or short story under
the work's title; thus, for example, all references to Jason Compson are under The Sound
and the Fury, rather than under Compson. In
this index the symbols (F) and (H) (for Faulkner and Hemingway) are used to identify author-
ship of book titles. No symbol is used for
books by others.